LEGENDARY
STORIES OF BLOOD,
SWEAT AND BEERS

DALLAGLIO'S
RUGBY TALES

By Lawrence Dallaglio and available from Headline

It's in the Blood: My Life
Dallaglio's Rugby Tales

LAWRENCE Dallaglio's
RUGBY TALES

headline

First published in 2009
by HEADLINE PUBLISHING GROUP

1

Cataloguing in Publication Data is available from the British Library

Hardback ISBN 978 0 7553 1973 2

Typeset in Stone Serif by Avon DataSet Ltd,
Bidford on Avon, Warwickshire

Printed in the UK by CPI Mackays, Chatham, ME5 8TD

Headline's policy is to use papers that are natural, renewable and recyclable products and made from wood grown in sustainable forests. The logging and manufacturing processes are expected to conform to the environmental regulations of the country of origin.

HEADLINE PUBLISHING GROUP
An Hachette UK Company
338 Euston Road
London NW1 3BH

www.headline.co.uk
www.hachette.co.uk

This book is dedicated to the memory of my mother, Eileen, who not only was an inspiration and made me laugh but who also brought great happiness to so many other people. Thank you Mum, for everything.

CONTENTS

Part Two
Tales from the Backs   141

LEGENDARY
STORIES OF BLOOD,
SWEAT AND BEERS

ACKNOWLEDGEMENTS

I'd like to thank all the players who contributed stories to this book. I have loved reading them and your generosity of time and effort has been wonderful. I know all the contributions were personal favourites and by way of concrete thanks for sharing these fantastic memories and observations I am delighted to be making a donation to the Rugby Players Association (RPA) Benevolent Fund for each of the tales told in the following pages. The Fund provides invaluable support for players who have been forced to retire prematurely from the game due to injury or illness and to the families of players who have passed away.

I'd also like to especially thank Damian Hopley and David Trick who have both worked incredibly hard in helping me collect the stories together and bring them to life in this book. Particular thanks also go to Richard Relton who was smart enough to remember the initial conversation that gave birth to this collection and who, alongside Rob Bennett-Baggs, has been very persistent and supportive and without whom this book would never have come into existence. Thanks also to Jo Whitford, Rhea Halford, David Wilson and the whole team at

Headline for turning a late manuscript into what I hope you all agree is a very entertaining read.

But most of all I'd like to thank everyone involved in the game of rugby. Without you all there would be no stories to tell.

Lawrence Dallaglio
September 2009

THE RPA BENEVOLENT FUND

The Rugby Players Association Benevolent Fund, The Players' Charity, was founded to provide financial support for professional rugby players who have been forced to retire from the game due to serious injury or illness, and support players' families in the event of untimely death.

Since 2001, the Benevolent Fund has helped several players including Leicester and England Under-21 prop Matt Hampson, former Bristol full-back Alastair Hignell, England 'A' centre Andy Blyth and England scrum-half Nick Duncombe, who died in February 2003 aged just twenty-one.

The RPA Benevolent Fund is especially close to the hearts of the players, as highlighted by the fundraising they themselves do for the charity. In recent years there have been a number of player challenges which include: climbing mountains, running marathons and cycling across entire countries in order raise funds and support for the charity.

In addition to the players' fundraising, the generous support of businesses and rugby supporters raises thousands of pounds for The Players' Charity each year. We are overwhelmed by the level of support and goodwill there is in the rugby fraternity for this cause, and we remain indebted to all who have donated, and continue to donate.

The RPA Benevolent Fund – Registered Charity number 1113160.

For more information visit www.theRPA.co.uk

INTRODUCTION
GRAPE, GRAIN AND GREAT TALES

I played nineteen seasons of senior rugby, which can be judged in terms of statistics, achievements and honours gained. All this information is available to any interested party via a simple search on the internet, but what is far more difficult to quantify is the amount of fun I had along the way.

During those nineteen seasons, spanning both the amateur and professional eras, I have met a host of characters who represent the wonderful diversity of our game. They come in all shapes and sizes, but whatever their background – be it carpenter, policeman or ridiculously posh public school boy – they all have one thing in common: they can reel off dozens of cracking stories, and I am lucky enough to have been a willing audience on many an occasion. I have even witnessed and participated in more than my fair share of these tales. Obviously I was never the butt end of the jokes of course . . .

During one particular evening when the beer and wine were flowing (I always mix the grain and grape – puts hairs on your chest), I was sat with my agent Richard Relton and my former Wasps and England colleague, Damian Hopley, who is the founder and chief executive of the Rugby Players Association (RPA). Several stories were being told, and as the night and the wine drew to an end we realised these tales were too good to keep to ourselves, so we stumbled and slurred upon a plan; we were going to contact a few rugby players, past and present, and ask them to contribute one of their favourite rugby stories for inclusion in a book. Some of the proceeds of this would then go to the players' charity, the RPA Benevolent Fund, which helps those players who have had to retire from the game due to serious injury or illness. Simple.

Now the essence of this book is honesty, and I should start by admitting that the following day I was not quite so chipper as I had been a few hours earlier. I did, however, have a vague recollection of a plot being hatched in the small hours regarding a collection of 'Rugby Tales'. 'Ah well, not to worry,' I thought. 'In a few hours' time my hangover will diminish and the recollection will disappear from my mind for ever.' Unfortunately, Richard is blessed with both a great attention to detail and the memory of an elephant, and he was soon on the phone with a plan of attack for the book. The rest, as they say, is history. Emails were sent, phone calls were made; players were persuaded, cajoled, blackmailed, even begged to write a story from their time in the game and the result, along with a few I penned myself, is the book now in your hands.

I thoroughly enjoyed reading all the stories as they arrived, many of which were new to me. Every now and again I would finish one and think 'that cannot be true'. A quick phone call to the contributor and I was left in no doubt regarding its authenticity, as the names and contact details of witnesses were gladly supplied. If you experience half the enjoyment I had reading them, you will consider your time well spent.

Having been reminded of all the great stories and infamous incidents which are included here, it occurs to me that club and international rugby might seem to anyone reading this book like one long jolly, consisting of nights on the piss, missed meetings and ridiculous antics. While the weight of evidence laid before you in the following pages may suggest this to be true, it is most definitely not the case. The countless hours of dedicated training are rarely covered by journalists but, believe me, every contributor to this book has put his body through hell (and looking at a lot of them, it shows) in order to be the best rugby player he could be. But stories of physical endurance don't make for a huge amount of hilarity, and as the matches themselves are covered extensively by TV, radio and the written word, they would in themselves hold few surprises for rugby fans. So this is not a training manual (I think I saw one of them once... might even have read it) or a series of match reports. Instead, the object of this book is to let the reader in on some of the stories that, until now, have rarely seen the light of day. As players, we worked hard and we played hard – this book, I hope, reflects the latter. Having fun, creating stories, is an important part of the game of rugby. It binds people together – fans and players – and I hope that remains the case for a very long time indeed.

So that's the origin of this book. If you enjoy it, it was all my idea. If not, blame Mr Rioja, Mr Hopley and Mr Relton. The cast of characters who have given up their time and tales for this book is wide (some of them very) and varied, and I'd like to thank all of them for their efforts. By way of introduction to each contributor, at the beginning of every story I've tried to give a flavour of who the author is, their achievements in the game and where I first met them, played with them or when I first admired them on the TV (if they are of an age).

But before all that, and to the get the ball rolling (or more accurately, bouncing around in weird directions), I thought I would share a few stories from my early playing days and the responsible, serious, senior players who took me under their wing and made sure I didn't stray too far off the path. Oh, and I might just slip in a couple of tales that happened around 2003. For no *particular* reason of course...

Deer hunting and dodgy jellyfish

Anyone who has ever met me would not be surprised to learn that I am a person with an ambitious outlook on life. I first broke into the spotlight as part of the victorious England team at the 1993 RWC 7s (Damian Hopley has some great anecdotes from that wonderful tournament which appear later in the book). At the time I was still on the fringes of the Wasps first XV, and even though I had enormous respect for the incumbent legends in the back row, such as Dean Ryan, Mark Rigby, Buster White, Matt Greenwood and Francis Emeruwa, all of whom played such a significant part in my rugby development, I was very hungry to make the step up to become a regular first-team player, and then press for full international honours.

After making the breakthrough into the Wasps starting line-up the following season, things began to go well for me, and I felt that my appetite to learn and gain valuable experience at the club were starting to make people sit up and take notice. My efforts were duly rewarded with my selection for the England 'A' team.

Now, the 'A' team remains one of the great enigmas of rugby. There are various schools of thought. Is the 'A' team England's second best team, the next best group of players from around the country who are selected to challenge and put pressure on the first XV? Or perhaps it is the stomping ground for the next generation of players who are emerging through the ranks, who are selected to gain that all-important ingredient in international sport – experience. Then again, it could be all about taking players out of their comfort zones at club level and throwing them, head first, into unusual combinations, testing their skills, application and big match temperament so that selectors can get a proper understanding of who is truly 'ready' for full international rugby.

To grasp fully the evolution of the 'A' team concept, we need to turn back the clock to understand the cultural nuances of this team of misfits. Back in the dark ages the RFU would arrange the final trial before the Five Nations got under way, when the 'Probables' would play against the 'Possibles' – which I'm sure inspired the latter XV to extraordinary depths. This archaic selection process, with the RFU selectors sitting in judgement like Simon Cowell and Piers Morgan in their version of 'Rugby's Got Talent', was formally abandoned under Geoff Cooke's management in the nineties.

The England 'B' team then evolved as the bona fide second team. In France they had the exotic sounding 'L'espoirs' . . . in England we had the 'B' team, until some RFU visionary had the Saatchi-esque foresight, after possibly several bottles of fine claret, to upgrade the 'B' to 'A'. Brilliant. Triple G&Ts all round, I'd say.

And so there was I, recently called up for the re-branded 'A's. The selectors had gone for a blend of youth and experience, even to the point of recalling my Wasps team-mate Steve Bates as captain to give some much-needed leadership and seniority to complement the youthful exuberance of the majority of the team.

Wasps had been playing at home that day, and quite a few of us had been selected for the 'A' squad. Following the final whistle at Wasps, a fresh-faced (well, it was a long time ago) yours truly, together with the other 'A' boys, dutifully drank our post-match tea, made our excuses and scarpered as fast as we could to Richmond, where we were staying for our Saturday night/Sunday morning training session.

You can imagine the chat when we arrived at the hotel. 'Drop bags in your room, boys, see you in the bar in ten – drinks are on Dudley Wood.' Now, Dudley Wood was secretary of the RFU which meant only one thing – free bar! Such 'hospitality' was the glue holding these training sessions together and we had already tucked into a few sharpeners when our team manager, the former Coventry and England

5

full-back, Peter 'Rosey' Rossborough (he of the exceptional sideburns in *101 Best Tries*), announced that we would be meeting upstairs in thirty minutes. Not wanting to miss out, we continued to sample the delights of the bar up until the very last minute, with all new arrivals being greeted like prodigal sons.

Knowing his audience was a mix of well-worn old timers, enthusiastic newcomers and a few undecided in the middle, Rosey was keen to bring all of his leadership talents to the fore. Rising to his entire 6ft 2in frame, he opened the meeting by revealing the first page on the flip chart. We all craned our necks as we saw in bold writing the letter '**A**'.

As he eyeballed each and every one of us in true 'Kennedy Sweep' fashion, he uttered the following: 'A is for Ambition. I want you all to play with unbridled ambition and fulfil your potential. You've got this far by being at the top of your game, but have that ambition to keep rising up the England ranks.' Sage nods all round. Impressive stuff.

'A is for Attitude. The only way we will perform to the level we know we are capable of is if we go out next week and play with a professional attitude. When things go wrong, as well they might, then we need to pick ourselves up and move forward.' Again, nods around the room, Peter was gaining the groundswell of support from his foot soldiers. 'Finally,' he continued, 'A is for Accomplishment. We go out there and finish off everything successfully. Then when we come off that ground we know the progress we have made collectively, and that's how we put pressure on those guys in the England team staying down the road.'

When it works, the relationship between the manager and his captain is a thing of rare synchronised beauty. You only have to think of Sir Alex Ferguson and Roy Keane, Clive Woodward and Martin Johnson, Kitch Christie and François Pienaar, to see the embodiment of two brains working as one. Having delivered his opening address with considerable gusto, Rosey turned to Captain Bates. Now Batesy had been round the block a few times, so was probably a bit long in the tooth for this motivational spiel. Staggering to his feet after a couple too many lagers downstairs, Batesy steadied himself on the chair in front of him, and slurred, 'Well lads, I've got a letter for you too. It's "R", and that stands for "Roebuck", which is the pub next door to this hotel. I'm off there right now and suggest you all show your captain your full support and join me for a beer!' Of course we followed him to a man and dutifully did our bit for the team.

Team bonding and inspirational leadership like that are crucial for success, especially if your team features a number of debutants or youngsters. They need guidance and to be shown how to behave, how to train and how to act sensibly. Exactly the role Graham Dawe took on for me that summer, on my first tour with the full England squad.

We were in South Africa and Graham was my first room-mate, one of the most durable players in the game – I believe he still turns out for Plymouth Albion aged 107. He was the oldest player on tour and I was the youngest. He was a farmer from Launceston in Cornwall and I was a Cockney wide boy. Not a natural mix, one would assume, but it was a good result for me. Graham was a brilliant room-mate. He was a man of few words – but each word counted – and from time to time he encouraged me to do things I would never normally consider.

We were staying in the Holiday Inn on the beachfront in Durban. Following the first training session most of the boys were in the local hostelry, Joe Cools, breaking the ice with a few cheeky shots. We got back to the hotel at about 2 a.m. and Dawsie tells me we are setting the alarm for 6.30 a.m. – lunchtime for him – and going for a run at 7 a.m. I was not feeling any pain at the time and assumed it was probably no more than a bit of bravado on his part.

At 6.55 a.m. I felt a tap on my shoulder, and my eyes opened to see Dawsie in full kit. 'Come on young Lol, we're going running,' he said. Grimacing, I pulled on my kit and as we walked out of reception we were greeted by a beautiful sunny Durban morning.

To put a few things in context, I need to tell you a quick story about Graham before I continue with this one, so please bear with me, it is relevant. This particular incident became part of England team folklore and has been repeated by so many players that I have no reason to doubt its authenticity.

During an England tour in the late eighties, a training session was coming to its conclusion. Being at the cutting edge of physiology, the team coaches had just been advised it was beneficial for players to warm down following exercise, so the squad was asked to gently jog around two laps of the pitch. The two hookers on the tour were Brian Moore and Graham Dawe. The rivalry between these two players was legendary; Graham firmly believes that all sixty-four of Brian's caps should have been his and, for the record, Brian believes all five of Graham's caps belonged to him. You get the picture. These two guys were adversaries and neither was on each other's Christmas card list.

Consequently, even though the warm down was no more than a gentle jog, Brian would not let Graham get in front of him and vice versa. The two led off and ran shoulder to shoulder, with the rest of the players following. Once that main group had completed their laps they made their way to the showers and changing rooms, as you would; the session was over after all. But not for Mooro and Dawsie, who continued to run shoulder to shoulder around the pitch, neither of them wanting to bend or buckle first.

As the rest of the boys left the changing rooms twenty minutes later, showered and changed, they were greeted by the sight of Moore and Dawe still running (well, that might be over-stating the physical movement, but they were still out there by all accounts) around the pitch. The pair were only finally brought to a halt by the forcible intervention of members of the management team – if they hadn't stepped in, the two of them would probably still be running today.

I'd heard this story prior to the morning in Durban so I knew it was probably not going to be a swift three-mile run and then back for a shower. I was right. The first three miles took place on the beach. Running in sand is not easy for anyone and at 6ft 4in, weighing nearly eighteen stone, it was certainly no piece of cake for me. We then hit the roads, and after a while it occurred to me that we'd been running for four or five miles and had not turned back for home yet. Eventually we reached a landmark, which Dawsie had obviously selected as the half way point. We stopped for a minute or two to take in the view and then started back towards the hotel. It's well known that when a horse heads for home it tends to move quicker than on the outward journey, and the same is true of Dawsie. He got quicker and quicker and quicker – I was blowing out of my backside by the time the welcome sight of the Holiday Inn was within view. It was at this point that he said, 'Well done, we're going for a swim now.'

The thought of a relaxing swim in the hotel pool was most welcome, until I noticed the mad West Country farmer heading for the sea. Foolishly I followed him, eyeing the crashing waves which were at least half the height of the hotel. This was utter lunacy! I am not very comfortable in the water at the best of times, especially so when I have no idea about the rips and currents that could at any moment drag me away from the shore and from safety. As each wave struck, I dived underneath and surfaced again, gasping for air; following the third or fourth wave I looked around for Dawsie, who was nowhere to be seen. I called his name but my voice was drowned out by the noise of the thundering sea. I'd had enough and headed back to the shallows, where I found Graham on the sand throwing up gallons of sea water. He was in obvious discomfort and struggling, and appeared to be suffering from some kind of anaphylactic shock. It transpired he had been stung from head to toe by jellyfish.

I helped him back to our room, where he remained for the next four or five days. Jack Rowell asked me what was wrong with his boy (Jack

9

had previously been the successful coach for sixteen seasons at Bath, Graham's club side). Dawsie had told me to tell anyone who asked he was suffering from food poisoning. 'Dodgy prawn sandwich, Jack,' I replied. For reasons beyond me, Graham laid the blame for his jellyfish encounter firmly at my feet. From my point of view I was reluctantly following the instructions of a senior member of the team; he seemed to think I should have warned him of the potential dangers lurking in the sea.

Two or three months later Wasps made the trip to the Recreation Ground in Bath for a Courage League match. At some point during the first half I was involved in a maul and felt some serious abuse of my face going on. I grabbed out at the perpetrator's hand and gripped it firmly. Fortunately there was only one person I knew in the entire game who had fingers like a bunch of Fyffe's bananas, by-products of his many years as a farmer. I knew it was my old room-mate Dawsie. 'Hello Lol, didn't realise it was you, the apology's in the post, see you later.' And off he ran.

Even though I didn't get a full cap on that South African trip (I sat on the bench for the final Test), I loved the experience and it only made me all the more determined to make the final jump to the next level. I managed to continue making progress the following season, but narrowly missed out on selection for the 1995 RWC. Surely if I just kept at it and didn't do anything silly, it was only a matter of time.

Keeping my head down

My chance duly arrived in the autumn of 1995, when I was selected for the match-day twenty-two against South Africa and I was invited to attend my first England squad session as a fully-fledged member. It was memorable for a number of reasons; firstly it was recognition of the work I had put in on the training field over several seasons and my personal performances for Wasps. It was also going to provide me with the opportunity to judge myself against the more established players to see if I was good enough to compete at this level, but most importantly it was a chance to get my hands on as much England kit as possible. 1995 marked the tail end of the amateur era when the major currency was kit. I was keen to check into my room, get hold of lots of stash, lay it out on my bed and look at it. I wanted to stare at the rose of England embroidered on each separate item and look forward to the days ahead when I could legitimately wear it.

As I entered reception at the Petersham Hotel, the England team HQ, I remember thinking, 'Don't blow it, you're going to be mixing with Will Carling, Ben Clarke, Brian Moore, Jerry Guscott . . . Be respectful, play it cool, don't panic. Observe, listen and learn.'

The first person I met was the legendary Saracens and Harlequins prop forward Jason Leonard, who had probably only gained five or six hundred international caps at that stage of his career. 'Hello mate,' he said, 'you're just in time for a flier up the road. Don't worry about checking in, you can do that when we get back.' Immediately ignoring everything I had told myself about not blowing it, the next thing I knew I was walking out of the Petersham thirty seconds after entering it, my bags already a distant memory, abandoned somewhere in the reception area.

'A flier up the road' was in fact a trip down the road to The Sun at Richmond (otherwise known as 'The Black Hole'). 'A flier' was most definitely plural, and ten pints later, at 3 a.m., Leonard and I arrived back at the team hotel and tested the night porter's knowledge of the computer system as we asked him to check us in. It was at this point that I noticed that Jase had four bags in the reception area. I had one kit bag containing all my clothes. What had I forgotten?

He hauled three of the bags up to the desk and asked the night porter to ensure his dry cleaning was delivered to his room before close of play the following day. Intrigued, I asked the great man what was going on. He informed me that as the game was amateur, the RFU were happy to pick up laundry and dry cleaning costs for the players whilst they were residents in the team hotel. With that said, he pulled out a pair of curtains and asked the porter to ensure the red wine stains were seen to. Even though I was half cut I couldn't help admiring Jason for his bravado. As it turned out, this was just one of the many perks the boys took advantage of to gain some additional benefits from the amateur system.

Having organised his laundry, booked a 9 a.m. alarm call, and ordered every daily paper, together with a tray of club sandwiches and two beers (which we obviously needed in advance of a 10 a.m. meeting followed by a training session), Jason looked relaxed and settled. I, on the other hand, wasn't in such a fit state, but I helped him with the sandwiches and beer nevertheless, before staggering up the grand old staircase and heading off to my room.

Unsurprisingly, with a gallon and a half of beer inside me, I slept very well and strangely did not feel too shabby as bright sunlight pierced the windows when I awoke the next morning. Then I looked at the bedside clock – 10.24 a.m. I was twenty-four minutes (and counting) late for my first ever England team meeting. I was about to ring reception and give someone an almighty bollocking for forgetting my alarm call when I noticed the phone was off the hook – I had obviously knocked it at some point during my drunken sleep.

As I hurriedly dressed in my tracksuit I knew I had a decision to make – either go home knowing my career at the top level was over before it had even started, or go and face the music. I decided on the latter, and as I sprinted down the stairs I also wondered why no one had come to get me. Was I part of the squad? Had I misread the letter and been selected as a non-travelling replacement? With these and other thoughts racing around my brain, I reached the door of the meeting room and could make out the voice of our coach, Jack Rowell. Should I try and sneak in unnoticed or wait outside? At that moment I heard my name mentioned and that decided it, I was going to wait outside. I listened to the rest of what was said through the oak door.

With the conclusion of the meeting, the boys filed out of the room to prepare for a training session. I will always remember the looks I received. Captain Carling gave me his renowned death stare of disapproval and shook his head. Ben Clarke smiled a knowing smile and Jason Leonard just shrugged his shoulders. I slipped away with the boys before Jack could notice that I was outside, and to this day I do not know if he was aware of my absence at the meeting. What I do know is I never made the same mistake again. Of course I still went out with Jason on numerous occasions but I always ensured I had several alarm clocks with me for the rest of my career.

Fare play

Any England rugby player from my era will tell you the Petersham Hotel has been the venue for a million great tales. It was where the England squad would gather after playing their club games, and the usual routine was to meet post-match, have dinner and a few beers, and then get ready for a meeting and training the next morning.

When Roger Uttley, the former Gosforth and England back-row forward and Harrow school teacher, was assistant coach of the national team he introduced the ever-popular run on the morning following our arrival.

The squad was to assemble in the reception area at 9 a.m. and participate in a run of considerable distance to help ease the bumps and bruises picked up during the previous day's matches. If you haven't guessed already, you will certainly know by the end of this book, that 95 per cent of players enjoyed a beer following a match. I would like to say 100 per cent but I have to account for players like Rory Underwood who was always committed to Diet Coke, something I will never understand (although I do remember during the '94 tour to South Africa that his brother Tony, who comes from the Rory School of Non-drinking, did take a night off from his full-time job as a saint and was spotted getting a couple down his throat when we arrived in Durban). Anyway, each to their own. In most cases one beer would lead to several more and I think it's fair to say that prior to the introduction of the run there could be several players who hadn't made it back to the team hotel before 9 a.m. So this inspirational idea of Roger's was not particularly well received.

One morning, the team assembled, in various states of dishevel-ment, with Mick 'The Munch' Skinner looking exceptionally rough. I decided to run with Skins as this would obviously not be too strenuous. While he was a phenomenal hard man and enforcer, Mick was not the world's most enthusiastic trainer. After a mile or so it was obvious that his heart wasn't really in it and he was unlikely to complete the exercise. This became certain when, a few hundred metres on, he hailed a cab and climbed in. Nowadays they call this 'training smart'; Mick was always a man ahead of his time.

What Skins had not factored into his cunning plan was that Roger would take the headmasterly approach and be standing on the steps of the hotel with a clip board, checking off the players as they finished. Having completed the route in his cab way too quickly, Mickey saw Big Rog at his command post, doing his impression of the BBC's Brian Hanrahan on HMS *Hermes* in the Falklands War: 'I've counted them all out, and I've counted them all back in again.'

Panicked by this sight, Skins ducked down in the back of the cab and told the driver to keep driving around the car park. From time to time he put his head above the parapet to see if any of the boys had turned up. Eventually the players started to arrive, and each received a few words from Roger and a tick against their name on his sheet. After much deliberation Mick chose his moment to 'finish his run'. His timing was exceptionally bad – Roger was staring directly at the Geordie culprit as the cab door closed behind him. He had no option but to eat humble pie and come clean. He walked towards Roger with his arms out-stretched, apologising profusely: 'I'm so sorry Rog, I think I must have a bit of food poisoning, I spent most of the night on the toilet but desperately wanted to give the run a go to see if I felt any better. Unfortunately it made me feel even worse so I had to get a taxi back.'

Roger looked more than a little sceptical, but reluctantly put a tick against his name. The approval obviously filled Mick with some confidence, as he looked at Roger, slapped his hands against the empty pockets of his shorts and said, 'Do me favour Rog, be a top man and sort out the cabby with his fare?' Pure quality from Mick.

Covering every base

Another top man is Sir Clive Woodward – although I bet he would have planned ahead and had his fare with him if he'd decided to take a sly cab like Mick. Clive is a wonderful family man who took England from being a good side in the late nineties and turned them into a great one. I have always had an extremely good relationship with him; he made me his first captain in 1997 after all. We went through an amazing journey together, not just me but the whole team, and he was at the forefront of that. Many people have questioned whether England's success was down to Clive or the team generally. But ultimately, when you see what's happened to the England team since he departed, you cannot underestimate the enormous contribution he has made to English rugby.

As a player, Clive was a bit of maverick, with his own way of doing things, and so too as a coach. He was leader and a pioneer, and he took rugby in a completely different direction. For many years England would look to the southern hemisphere to copy everything they did, and I think Clive turned that on its head by forcing those rugby powerhouses to start dancing to England's tune. Aside from winning the World Cup, in my mind his greatest achievement was probably leading England to fourteen consecutive victories, home and away, against the southern hemisphere nations, something that he can rightly feel proud of.

It's fair to say Clive was always a man to think outside of the box and he always had 'the big picture' in mind. In order to achieve this, he was constantly looking for anything that would give the squad a slight edge. You often hear football managers in post-match interviews say something like, 'We are going to have to improve 100 per cent by next week to stand a chance of winning.' This is clearly not possible, and indeed success is not about 100 per cent improvement. The edge comes from all the little things in a team's preparation, and the mental strength of individuals and the team as a whole. The real advantage comes when a team is concentrating on something the opposition knows nothing about, giving them a 1 per cent advantage in a particular aspect of play. Clive's philosophy was based on small percentages making a big collective difference.

To give just a few examples, it was Clive who employed an 'eye coach', Sherylle Calder, to assist with the English preparations for the 2003 World Cup campaign. He was widely ridiculed in the press for this appointment, but the truth is she was excellent and the techniques and exercises she gave us definitely improved our spatial awareness and peripheral vision, both of which are crucial in top-class sport. The eyes are like any other part of the body, they improve with exercise. But I'm afraid some of the squad were a little unconvinced.

Each player had a one-on-one consultation with Sherylle and was then given a series of exercises to do on a daily basis. Many of the exercises necessitated the use of a laptop so that we could identify different shapes and sizes appearing randomly on the screen. As a forward, it was good to know our half-backs could learn to use their eyes, because we all knew they couldn't hear or catch!

By the time we reached Australia for the World Cup finals, there was a permanent chart in the team room and every player had to write next to their name the number of minutes of eye exercise they had completed each day. On top of all his training, kicking practice, eating and resting, I'm still at a loss to see how Jonny Wilkinson could manage two hundred minutes each and every day throughout the tournament!

Our first port of call was Perth, and anyone who has flown to Australia will know jet lag is a serious issue. I lay in my bed on the first night with eyes wide open, so I sent a text to Jason Leonard: 'R U awake?' Seconds later came the reply, 'YEP, fancy a beer?' A few texts later and we had a small crew of boys – Matt Dawson, Mike Tindall, Mike Catt, Jason and myself – and we disappeared into Perth for a few pints. (Low alcohol of course.)

On arrival back at our hotel, we decided a quick visit to the team room was in order, to see if there was any leftover food we could scavenge. As we entered the room, the eye chart was in a prominent position and there were some spectacular postings by many of the team. Trevor Woodman's forty minutes in the morning, thirty minutes in the afternoon and thirty minutes that evening was one I particularly recollect. 'Put me down for another forty-five minutes,' shouted Jason. 'Yeah, I'm good for another thirty minutes,' chipped in Dawson. I think we all added a few minutes to bring ourselves into line with the other boys in the squad.

One member of the team of course was Martin Johnson, the best captain any of us have played under, a giant of a man and an inspirational leader. All of us would follow him to the ends of the earth.

Scott Quinnell once said on a Lions tour that if Martin Johnson asked you to run through a brick wall, you would do it without thinking, and it would be easy because there would already be a bloody great hole where he had previously run through it himself! Johnno never asked anyone to do something he would not do himself.

Having said that, he was not necessarily a fully paid up member of the eye exercise fan club. He rarely posted any minutes on the flip chart, and generally refused to take on any of the exercises, although no one was brave enough to confront him and draw attention to this fact.

The day after our quiet night out, having resorted to our own technique for adjusting the body clock, several of us were in the team room having an informal chat with Clive. During this meeting Clive noticed Johnno at the back of the room tapping away on a laptop. 'Look at that, lads,' he said nodding towards our revered leader. 'Isn't that typical of the man, spending his downtime doing more eye exercises. What an inspiration.'

We looked over at the great man, and those of us with better eyesight than Clive could clearly see he was not toiling through eye exercises at all; he was in fact embroiled in a giant game of Minesweeper. What an inspiration indeed.

Another example of Clive's attention to winning details can be seen from his reaction to witnessing Jason Robinson being prevented from scoring a try because a defender had managed to grab hold of his shirt, hang on and bring him down. Within a relatively short period of time Clive had developed the 'skin-tight shirt' with our kit sponsor, Nike, and all international teams and senior club sides have since adopted this shirt. There was a downside to this initiative, though: the bottom almost dropped out of the replica shirt sales market when it became apparent that the only people who could carry off this style of shirt were finely honed athletes, which, to be fair, the majority of rugby supporters are not (unless you count spending years dedicating oneself to the consumption of beer a daily training regime). In fact, Jason Leonard and Dorian West weren't too happy when they first put their shirts on, especially when I pointed out that I thought they bore a passing resemblance to the *Viz* characters The Fat Slags. Come to think of it, they never stood next to each other during the national anthems again.

Clive adopted a 'hands-on' approach when it came to building up the confidence of his players. One technique he utilised from time to time was comparing his England team with the opposition. During the build-up to a fixture against the All Blacks he held a team meeting, and at the appropriate moment removed a sheet from his flip chart revealing the New Zealand team down one side and our team down the other, each player matched up against his opposite number.

He asked all of the squad to have a look at the New Zealand team and at each individual player. As we were doing this he told us that not one of the New Zealand team would make it into his England side. To emphasise this, he started with the front row and picked on tight-head prop Olo Brown. 'There is no way he would get in above Jason Leonard.' Then the hooker Norm Hewitt: 'Not a chance of getting in my team, he couldn't hold a candle to Richard Cockerill. Loose-head prop Craig Dowd is probably in the All Blacks team hotel as I speak, quaking in his boots at the prospect of facing Phil Vickery.' And so on down through the team.

With each name and damning comparison, the nods of approval and positive feeling spread through the squad like wildfire, and chests were filled with national pride as Clive fired us up for the pending encounter. We were getting swept along with this stirring speech. Well, most of us were. By the time Clive reached scrum-half, Jason Leonard had scanned the entire NZ team and leant over to me, whispering in my ear, 'I'll give you a clue Lol, that 6ft 5in nineteen-stone winger who runs the 100m in 10.8 seconds [Jonah Lomu] would f***ing well make it into my team.'

On another occasion, prior to a match against Australia, Clive was talking to the squad about some of the Australian strengths. He had studied the team in depth and was giving his opinion as to how he thought Australia would play.

'Having studied the Aussies, I believe they will run the ball from everywhere, and at every opportunity. They have a lightweight pack and backs with the speed and calibre of Gregan, Latham, Burke, Roff and forwards with the mobility of Kefu, Strauss and Wilson. Whether they are in our half or on their own tryline they are likely to run, run, run. So we need to make sure we pressurise them when they have the ball, and it's critical to get all our first-time tackles in. We need to snuff out their running game before it even gets a chance to get started because, believe me, they are going to run from everywhere.'

At this point, it was like a little cartoon light bulb lit up above Clive's head, and he looked at the squad and said, 'Or . . . they may kick it.'

No shit, Sherlock, that's what I call covering all the bases.

Careful what you wish for

There is no doubt in my mind that Clive's attention to detail played a major role in bringing the World Cup home to England in the winter of 2003. To have been a member of that squad is something that has shaped the rest of my life. But for me, victory in Australia brought even more than a winner's medal and a deeply grounded sense of achievement. It also provided me with pub quiz immortality. Well, that's what I tell my kids anyway. (They keep saying the question is bound to crop up on *The Weakest Link*. Not sure if they are trying to tell me something by picking that particular quiz show.) Anyway, the question for which the correct answer is Lawrence Dallaglio is: Which English player played in every minute of every game in the 2003 World Cup?

It was never an intention of mine to try and play every match, although with hindsight I am proud of the fact. The last of the group games was against Uruguay, which, with all due respect, is not a country which readily springs to mind when discussing the giants of the world game. I fully expected a rest, along with a number of other players, particularly as we had beaten South Africa 25–6 in our previous match to decide who would top the group, thus giving us the supposed 'easier' quarter-final against Wales (how wrong we were!). However, Clive Woodward had different plans. He announced his selection to the press and, when asked about my inclusion, he said I still needed to secure my place in the team. I would have been happier with something like, 'Lawrence needs to get as many games under his belt to ensure he reaches peak fitness during the latter stages of the tournament.' You can see why. And just to make things extra special, I was in a team without the presence of our captain, Martin Johnson, and I was not even asked to fulfil his role (of course I just brushed off the disappoint-ment like the professional I am . . .).

To give you a clue regarding the strength of opposition Uruguay provided, England won the match 111–13. A one-sided affair but as is often the case, the score-line does not give the full picture. Within their side there were a few individuals who knew how to play, notably their full-back, Juan Ramon Menchaca, who had a siege gun boot and could not only kick the ball prolific distances, he could also get incredible height on it. This allowed one of their other decent players, Rodrigo Capo Ortega, the nineteen-stone man of granite who played No. 8, plenty of time to follow up his kicks and cause as much disruption to our defence as possible.

I don't believe it was personal but almost without exception, every towering kick Menchaca made seemed to be directed towards me. Or perhaps it was just that the other English players in the vicinity had been instructed by Clive that I needed the practice and that they should leave me to it. Whatever the reason, time after time the high balls came my way and I caught them, and more often than not the catch coincided with the imminent arrival of Ortega, who flattened me with alarming regularity. On the odd occasions when I was allowed a bit of time to secure the ball before my opposite number's arrival, the opportunity merely gave me the chance to build up some speed before Ortega clattered me. Having said that, I was doing my job, taking the ball, which was recycled and passed to our backs who, I'm thrilled to say, all looked great, showing off their moves, swerves and sidesteps (they made us forwards feel so proud – just what we live for . . .).

The one English back who did not seem to get much ball was Iain Balshaw, and he clearly felt he was missing out. The northern monkey is one of life's real good guys. He likes to have a lot of fun and is infectious with his enthusiasm. He announced himself on the England scene in 2001, gliding through gaps and tearing holes in every defence, which is why he was probably so desperate for the ball in this match, so he could demonstrate his silky skills. Iain ended up winning thirty-five caps for England and was always at the heart and soul of all the parties we had. The fact that he is still playing now is testament to him as an individual and his abilities as a player . . . and is powers of recovery after this match.

Iain had astutely worked out that I was getting a lot of attention from the high ball specialist, so he said to me part-way through the first half, 'Lol, give me the ball, when you take a high kick look for me and give me the ball.' Now 'Balsh' is not a small man but he was one of the English fliers and I knew he would doubtless come into his own during another match. 'Don't be stupid, Balsh,' I said. 'Do yourself a favour and leave the donkey work to me. You don't want a ball covered in ice coupled with that monster from Montevideo smashing you into the dirt.'

Throughout the rest of the first half Balsh kept asking me to give him the ball from the high kicks. I (honourably, I might add) continued to keep it to myself, take one for the team and continue my flourishing relationship with the enormous Uruguayan.

At half-time I'd have thought the management would be reasonably happy. We had a comfortable lead and the only player who looked like getting injured was me, and as my place was not even secure, presumably Clive had someone in mind that was at the very least equal to the task. I was looking forward to a cup of tea and a 'more of the same' speech from the coaching staff. How wrong I was. We actually managed to provoke a bit of a bollocking from them. 'We need to change this and that, we need to tidy up in these areas, we need to be quicker to the breakdown, we need to recycle the ball a lot quicker.' All sorts of suggestions were coming from all coaching quarters. In truth, you can only play against the opposition in front of you, and in terms of preparation, playing Uruguay is not ideal since most of their players were in positions you would never find some of the more traditional rugby playing nations. It was just a game to get through, win the group and move on to the knockout stages.

The second half was similar to the first in all respects; we kept scoring, I kept getting hammered and Balsh constantly pestered me to give him the ball. Eventually, I had a word with Andy Gomarsall, our scrum-half, and told him if the ball came to me from the kick-off I was going to unload it to Balsh, allowing Andy to change his position for the re-start. The ball was duly delivered and this was one of those occasions when I had a little time before the arrival of the juggernaut. I took two paces and passed to Balsh, who in turn took two paces and met the advancing 119kg of prime Uruguayan beef who smashed into him at full tilt.

Following the necessary treatment, Balsh was stretchered from the pitch. As the stretcher passed me, I looked at Balsh, who looked back through very hazy eyes and said, 'Why the f*** did you pass me the ball?!' That's the problem with backs; they never really know what they want.

The squad already had a few niggles and injuries including Josh Lewsey (full-back/wing) and Kyran Bracken (scrum-half). And now Balsh (wing/full-back). Clive needed to call up a player for cover. The obvious choice was Austin Healey, who has been capped by England or the Lions in nearly every position in the backs.

The phone calls were made, the travel arrangements organised and Austin flew out to Australia. The rules of the tournament dictated that no additional players can join a World Cup squad until a player has departed. The players in the squad were being assessed and treated as Austin arrived. He checked into a hotel (different hotel to the team hotel), played a round of golf and was then, much to our amusement, informed that all England players were fit to carry on with the campaign. He then travelled to the airport and flew back to the UK to play for Leicester Tigers against Rotherham. I admire Austin for his efforts; it just shows how things can change in an instant. Had one of the players been unable to continue, Austin would have been welcomed into the squad and would doubtless have made his way into the side, and would probably have played in the World Cup final. As it was, he had a 25,000 mile round trip for a game of golf.

Urbane myths

So that's a taster of the type of stories to follow in this book – ones that I have personally been involved in. But there are others that you might find attributed to me, or to any number of other players. They crop up across bar tables in clubhouses up and down the land. Are they all true? I don't know. But I like to think they are; that they actually happened to someone. Just don't ask me who. Here's a few of my favourites which, purely for the purposes of this book, I've arbitrarily allocated to certain players purely so I can recount the tales.

Happy hour

The game of golf is played by many rugby union players of all levels. Given that professional players have a fair bit of spare time on their hands and are all extremely competitive by nature, there is nothing that many enjoy more than the opportunity to haul out their clubs and play a round. Indeed several rugby players have very respectable handicaps. It is always fascinating when different generations of famous players compete in charity golf days, as the old guard always enjoys showing their successors a thing or two on the course. Following one such benefit day held at the Buckinghamshire Golf Club several years ago, a member of the public witnessed the following conversation.

Standing in the bar after a round were Gavin Hastings, Jason Leonard and an Irish international who, even for the purposes of this story, I am not going to name (that gives you a clue to how big and fierce he is!), and each seemed keen to buy the others a drink. The reason for this show of generosity, of course, was that the bell had just rung to announce 'happy hour'. The deal was that if you bought three drinks, you would receive a fourth one free, and judging by the look on the faces of Gavin, Jason and their Irish friend this was not the happiest hour they had ever spent.

After a couple of sips Gavin looked at the other two and said, 'This is rubbish. Back in Edinburgh in my local, The Welded Wallet, you only need to buy two beers before receiving a free one. Far better than this.'

Jason nodded his head in agreement, 'In my local in Barking, The Cock in Hand, it's very simple. You buy one drink, you get another one free and happy hour lasts for two, I repeat, TWO hours.'

The Irish international then looked at Gavin and Jason and said,

'Now boys, if you really want to experience an Irish style happy hour you need to go to Maxwell Plum's in the middle of Leeson Street, Dublin. When you walk in there during the appointed hour they buy you a beer, then they buy you a second, a third and a fourth. And when you've finished they'll take you out the back and get you laid!'

Jason stared at him with a look of complete disbelief on his face, 'Blimey! That is incredible – did that happen to you?' he asked.

'Well . . . no,' admitted the Irishman. 'But it happened to my sister.'

Picking on the wrong man

This next one I've heard told about Martin Johnson, Jason Leonard, Dean Richards and Gareth Chilcott. I'm going for Gareth.

During the early eighties, Bath were playing Newport at home on the Recreation Ground and three or four minutes into the second half Newport had a line-out. At exactly the moment the Newport hooker was throwing the ball in their prop was delivering one of the finest punches ever seen at the Rec. The punch ended up on Gareth Chilcott's jaw, and he was out for the count, a fine punch when you consider Gareth never left the field of play in his entire career (apart from the six times he was sent off). This particular day was to be no different.

The referee ran over to see what was happening just as Gareth began to stir. Slowly, as his eyes opened, the mist began to clear and he fixed the official with his steeliest stare and said: 'Referee, do not, under any circumstances, send that little twat off.'

The referee then went to have words with the offending player and as he approached, the prop, with a look of resigned fear and terror on his face, rather meekly said, 'I suppose I'm off then, Sir.'

The response was not, I suspect, what he was anticipating. 'Not yet, you're not! But since you've taken the trouble to bring the topic up, knowing Gareth as I do, I guarantee you'll know f*** all about it when you are.'

Matter over mind

I'm attributing this beauty to myself and Wade Dooley in the hope he still considers it a compliment and also due to the fact he lives over 200 miles away.

Many years ago I was in a gym in London and had just completed fifteen minutes drifting on a rowing machine. I was just about to take a break before mounting the bike, with the aim of pedalling fast enough to power the TV screens at the front, when Wade Dooley walked in to the gym. For those of you who have never seen Wade in the flesh, he stands at 6ft 8in tall and weighs in at almost nineteen stone (playing weight). A quite frightening physical specimen, certainly someone you would want on your side and not against you.

It is also fair to say he is not the 'fizziest drink in the fridge'. Rumour has it that on the Lions tour of New Zealand in 1993 he walked into breakfast and ordered bacon, egg and toast, at which point the poor waitress informed him they did not have any bacon. Wade stared at her and said, 'You live in a country with thirty-seven million sheep and you're telling me you've run out of bacon?' It's also been said of Wade that he doesn't know the meaning of the word fear. To be honest there are another thirty thousand other words he doesn't know the meaning of.

But I digress. Wade walked into the gym and for forty-five minutes proceeded to use every single piece of apparatus, shifting herculean poundage. He then moved on to the bars, and for another forty-five minutes he lifted unbelievable weights, culminating in 'arm curls' in front of the mirror.

For ninety minutes I had not taken my eyes of him, and I think he noticed this. He caught sight of me in the mirror, put the bar on the floor and made a beeline in my direction. From his great height he looked down at me, his brow dripping in sweat and his veins pumping, and growled, 'I can bench press 350lb. I can run on the top level of the running machine at a 15 per cent incline for twenty minutes and I can leg press 500lb on each leg. What can you do, old man?'

To be honest I was pretty intimidated. Slowly edging around the granite frame in front of me I congratulated him on his undoubted athletic prowess and replied, 'That's very impressive but, at the risk of appearing a touch arrogant, I'll tell you what I can do . . . I can read.'

Needless to say, I was then gone in a flash. There was no way I was hanging around to feel the full force of his comeback.

Hooligans and gentlemen

This story comes from Martin Bayfield and I think the observation he makes is spot on. Even if the event described didn't actually happen in the game Martin says it did, I can assure you something very similar will have happened on many occasions in many different matches.

Most people will have heard the old adage, 'Football is a game for gentlemen played by hooligans and rugby is a game for hooligans played by gentlemen.'

The sports have often been compared; indeed recent years have seen the media highlight the intimidation of referees by footballers with some pretty shocking scenes, and yet rugby union players seem to accept every decision and just get on with the game. The following story illustrates a major difference between the two sports and how referees deal with similar circumstances.

During the 1998 World Cup finals, England played Argentina in the last sixteen knockout stage. On the pitch that day was a young lad some of you may have heard of, David Beckham. Those that watched the match will remember the brutal assault Beckham perpetrated on the Argentinian midfielder Diego Simeone. I have to say that having watched it from six different camera angles, I firmly believe from one particular angle it looked as though Beckham might possibly have actually *touched* Simeone. We have to assume he did because Simeone crashed to the ground, rolled around in apparent agony; his shirt was untucked, and to this day they have never found his 'Alice' band. Poor lamb.

The referee had no option but to send Beckham off, the game finished in a draw and England (uncharacteristically) lost the subsequent penalty shootout. Inevitably, Beckham was blamed by many supporters and journalists for the major role he played in England's elimination from the tournament and he became the number one public hate figure for a while, suffering torrential abuse for many months to come.

A few days later, on 4 July 1998, the England rugby union team were in Cape Town playing a Test match against the mighty South Africans, having taken part in the 'Tour from Hell' to Australia where they lost by a record margin of 76–0. During a scrum three minutes into the game the two packs broke up and the English hooker Richard Cockerill (man voted most likely to marry outside of his own species) stood up and punched his opposite number James Dalton in the face, causing a nasty cut above his eye. Dalton reacted by catching Cockerill with a superb effort right on the jaw. At this point the referee saw fit to get involved.

He looked sternly at both players, pointed at Dalton and said, 'You!' He then pointed at Cockerill saying, 'And you! Shake hands!' Perfect. Five seconds earlier these players had committed two pieces of 'actual bodily harm' and their punishment? A personal introduction. God I love rugby.

The press the following day called it a minor altercation.

Don't shoot me, I'm only the piano pusher

I hope these few stories have given you a flavour of just how diverse the characters in rugby are and yet how much they all have in common – a love of the game and its traditions, and a sense that what happens on the pitch is not the only thing that keeps the spirit of the sport alive.

So now it's time to hand over to a few of those characters and let them tell you their favourite rugby stories. But before I do, I'll take a moment or two to introduce the diametrically opposite breeds that make up a rugby team: the piano pushers (fat boys) and the piano players (girls).

Historically, the forwards were bigger and stronger, the backs quicker and more nimble. As a consequence any argument between these two groups of gentlemen, when reduced to its base level (a fight), was always going to see the fat boys prevail. However, with the arrival of the devastating All Black winger Jonah Lomu in the early nineties, together with the beginning of professionalism on 26 August 1995, when the IRB declared rugby union an 'open' game, things changed.

Jonah proved to the world that even if you are 6ft 5in tall and weigh somewhere in the region of nineteen stone there is a place for you in the back line. That was news to us all. He ran around, and indeed through, opposition backs at will, and caused equal problems for the forwards, who no longer had the comfort of stopping 'big guys' running at a slow pace from close quarters. Believe me, I am talking from personal experience.

Professionalism enabled players to train full-time. A natural consequence was not only a greater level of fitness, but also increased bulk. I do not have any statistics to hand but I'm certain that within just one generation, backs became on average at least two stone heavier. I noticed earlier in the year that Matt Banahan from Bath made his full

England debut in a comfortable win over Argentina at Old Trafford, where he also scored a try and was named man of the match. Matt is 6ft 7in and according to the font of all knowledge – Wikipedia – weighs 18st 1lb. His position? Winger. Matt is by no means alone. There are numerous 'piano players' with similar dimensions participating in rugby at a senior level. The fights are no longer the foregone conclusion of years gone by.

One conversation which epitomises the difference between the fat boys and the girls was relayed to me by David Trick (a girl who, like Matt, used to play on the wing for Bath). David was considered a decent size for a winger in his day, 6ft and 13st 7lb. Fifteen years on from retirement he is now 5ft 11in, and weighs a healthy 14st 10lb.

He was sitting next to Gareth Chilcott on the team bus, travelling to a fixture, when the following conversation took place. Gareth was front row through and through, playing at both tight-head and loose-head prop during his illustrious career. David was thinking about the possible outcome if the person playing opposite him was a better player than he was. He said to Gareth, 'Hypothetically speaking,' to which Gareth replied, 'What do you mean hypertheticlee speaking?'

David started again.

'I was just thinking about the possibility of the player playing opposite being better than me. I know it will never happen, but if it did, what's the worst thing that can happen to me? I can only imagine it would be nothing more than personal embarrassment, it would definitely not cause me any physical pain. If, however, the player opposite you was better than you, I KNOW IT WOULD NEVER HAPPEN, but if he was, you would have nothing but eighty minutes of complete agony to look forward to as he forced your head up your backside during every scrum. How on earth would you cope with a situation like that?'

Gareth just looked at Tricky with absolute disbelief and said, 'The mere fact you have asked that question just shows me exactly why you are a f***ing back, you f***ing girl!'

They continued to sit next to each other in total silence, both equally happy they played in their respective positions.

One thing is certain; one group cannot do without the other. They are bound together, two essential ingredients that constitute a team. Neither breed will ever understand the enjoyment the other derives from the sport, but both know that at some stage in a game a forward or a back will make a contribution that has a major impact on the outcome of a match, whether it's a bit of magic from a centre as he beats his man, glides past the first line of defence and gives a scoring pass to his full-back who he knows will be 'on his shoulder', or a shuddering tackle from a second row as he drives an opposition prop up and back, depositing him in a crumpled heap on the floor.

The banter will continue for ever, and secretly, so will the respect.

PART ONE

TALES FROM THE FORWARDS

I'm often asked what I think the biggest difference between forwards and backs is. Easy answer. Leave aside for a moment raw power, nerves of steel, match-winning guts and determination, quick wits (sorry, that was meant to go into the next introduction), a willingness to lay your body on the line for the team – yes, leave them all aside.

The biggest difference in my view is that the forwards throw more punches. Oh, and I suppose we're more likely to open our mouths when we should keep them tightly shut. And there is that tendency to, er... lose our... er... thread in conversation more than the other lot (I wonder, is that down to that first difference I mentioned?). But most of all, there is the one thing forwards would never, ever do and that is strike a pose in front of a mirror. I think the following stories illustrate my point.

But before I proceed, I must make special mention of the front row union. Of all the characters within the forwards, they are the most endearing yet simultaneously frustrating group of men. At the genesis of this book I made a fatal mistake when attempting to gather stories from this unique breed – I wrote them letters. Reading? What was I thinking?

No doubt many of those requests are still in colouring-in trays up and down the land. So to save them embarrassment and to give the front row the recognition they deserve, I've also included some particular gems about a couple of men who play their rugby at the coalface. To be fair, I must admit that I have heard a few shocking tales showing that some members of the front row do actually possess quick-witted brains. Fran Cotton, a prop himself, who has given so much to rugby as a player (thirty-one caps for England and seven Lions Tests), as a manager (of the successful 1997 Lions tour to South Africa) and as an administrator (RFU council member), told me a story about Phil O'Callaghan, who played for Dolphin, Munster and Ireland in the seventies. During a scrum in an England v Ireland fixture at Twickenham, the referee blew to give a penalty against Ireland when England was putting in the ball. 'Penalty against Ireland. You're boring,' said the ref as he tapped the Ireland tight-head O'Callaghan on the shoulder. 'Ah Jesus, ref, you're not too f***ing interesting yourself!' retorted an indignant O'Callaghan.

Coppers and bag snatchers

During fourteen seasons as a senior player and several more prior to that, participating at various age group levels, I have seen many punches thrown and received. But perhaps none as devastating as the punch thrown by the young Argentinian prop forward Federico 'Freddie' Mendez, who I believe was eighteen years of age in 1990 when the incident occurred.

Freddie went on to have a long and distinguished playing career, representing Argentina in no fewer than four World Cups, and he also played for Natal Sharks, Bath, Northampton Saints and Bordeaux-Begles in a globetrotting career that saw his eventual return to his beloved Mendoza RC where he now coaches.

It was, however, in his first game at Twickenham that Freddie announced himself to the international stage with one of the most spectacular punches thrown in rugby history. England were playing Argentina on 3 November 1990 at Twickenham, the result a resounding 51–0 victory to the home side. In fairness, Argentina were not the force in world rugby back then that they have become today. It was a stroll in the park for the England team, with the exception of Paul Ackford – that's *Police Inspector* Paul Ackford at the time, although he has now been reduced in rank to chief rugby correspondent for the *Sunday Telegraph*.

There has been much speculation as to the event which caused Freddie Mendez to lash out as he did on that day. The general consensus is that his head was mistaken for a trampoline by a member of the opposing front row – Jeff Probyn. In defence of the Wasps prop, he only placed his size tens on Mendez's head when the Argentinian apparently grabbed his testicles, for what is known in the trade as some friendly 'bag snatching'. What became clear as this melee broke out was that Mendez got up thinking of only one thing: retribution.

Looking to seek and destroy, Big Freddie jumped to his feet and spotted his unassuming target, Paul Ackford, who incidentally had not been anywhere near the Argentine's head and, more alarmingly, was looking in the opposite direction when Freddie stretched himself up and delivered a knockout blow. It was a punch which started off in Southend, gained speed through Mile End and reached terminal velocity in Bourne End, just before connecting with the chin of the totally unaware England second row. Paul is 6ft 6in tall and weighed in the region of seventeen stone, a sizeable man. For a split second, Inspector Ackford stood rigid, before crumping in a heap on the ground.

Seeing this heinous atrocity, the touch judge intervened and Freddie was given his marching orders. Ackford received immediate treatment as several members of the England team wandered over to see if he was still alive. Upstairs, Nigel Starmer-Smith and his co-commentator Bill Beamount replayed the incident to try and identify how events had unfolded while Ackers still lay unconscious on the pitch.

As they returned to real time, Wade Dooley – that's *Police Constable* Wade Dooley – walked into camera shot to observe the damage. Beaumont, himself a former second row, looked at the TV monitor in front of him and told the nation what a great act of brotherly compassion they were all witnessing. As well as being team-mates, Dooley and Ackford were also both in the police force – what a wonderful sight it was to see Police Constable Dooley kneeling down and checking on the well-being of his colleague Police Inspector Ackford. The care and concern being shown by one policeman to another was clear for all at home to see, Bill Beaumont insightfully pointed out.

But those on the pitch within earshot know the truth. As Wade walked into camera shot he leant towards Ackers and said, 'You can tell which f***ing copper works behind a desk!'

Later, at a disciplinary tribunal, Federico Mendez admitted his part in the incident – difficult to deny when BBC cameras caught it from five different angles. However, he did say it was a case of mistaken identity: 'I had intended to punch the England prop Jeff Probyn who was in the process of stamping on my bollocks!'

No mean City

When the game turned professional, one of my first England coaches, Dick Best (it was Dick who gave me one of my first breaks in rugby when he came to a Wasps training session and on the back of that picked me for the England 7s team in 1993) found himself catapulted into the role of director of rugby at Harlequins, which brought with it the whole new ball game of signings, transfers and sponsorship deals.

Across the rugby board, it was the London clubs who faced some of the toughest challenges in the new era as they had to recruit players to come and 'work' in London, with its exorbitant cost of living, and then pay them suitable wages to make them competitive with the wage levels of the other clubs around the country, such as Newcastle.

Richmond had been purchased lock, stock and barrel by Ashley Levett, a copper trader who resided in Monaco and bought in household international names such as Ben Clarke, Scott Quinnell and Alan Bateman in an attempt to gain promotion to the top league. Saracens was purchased by property magnate Nigel Wray who remains chairman to this day and is very highly regarded. Wray bought in a host of his very own 'Galacticos' from then world record points holder Michael Lynagh, to the 1995 RWC winning South African captain François Pienaar, and then the pièce de résistance, perhaps the greatest of centre three-quarters to have ever graced the game, Philippe Sella. Wasps themselves were purchased by Chrysalis Records chairman Chris Wright, as part of a joint deal with Queens Park Rangers.

But it was Harlequins, the aristocrats of English rugby, who were most up against it. They already had a successful recruitment conveyor belt whereby the likes of Winterbottom, Skinner, Leonard, Moore and Carling amongst others had all converged in the club in the early nineties, but the club was also famed for their connection with the 'Square Mile' and boasted a list of aristocrats, bankers and brokers amongst their biggest supporters.

Now two of the players who were first team regulars at Quins around that time were Alex Snow and Jim Staples. Snow, a 6ft 7in second row whose baby-faced looks belied a steely interior and a world-class line-out technique, was an Old Harrovian who had come down to London to start what was to become a stellar banking career in the City. At the other end of the team, if not the social continuum as he also had a successful City career, was full-back Jim Staples, born in Bermondsey, formerly of London Irish and a fully fledged Ireland international. The advent of professional rugby was set to cause these two high fliers serious issues about their career plans.

Best was adamant that he wanted the entire squad to go full-time, so that he could get the best out of his players and challenge for honours in the domestic league. This meant that Best had one-on-one meetings with every member of his squad to thrash out salaries that would deliver his full-time goals. Most of these meetings had gone relatively smoothly and according to plan. However Best knew that he was going to struggle to convince the bankers of the merits of a career as a professional rugby player.

This became all too clear when he encountered a belligerent Snow for the first time. Best was a shrewd, straight-talking operator, but he knew how to win people over and he promptly set about laying out to Snow – a key member of his squad – his vision to make Harlequins a powerhouse in Europe, indicating that Alex was at the heart of that ambition. Intrigued, Snowy began to warm to this idea and the ladling of international honours as the topping of Besty's all-consuming vision was starting to bring the Old Harrovian round.

At the crucial moment Best sensed the kill was imminent and decided to strike the fateful blow. Without any further hesitation, he produced the full-time contract that he wanted Alex to sign. Being a fine product of a capitalist environment Snow quickly thumbed through the first few pages and got to the business end of the contract: the offer.

After what seemed ages considering what was written in front of him, Snow looked up and fixed his director of rugby firmly in the eye *mano a mano.* 'Thirty-five grand a year?! Richard dear boy, that would barely cover my dry cleaning bill!'

The City 1 – Harlequins 0.

A few days later Best had come to terms with the fact that full-time was definitely *not* the way for these City types and he completed a tactical *volte face* when he met up with Staples to thrash out the terms of Jim's contract. Anyone who encountered Jim knows that he is a fearless character, rarely flustered, and this showed in a number of outstanding performances for club(s) and country. He won twenty-six caps for Ireland and would have won many more were it not for a couple of horrific injuries he sustained during his career.

Having made the move to Harlequins, Staples was only too aware of Best's reputation as a no-nonsense negotiator who didn't suffer fools, and was genuinely concerned about the confrontational negotiation that lay ahead. On the way to the ground to meet Besty, Jim was psyching himself up, so anxious was he to get in the right frame of mind. He and Best had already agreed on the phone that he would only settle for a part-time contract.

Best was stuck in a meeting when Jim got to his office, and Jim had already decided on the number that would work for him and he wasn't prepared to take a penny less. As he waited nervously outside the office Jim was pacing up and down repeating the mantra over and over again. 'Twenty grand a year, Jim, twenty grand a year. Do NOT accept any-thing else. You are worth every penny. You have come here with a big reputation. Twenty grand, TWENTY GRAND A YEAR!'

At the very height of his focus and intensity, Besty's door opened and Jim was beckoned in. After exchanging pleasantries Besty decided there was no point hanging about and got straight down to business. 'Jim, we're not too happy with you going part-time, but we reluctantly accept that you have a successful career outside of rugby. As a result we can only offer you forty grand a year.'

On hearing those words and realising he'd just got a 100 per cent pay rise, Jim leapt out of his chair, thrust out his hand and said, 'Thanks Dick, that'll do for me!'

The City 2 – Harlequins 0.

The bus stops here

Jason Leonard and I have always got on well together; we share a similar philosophy towards the game of rugby, life in general and most things in between.

I remember a conversation I had with Jason during the early stages of my involvement with the England squad. It was in the amateur era and he had been around for a while (even then) and witnessed several regimes. From the 'outside', the England set-up appeared to have become a lot more professional (with a small p) in its approach to training and matches. I asked Jason if he could identify when the change had taken place from the shit-or-bust days to the more intensive approach which had been adopted for a couple of seasons by then.

He said, 'Not only can I tell you when it occurred but if I put my thinking cap on I could probably give you the date.' He then proceeded to tell me a story which, in his opinion, identified the moment the approach to English rugby changed for ever.

It was during the World Cup in 1991 and the England squad had taken part in quite possibly the worst training session ever. Every ball that could be dropped had been dropped. Players were running into each other during the rehearsal of moves. It was nothing short of a complete shambles. The group stages had been completed and England were preparing for the quarter-final in Paris against France. When they returned to their hotel, an urgent team meeting was hastily arranged by the management.

Geoff Cooke held the title of team manager, which is somewhat misleading as he was coach at the time. He had sole responsibility for the style of play, indeed all rugby-related matters, and he was not happy! A dour Yorkshireman, he had a terrible scowl across his face when he stood up in front of the squad and launched into them, holding nothing back. He let them know exactly what he expected and left everyone in no doubt the performance he had just witnessed was not good enough. The severity of his speech came as a shock to everyone. A bollocking was in order, sure, but this was a different league. Geoff was, and still is, a calm man with a measured approach. His absolute fury was something new to the team, but it left them knowing they really needed to concentrate and tune in if they were to progress any further in the tournament.

Following Geoff, the captain of the team, Will Carling, stood up and gave everyone more of the same. Slightly trickier for Will because he had taken part in, indeed had contributed to, the crap session that they had just finished. However, he did a great job of removing himself from 'the boys' and telling it as it was. Everyone needed to switch on and pay more attention to the rugby than to the peripheral activities that go hand in hand with being an international rugby player. The room remained silent when Will finally sat down, each player mulling over how they could improve their own team performance and approach.

It therefore came as a surprise when Geoff took to the floor again and spelled out a few more home truths, as if they had not heard enough already. He finished by saying, 'If anyone gets on the Judge's bus tonight . . .'

I will finish that sentence in a moment, but first I should explain that the 'Judge's bus' was something organised almost daily by the legendary Wasps prop forward Paul Rendall (aka 'the Judge'). It would wait at a pre-appointed time at the end of the drive leading to the hotel and take a number of the squad to The Sun at Richmond, where they would be deposited for a few quiet beers, enabling them to foster good relations with members of the public, and then pick them up a couple of hours later and return the crew to the hotel. These days it's called a PR campaign.

The players all thought, naively, that their little jaunts to The Sun were a secret. So it came as a shock when Geoff said (and here I pick up the sentence again), 'If anyone gets on the Judge's bus tonight, those people will effectively leave the campaign forthwith.'

There was something approaching shock in the room at Geoff's statement, and the silence endured until it was eventually broken by a lone voice from the back of the room.

'What time does the bus leave, Judge?'

Everyone turned, tried to stifle their laughter and looked in amazement at Dean Richards, who had just uttered the sentence.

Dean was not actually removed from the squad but he was replaced by Mickey Skinner for the remaining matches, with Mike Teague moving to No. 8. The first of these matches was, as I mentioned, against France in Paris the following Saturday. It was during this match Mickey put in one of the most impressive tackles I have ever seen, on the French back-row forward Marc Cecillon. Mickey hit him so hard even the Frenchman's teeth rattled. It was following that tackle he picked up the nickname 'Munch'.

High-performance training

In the run-up to the 1995 Rugby World Cup, the England team and management were looking at a number of ways to professionalise the approach and attempt to go one better than in 1991 at Twickenham when Australia won the final 12–6.

One of the areas targeted was the need to speed up the players' adjustment to the South African climate and altitude. The result: specially created training suits, complete with hoods and visors, designed to raise the core body temperature by just one degree, which would, apparently, make a significant difference to reaching the competition in peak condition. Picture if you can the scenes at the England training ground at Marlow RFC when the squad were handed boiler suits. Damian Hopley describes the boys as looking like misfits from a *Star Wars* convention as they tried on the poor-man's Darth Vader outfits. I understand that Jason Leonard sold his to his local Domino's Pizza delivery boy for the winter, so at least some practical use came from them.

Fast forward several weeks and the boys arrive in Durban, the base for the pool stages. Their beach front hotel beckons and they have twenty minutes to drop off their gear and meet downstairs, ready for a quick training session.

Keen to make a good impression, they all jogged round the corner to a training field. The facilities were adequate and certainly put the squad in a relaxed frame of mind as the waves came crashing in on the beach a couple of hundred yards away. The locals were strolling past in their board shorts and bikinis, enjoying the sight of twenty-six Englishmen limbering up. Physio Kevin Murphy (aka 'Smurf') was in charge of warm-ups – no extensive back-room staff here. In fact Smurf probably worked harder than anyone on the management team, and rightly enjoyed tremendous respect. He set off on the first lap of the pitch, and whilst it was fairly hot, it wouldn't have been any worse than the conditions most of them had encountered on previous tours.

Having completed the first lap, the boys partnered up and did some stretching exercises to help loosen up; all except Victor Ubogu, who could be seen struggling at least fifty yards behind everyone else. That didn't bode well for the man who dubbed himself 'Pop! Pop!' on account of the noise champagne bottles make when opened. Make no mistake, Victor was cut from a very different cloth to most props. A part owner of a trendy bar on the New Kings Road named Shoeless Joe's and renamed 'Clueless Vic's' by his England team-mates, Victor definitely liked the finer things in life.

Hamstrings stretched, they all set off on their second lap and to everyone's delight Victor seemed to be lagging further and further behind. Sweat was streaming out of every pore, and he was blowing like a wounded buffalo as he struggled with the mild heat. Some cynics wondered if he had been neglecting training in his suit in a show of defiance. As the rest of the boys began more stretches, Victor made it to the end of his second lap and joined the squad, only to exclaim in between breathless gulps of water, 'Jesus Christ! This altitude training is killing me!'

Fact – Durban is eight metres above sea level.

He will never live that one down. Ever.

Fishing for the right line

The British and Irish Lions tour in 1997 was the first in the professional era, and had generated a lot of media interest as those of us fortunate enough to be selected to represent the four home countries were travelling out to South Africa to play against the reigning world champions in their own backyard.

Prior to departure we had a week of training at Oaklands Park Hotel in Weybridge, Surrey. From a physical point of view it was brutal, as we experienced the training methods of the coach, Jim Telfer, some of us for the first time, and by the end of that week we were fully aware of the high standards expected from all of us in the weeks to come.

There was, however, one ray of sunshine on the horizon when our tour manager, Fran Cotton, invited the squad for a beer on his last night prior to departure. He was booked to fly out twenty-four hours ahead of the team to check on final preparations and make our arrival as smooth as possible. Fran's experience of what it took to win in 1974 on 'The Invincibles' tour of South Africa (when the Lions won twenty-one of their twenty-two matches — the final Test being drawn 13–13 under highly controversial circumstances, with the home referee disallowing what is seen by many as a blatant try by Irish flanker Fergus Slattery in the last minute) was a crucial ingredient in helping us all understand the size of the task that lay ahead. We all felt the manager's invitation for a beer was well deserved and we accepted with glee.

Standing at the bar and ordering the drinks, Fran seemed very much at home. I have a vivid memory of him holding his pint, which looked no bigger than a sherry glass in his massive hand, and watching in amazement as the liquid disappeared in one go, before most of us had even taken a sip. 'Right lads,' he said, 'who needs another?' Let me just say it was a great night and helped to break the ice amongst all the boys.

We flew into Johannesburg a day later and then on to Durban where we were deposited in one of the best hotels in the area, the Beverly Hills at Umhlanga Rocks. Shortly after our arrival a team meeting was called, and sitting behind a table in front of all the boys was Fran, who had clearly spent all of the previous day either lying by the swimming pool, or out on a boat without any sun cream on to protect himself.

Just prior to the start of the meeting one of the lads exclaimed, 'Bloody hell! Fran looks like a massive salmon!', which caused a ripple of laughter as players realised the pinpoint accuracy of the description. Fran then called the room to order and, eyeing each and every one of us, he delivered the immortal first line of his prepared speech which was to set the tone for the rest of the tour.

'Right lads, this is not going to be a f***ing fishing trip or a holiday.' There were players chewing on shirt sleeves as we tried to contain our laughter – it may not be a f***ing fishing trip for us, but it clearly had been for Fran.

We recovered and were soon hooked into what Fran had to say. His well prepared speech contained motivation without going over the top. He knew even more rousing words would be required as the trip progressed, so there was no point in peaking too early. Less was more, and Fran was getting this address spot on – that was until he reached the part about Napoleon.

Fran held everyone's attention. Most impressive of all, he had not looked at his notes once. It was clear he had thought this through and believed in everything he was relaying to us as he reached his climactic finale.

'As Napoleon once famously said . . .' At this moment Fran left a pause for dramatic effect, and then repeated, 'As Napoleon once famously said . . .' The pause was now beginning to feel uncomfortable with most of us racking our brains for relevant Napoleonic quotes. (Well, I say most of us but truth be told, that didn't include many of the assembled forwards.) After the longest of gaps, a look of frustration appeared on Fran's face as he scrambled through his notes and said, 'What the f*** did that little French git famously say?!'

The boys completely cracked up as he tried to find the not quite so famous quote from the commander of the French army amongst his copious sheets of paper.

Mind you, whatever Napoleon did or didn't say, Fran's speech had the desired effect in the end. We went on to win that tour triumphantly. The little Frenchman would have approved.

Reflected glory

During that Lions trip to South Africa, Doddie Weir, the giant Newcastle and Scotland second-row forward, suffered a horrific injury to the medial ligament in his right knee while playing for the British and Irish Lions against Mpumalanga Province. It was a massive blow that this very popular player's tour was over and a replacement had to be called for. The management had a meeting and decided the Bath and England second row Nigel Redman was the man for the job. Nigel has been known by all players of his generation as 'Ollie'. Why? I don't know, perhaps something to do with a vague likeness to the famous Hollywood actor Oliver Hardy?

At the time of the injury to Doddie Weir, Ollie was on tour with England in Argentina under the guidance of Jack Rowell, who was Ollie's former coach at Bath during the height of the club's success. For those of you who have never met Jack, he is a man with a sharp mind and even sharper tongue. His acerbic wit is famed throughout the rugby world.

When Jack received the call from Fran Cotton informing him that Nigel was required by the Lions in South Africa, one assumes he was happy for the good fortune the news would bring to Ollie, and at the same time disappointed to be losing a key player from his squad.

This is how Ollie told it to me.

'We had returned to our hotel in Buenos Aires from a training session, and during lunch I noticed Jack was on the phone. He seemed a little perturbed, and from time to time I heard the names of various second-row forwards being mentioned. I moved closer to Jack to try and pick up more information. I gained nothing, other than the names of yet more players who played second row.

'When the call ended, Jack looked a little disappointed and continued to eat his meal. About an hour after lunch I received a call from him asking me to come to his room. As I entered, Jack was seated in the only chair and I perched on the edge of his bed. He thanked me for coming and asked me how I thought the tour was going. We were unbeaten at the time and our performances had been promising, we were looking good to win both of the forthcoming Test matches and I expressed this opinion to Jack.

' "How do you think your own form has been?" he enquired.

'At this point I started to get worried; was it possible to send a player home if his form did not warrant a place in the team? Why had he been talking about other second-row players on the phone? Was he going to replace me?

' "I think I have been playing well Jack," I countered. "I'm winning all my own ball in the line-outs and definitely making inroads into the opposition ball. Our scrum has been solid all tour and I think my contribution around the pitch has been excellent."

' "Well, it appears you're not the only person with an inflated opinion of yourself. Fran Cotton has just been on the phone and informed me he would like you to fly to South Africa and join the British and Irish Lions."

'I was absolutely stunned. I started my career with Bath during the 1983–4 season and thirteen years later, out of the blue, I was going to become a British and Irish Lion, the highest honour in the game. After several moments of silence I looked at Jack and said, "I don't believe it!"

' "Neither do I!" replied Jack

'I am sure he was referring to the disruption my departure would cause his England team . . .'

Ollie did fly out to South Africa and became a Lion, captaining the side on two occasions during the midweek matches. Wearing that famous jersey means a lot to any rugby player who has been privileged enough to pull it on. Ollie was no exception. The first thing he did when he got to his hotel room in South Africa was to phone his wife to tell her the great news. He gave her a brief rundown of the events of the last eighteen hours or so and then uttered these fateful words. He claims he couldn't help himself. 'Darling, promise you won't tell anyone, but I'm sitting on the edge of my bed in my room, looking at my reflection in the mirror and I'm wearing all my Lions kit and it's brilliant!'

Mmm. Ollie, are you sure you weren't meant to be a back?

BUSTED TEAM-TALK
BILL BEAUMONT

'A good Lancashire lad, Bill is an absolute legend of English rugby with thirty-four caps from 1975 to 1982. Probably his greatest moment was captaining the England team of 1980, winning the first Grand Slam in twenty-three years. He played for Fylde Rugby Club his whole career and he took part in two Lions tours, in 1977 and 1980. Bill skippered England at a time when they struggled to win games, though he was always a very inspiring captain and led the North of England to victory over the All Blacks in 1979. He retired from rugby in 1982 because of injury and I remember very fondly when he became captain of *Question of Sport*. I went on the show for the first time and Bill was captain of one team and Ian 'Beefy' Botham was captain of the other. Bill was always very reassuring but was keen that I get my rugby questions correct. He has since worked with the IRB as England's representative. Loved all over the world in our sport, his name and face become synonymous with success in English rugby.'

Most readers of a certain age will know the name Erica Roe. For those who don't, or are too young, in 1982 Erica became the first streaker at Twickenham. It happened during an England v Australia international, on my watch as England captain.

I would guess there are two things related to that match you won't remember, and there's certainly one thing you couldn't possibly know. How sad that so many people can name Erica Roe and no one can remember her friend, who took to the pitch topless at the same time. The friend was less well endowed than Erica, and slipped from memory even before the final whistle. Her name? Sarah Bennett. The second thing that has been long forgotten, lost in the mists of time, is that England won the match 15–11. And as for the third thing, that was something only the England team was party to at the time.

Rugby union rivalry between England and Australia started on 9 January 1909 at the Rectory Field, Blackheath (Australia won 9–3). Seventy-three years later, on 2 January 1982 at Twickenham, little had changed apart from a try being worth four points instead of three. The kit was remarkably similar; the temperature was close to freezing; and the game had a 2 p.m. kick-off due to the lack of floodlights.

Half-time was still spent out on the pitch. We didn't have the luxury of warming ourselves up in the changing room with a cup of tea. We stood there enjoying a slice of orange brought to the players by 'Scowling Ken'. Ken was principally in charge of the dressing room (where he was reluctant to give you even a new pair of socks!) with the added responsibility of the half-time refreshment and had perfected the art of cutting a single orange into fifteen segments.

Not only did we win the match, we were also leading at half-time, which was my moment to get the team together and calmly issue instructions for the second half. Luckily, half-time was no more than a two-minute interval, and even I could hold the attention of my team-mates for that length of time, or so I thought.

I was in full flow, emphasising all the things going well and identifying a couple of areas where we needed to tighten up a little. What perturbed me was the simple fact that not one player was looking at me, they were all looking in my direction but seemed preoccupied with something going on over my shoulder.

In perfect English I demanded to know, 'What the f*** is going on?' Even these stern words failed to gain me any recognition, with one exception, our scrum-half Steve Smith. Smithy still didn't look me in the eye but at least he was engaging with me, unlike the rest of them. 'Hey Skuttle [a nickname he had bestowed on me after watching Benny Hill one night and noticing I bore a resemblance to one of his characters – the one with the thick glasses, a strange left-handed salute and a big backside!], someone's on the pitch taking the piss out of you.'

I refused to turn around, and said, 'What the f*** are you talking about?'

'I'm not sure how to say this, Skuttle, but there's some bloke on the pitch running around with your arse on his chest,' replied Smithy.

The entire team collapsed into fits of laughter as I turned to see Erica Roe running towards me being chased by several stewards in fluorescent yellow jackets.

End of team-talk.

BAYFIELD OF THE YARD
MARTIN BAYFIELD

'Well you can't miss him, really. Martin is just a legend of the game. I was trying to explain to my children that he is now actually Hagrid from Harry Potter. He hasn't got a Scottish accent and his name is not Robbie Coltrane but he is actually Hagrid! At least, he is for the scenes when Hagrid's in the distance. Baffs was a fantastic player for Northampton and for England, winning thirty-one caps, and he was very unfortunate to have to retire prematurely due to a serious neck injury. He might not have scored any points for his country (sorry to mention that, Baffs), but he certainly played his part in many famous England victories. He is one of the funniest guys, on and off the field, you could ever meet. I'll never forget the time when, unfortunately, he was one of five England players to be given the bullet following one particular match. At Marlow, after the announcement of the England team selection for the next match, he was surrounded by hacks, microphones in hand, all desperate to question him and hanging on his every word. "Martin, what does it feel like to be omitted from the England team against France next week?" asked one journo. And Baffs replied, "Well, me being dropped and Take That breaking up on the same day has all been too much to take, really." Spot on.'

The force's sweetheart

There are many and varied ways a rugby player can embarrass himself on the field of play. I have contributed personally to the amusement of team-mates, opponents or spectators (occasionally the entire ensemble), and I have also witnessed the great and the good slip up on 'The Webb Ellis Banana Skin'. Watching the legendary Buck Shelford launch himself from the base of the scrum and dive triumphantly over the 'tryline' only to discover it was in fact the five metre line is one brief example.

Fortunately, though, one unforgettable moment in my life has ensured that, no matter what nonsense I have managed to get up to on the field of play, I can comfortably shrug my shoulders and proclaim, 'I've had worse.'

It happened during the wondrously shambolic days of amateur rugby and in my capacity as PC 546 of the Bedfordshire Constabulary. I was assisting in the early morning raid on the house of one of Luton's many undesirables. Full of excitement at the thought of actually doing some police work, I made my way with several of my colleagues to Luton's Latin Quarter (only joking) and took up position outside the plywood and bottle-glass front door of the aforementioned suspect – a man believed to be involved in burglary and the supply of drugs. He was also homosexual, which is relevant to this story.

An almost undetectable utterance of 'Police, open up!' was followed by the splintering of the door as a well-placed size fourteen was hoofed somewhere near the flimsy Yale lock. As we bundled into a living room that would have made Kim and Aggie retch, we split into two search teams. I remained downstairs with some other officers while the supervising sergeant and his motley crew headed upstairs.

For a while it seemed to be a normal police search. Evidence was sought and occasionally found, private photos were rifled through and the kettle was put to use in double quick time. As the morning meandered towards a dull but satisfactory conclusion, my sergeant barged his way down the stairs and my benchmark for any future embarrassment was set monumentally high.

The first thing I noticed was that he had tears in his eyes. 'Good God!' I thought. 'What on earth have they found upstairs to make this granite-hard copper cry?' Even as I thought this, it became apparent that he was crying from laughter, and he grabbed me by the wrist and launched himself back up the stairs, giggling like a naughty schoolboy.

As we headed north two officers passed us heading south, their hands over their mouths, tears also pouring liberally from their eyes. I just caught the word 'brilliant' escaping from their mouths as they crashed back through the front door and out into the street.

Once in the suspect's bedroom, all hell broke loose. The final three remaining officers dissolved into fits of laughter as I entered the room and my sergeant now gave up all pretence of any self-control and fell to his knees, sobbing. The miscreant remained impassive throughout, hands handcuffed at the waist but with an uncomfortable twinkle in his eye. A quick glance out of the window revealed the previous two coppers now rolling around on the grass outside, almost incontinent with laughter.

It was then, as my gaze returned to the confines of the bedroom that it all became agonisingly clear. As my startled eyes established focus on the damning evidence, I realised that while I was, for that moment and indeed many weeks to come, the butt of a thousand crude and cruel police jibes, I was in fact for ever protected against any further embarrassment. For, you see, above the man's filthy, stained bed was a poster – of me resplendent in my England kit! I rest my case.

The afterlife

With that little classic reverberating around the station locker room for years to come, a return to the force was never going to be an option when I had to retire from rugby. But what was I going to do? How was I going to survive the 'afterlife'?

I'll never forget the look on Keith Barwell's face when I uttered the ridiculous statement, 'I'm going into the movies!' The Northampton Saints chairman, a great supporter of the game and the heartbeat of the rejuvenated East Midlands club, looked at me as if I was a gang of teddy boys.

Retirement had come a few years earlier for me and I was in that awkward position of still working at the club where I had played for eight seasons. While I grew more rotund in my coaching tracksuit, my former colleagues went about their business preparing for the next big game. I didn't like the feeling of not being involved and I knew that it was time to move on. But, 'Move on to what?' was the big question.

A fortuitous meeting with a 'suit' from the film fraternity gave me a new focus and a way out. I had absolutely no idea what I was letting myself in for but, with Keith's blessing, I was off to Hollywood (okay, it was actually Watford) and life as Robbie Coltrane's stunt body double in the Harry Potter films.

Now, as you might expect, life as Coltrane's arse does not require a great deal of talking. So, while I was having, and continue to have, a fantastic time, I'm afraid I fell into the classic trap of believing my own press and, as ashamed as I am to admit it, I started to nurture ideas well above my station – I wanted a speaking part. With a theatrical agent now in tow (daahhling!) equipped with the ludicrous brief of finding me a leading role, I sat back and waited for the big offers to kick my door down. I dread to think what the Franklins Gardens faithful would have made of all this carry on.

As us luvvies in the film game say, 'things went very quiet' and my door remained intact for many months, years in fact, until the spring of 2005 – 2005! A remarkable year indeed. At the risk of ruining the surprise, my acting career mirrored the achievements of that year's Lions tour to New Zealand – promising much while delivering abject embarrassment, on an Olympic scale.

One bright morning a wheezing postman handed me a surprisingly large package. A note slipped from the ripped manila and I scanned the brief instructions written thereon. The package contained the script of a new film and in two days' time I was to head off to London to read for the part of 'William'.

Read! That implies words! Words! That implies dialogue! This could be it, my big moment. I rushed inside, poured myself a G&T, adjusted my cravat and crushed velvet smoking jacket and settled into my wing-backed chair. For the briefest of moments, as I held the script – two hundred pages of potential Oscar glory – in my trembling, sweaty hands, I imagined Robert de Niro or Al Pacino doing something very similar in their Beverly Hills mansions and momentarily we were joined in an acting fraternity that spanned the thousands of miles and yawning gulf in talent that separated us.

I savoured every syllable, devouring every page as I made my way through this classic low-budget British comedy horror. It became apparent very early on that 'William' played very little part in the opening scenes of the film – none in fact. To be honest, he was glaringly absent through the middle of the film as well. Just as I was beginning to lose faith, 'William' finally made his appearance, on page 198 of this 200-page epic.

'*Enter William – a tall* [oh yes], *powerful* [on a good day] *DEAF MUTE*'!

Ouch! Oh well, as Lao Tzu, the Chinese Taoist philosopher, once famously said: 'The journey of a thousand miles begins with a single step.'

The film was made, it's never been released and I've yet to be paid. I think the common term used is 'straight to video'. Am I going to give you the title? Not a chance.

CRIME AND PUNISHMENT

BRIAN MOORE

'Brian "the Pitbull" Moore is a legend of England's successful team of the early nineties. I used to spend hours watching that team when I was young. Brian was a real leader and a driver in taking them forward to win Grand Slams in 1991, 1992 and 1995. In 1991 he was voted *Rugby World* Player of the Year. Always wonderfully good at winding up the French, he was a typical English bulldog who gave everything to the cause. He's also an incredibly funny guy. To have combined two careers as a litigation lawyer and England hooker – I mean, you'd have to have a split personality to do those two jobs! Or would you?'

Some eight years after the end of the Falklands War, the England rugby team's tour to Argentina brought about a cultural dilemma. The war had lasted just over two months and 255 British and 649 Argentine military personnel and three civilian Falklanders had died. There is no doubt that the political impact of the war was felt strongly in both countries, but perhaps more so in Argentina, where it was still a topic of discussion in 1990 and remains so to this very day.

This was the first time that the any team from any sport had set foot on Argentinian soil since the conflict ended in June 1982. Having been fully briefed by our consulate in Buenos Aires about possible underlying ill feeling that still lingered towards the English, it was obvious to us, the senior players in the squad, that we would need to show tremendous moral fibre and provide pastoral guidance on this tour to ensure the squad remained resolute regardless of what came our way. The most immediate problem that faced us was of vital significance to the harmony and bonhomie of the trip – who was to be the 'Judge' in the kangaroo court?

For quite possibly the first and last time in his career, the presiding Judge, Paul Rendall, did not make the tour. Geoff Cooke, the England manager, had selected a mixture of callow up-and-comers and old-stagers to enjoy a baptism of fire in Argentina. Many of the party were on their first tour with the full international team. When casting an eye over the squad, it was a challenge to find a person capable of filling the large and, dare I say it, rather ill-fitting shoes of His Honour Justice Rendall, who had a fearsome reputation as harsh, but fair. We didn't have to look too far, though, since a shining light emerged from the darkness of the front row as the heir apparent. Enter stage left one Mark Linnett, the nineteen-stone policeman who also played prop for Moseley RFC. It was clearly a gamble, adding a custodian of the law to an already suspect kangaroo court set-up, especially when you saw which other underworld characters were involved. Given my ability to talk the hind legs off a donkey and baffle even the noblest of people with my legalese, I was the natural choice to be the Prosecuting Counsel. Wade Dooley was by far the biggest and nastiest court enforcer in the land and Jon Olver, my fellow hooker, was the appointed Chief Sneak (otherwise known as Mr X in the court room, where he had to protect his identity by wearing a black trilby, dark sunglasses and a false moustache and beard, thereby ensuring total anonymity). And so it was that we three court incumbents set about interviewing the replacement judge to test that his integrity was of an equally low standing and ensure he would fit in well.

In the course of one of his answers to a question about his previous judicial experience, Linnett managed to inform us that one of his first memories was of rolling about in a tray of Swarfega heavy duty cleaner and ball-bearings; also that, when young, he had experienced an incident with a dog and a furry glove. So convulsed were we as interviewers at these bizarre, not to say perverse, revelations, that no one thought to question their relevance to the job in question. We simply agreed that he was a most excellent candidate.

During the post-interview discussions (if truth be known there was no one else whom we even considered for the role, but we had to make Mark sweat it out), I reminded the court officials that at a previous training camp at the infamous Club La Santa in Lanzarote, Linnett had, along with Mr X, climbed over the wall of the apartment of Merlene Ottey, the Jamaican sprinter, 'borrowed' her one-piece running singlet and appeared in the bar to perform a pole dance. The incident remained unknown to Ms Ottey because he returned the item – he was, after all, a policeman with the West Midlands Constabulary. For the record, Ottey went on to win eight Olympic medals, the most by any woman in track and field history. These include three silver and five bronze medals. However, she never won an Olympic gold. Indeed, she famously lost by as little as a thousandth of a second to Gail Devers in the 100 metres in Atlanta in 1996 and by a hundredth of a second on numerous occasions to different athletes. In hindsight, I fear that the prop forward's comedy moment on that trip may well have triggered Ms Ottey's downfall in the following years.

That aside, Linnett turned out to be an inspired appointment, dispensing justice in a firm but fair manner, as befitted his station. Aided by Mr X, he successfully sent down nearly every player charged at some point in the tour and was highly inventive in his sentencing. Respect, rather than popularity, is the quality most needed with a judge, but in those few short weeks HH Linnett J achieved both with a measure of ease. Bravo.

It must be noted that the Counsel for the Defence on each occasion was a local guest especially brought in from the surrounding area in an attempt to engender good Anglo–Argentinian relations. Typically, he would be a kitchen hand or workman in the hotel – the only proviso was that he did not speak a word of English. This tended to make for some compelling cases for the prosecution, m'lud.

However, there was one member of the touring party who was a constant thorn in the side of Justice Linnett. The Judge could do little about the timekeeping of Mr Michael Skinner, but then again neither could the tour management. He did, however, come down heavily on the said miscreant for his fabrication of one excuse for missing yet another early morning pre-training meeting. He was rightly unimpressed by the fact that Skinner claimed to have foiled an attempted burglary from one of the player's rooms, and had 'persuaded' Fafa, our 4ft 10in liaison officer and impersonator of the character Tattoo from

Fantasy Island, to corroborate his story. It must be noted that Mr Skinner did actually spend a lot of his time at New Scotland Yard where he was an IT programmer for the Metropolitan Police, so he had learnt from the very best.

The primary threat to all the officials of the tour court is that, in the final session, us infidels are overthrown by a players' revolution. It was, perhaps, befitting that in the birthplace of Che Guevara, the icon of revolution and liberation, we officials were held to account for our performances during the previous hearings. Punishments were invariably harsh and most cannot be repeated in such a worthy collection of rugby folklore. Linnett's punishment was one of which he would have approved, being inventive, embarrassing, but not malevolent.

On a limited number of occasions, and at the call of a specified word from one of the court officials, Linnett had to perform a striptease, to reveal a micro-bikini of the Copacabana variety, which was a lurid green with black polka dots. After performing the punishment twice – once in the hotel reception and then in the airport check-in area – the sentence was withdrawn on the grounds that he was enjoying it and therefore it was no retribution at all.

And they wonder why the tour results left something to be desired.

AMATEUR HOUR

PETER JACKSON

'Peter has recently retired from his job as the *Daily Mail* rugby correspondent. He is one of the hardest and most professional journalists I have ever come across. He will do whatever it legitimately takes to get a "scoop" and invariably he gets his stories and facts 100 per cent correct. He is a tirelessly hard worker, a straight-talking guy and has given a huge amount to the game of rugby. And he knows pretty much everything that is going on at any time. I like to stay on his good side ...'

Irish rugby swept the board in 2009. You name it, they won it – the Grand Slam in Cardiff in March, the Heineken Cup at Murrayfield in May, the Churchill Cup at a place called Dick's Sporting Goods Park in Denver in June.

For good measure, they also provided the Lions captain, Paul O'Connell, as well as the three outstanding players on the tour in Rob Kearney, Brian O'Driscoll and Jamie Heaslip. Never, in a single season, has Irish rugby owed so much to so many with the Six Nations clean sweep worth not far short of £3,000,000 in prize money alone.

Whatever the exact amount generated by the second

Shamrock Slam, it was more than enough for the Irish Rugby Union to have settled Jim McCarthy's modest expenses claim for the first. It has been outstanding since their former captain ordered six raw eggs before he went to work on Wales at Ravenhill on Saturday, 13 March 1948. When McCarthy, not unreasonably, sought reimbursement for his pre-match lunch in addition to the rail journey from his native Cork to Belfast, via Dublin, they came back minus the cost of the eggs and the phone call he had made to his parents to assure them of his safe arrival on the northern side of the border.

Instead of £4.10s in old money (£4.50 in new), they paid him £4.7s (£4.35). Three shillings may not sound much except that back then it represented roughly one-twentieth of a weekly wage of £3. Factor in the compound interest over six decades and any accountant worth his percentage would have had no bother pushing Jim's six raw eggs and one cross-border phone call into three figures. In the finest Corinthian spirit, McCarthy has long since written it off as a trivial price to pay for the privilege of achieving something which no subsequent Irish side had achieved until Brian O'Driscoll's team finally consigned the pioneering 1948ers to history.

The notion that Jim could always make a retrospective claim and cash in on the mood of national euphoria had him in fits of laughter. 'I'd say it's probably a bit late,' he said from his home looking out across Dublin Bay. 'Sure, most of the guys on the Irish Rugby Union back then are dead now. When I got my expenses cheque from the IRFU they sent me a letter which said: "McCarthy, we have deducted three shillings for the eggs and the phone call. We would remind you that the Union does not look kindly on such antics." I felt a very naughty boy about that . . .'

The players had been told to stick strictly to the table d'hôte at the long-gone Grand Central Hotel, their base in Belfast, but their tearaway flanker from Dolphin had to go à la carte for his pre-match diet of raw eggs. In the austerity of the late forties, eggs were considered a luxury. 'I'd crack each one on the side,' he said. 'It would go straight in and straight down. I used to have three or four a day but I'd put it up to six before a match. You persuaded yourself that it was good for you, although the Union were not interested in the medical aspects of it.'

McCarthy and his team-mates belonged to a generation who never complained, at least not publicly, about the rugby unions and their fanatically rigid adherence to the amateur regulations at what was then the height of the cold war between league and union, when a player could be declared persona non grata merely on the suspicion of having talked to a league club. In a cause célèbre which still beggars belief, George Parsons suffered precisely that fate after being picked to play for Wales in the second row against France at Stade Colombes in March 1947. No sooner had Parsons joined his team-mates at Newport than he was ordered off the train seconds before it steamed out of the station.

It took the Welsh Rugby Union more than thirty years to right the wrong and finally present Parsons with the cap which he had won during the first post-war international, against England that January, but which they had confiscated as punishment for the player turning professional. It probably never occurred to those in charge that, by leaving him stranded on the platform, they gave poor old George no alternative. The unions ruled with a rod of iron and woe betide any player who dared to question their authority. Ireland's original Grand

Slammers, for example, were forbidden by the IRFU from talking publicly about their feat.

'We were not allowed to give interviews to newspapers or to the radio,' Jackie Kyle, their revered fly-half of the immediate post-war era, said. 'It was frowned upon because you were part of a team, not an individual.' Which is why Jim McCarthy has long since abandoned hope of ever being reimbursed for those six eggs . . .

YOUTH DEVELOPMENT
SCOTT QUINNELL

'A proud Welsh international and Lions man, Scott is the son of Derek Quinnell, one of the stars of rugby in the seventies. I first came across Scott when he played for Wales Colts and I played for England Colts, which means we were both about eighteen years old. The frightening thing about Scott then was that he looked about twenty-nine years old. He had a beard and probably weighed twice as much as I did! We were playing opposite each other at No. 8 and that was about the only thing we had in common that day – he went on to score four tries and I scored ... four less! It was clear to me that he was a guy I would be coming up against on a regular basis in the future. And I did.

'Scott was a wonderful player for Wales, winning fifty-two caps and scoring eleven tries. I roomed with him on the 1997 Lions tour (he also toured in 2001) and was very impressed with what a lovely guy he is ... off the field anyway.

'One of the proudest, and funniest, moments in Scott's career occurred following his last-ever game at the Millennium Stadium, when he captained a British and Irish side against Rob Howley's Rest of the World XV on 5 June 2005.'

Rob Howley, a former captain of Wales and one of the great Welsh scrum-halves, and I were granted the honour of a testimonial game in 2005. The match was to be between a Rest of the World side and a British and Irish side, and we were to be the captains. Rob immediately opted for the Rest of the World (small man syndrome in my eyes) so I was left with the British and Irish side. I immediately saw an advantage in this because it gave me the opportunity to pick my brothers, Gavin and Craig. This was very important to me because, while we'd played on the same pitch before, all three of us had never previously been on the same side. As the team started to take shape, another thought crossed my mind. Why not pick my father, Derek? Having been capped twenty-three times by Wales and toured on three occasions with the Lions, he had huge experience and at fifty-six years of age would make me look quick! With one place remaining, I selected another Quinnell, my six-year-old son Steele to complete the quintet. The plan was for Dad and Steele to come on to the field of play with a couple of minutes remaining of the match so three generations of Quinnells would be on the pitch at the final whistle.

The start of the game was unusual. Rob and I had to abseil from the roof of the Millennium Stadium. This exercise emphasised the difference between forwards and backs. Rob was at one end of the ground with me at the other, the fireworks were lit (our cue to start the descent) and we were off. We both had a clever piece of equipment called a 'descender' or 'figure eight'. Quite simply, this is a friction device which controls the rate of descent. I wish I'd paid more attention during the briefing. I had assumed someone would be controlling my downward progress from a remote position, and it wasn't until halfway down, and approaching 50mph, that I started to pull every rope

I could find. The result was I touched the ground (severely testing the foundations of the stadium) almost before Rob had left the roof. Then I sauntered through the stand and on to the pitch, arriving at the centre spot while Rob was still inching his way down. Quite honestly, that was the only time in my entire career I beat Rob Howley for speed off the mark, or at any other pace-related activity come to think of it.

I have no doubt that somewhere in this book there will be a well-known, high-profile back committing to print a story showing a forward, or indeed an entire pack of forwards, in a bad light. What they fail to remember is that they would all be unknowns without the grit and determination of forwards, which reminds me, 'What do you call those blokes who keep hanging around with rugby players?' Ah yes, that's it . . . backs!

Anyway, back to the game. The match was a festival of open running rugby and a few minutes prior to the final whistle, my dad and Steele took to the pitch amid rapturous applause. Dad took up his customary position at No. 8, leaving me to find a place in the second row. Steele, having watched me play on many occasions, decided to copy his dad and took up a position in the centre!

My British and Irish side were a couple of tries down, so with victory assured, Rob allowed a previously discussed plan to go ahead. We had an attacking scrum on the twenty-two metre line, Kyran Bracken put the ball in and it was filtered back to Dad's feet at No. 8. He scooped it up one-handed straight into Kyran's hands (even I had to take a step back and admire his skill). Kyran passed the ball to Alex King, who placed it in Steele's hands and pointed him in the direction of the tryline. The plan was for Steele to run over the line and score a try, which would have been a lovely end to what had been a marvellous occasion. However, between Steele and the tryline stood the Tongan centre, Salesi Finau, who, at 5ft 9in tall and 5ft 9in wide, obviously appeared as an imposing figure to my young lad. In fact, Steele did what any six-year-old (and several Guinness Premiership players) would have done and handed Salesi the ball. Fully aware of the situation, God bless him, Salesi managed to stumble forward and place the ball back into Steele's hands as he fell to the ground. At this point Dad and I arrived, and with one of us holding each arm, swept Steele up into the air and over the tryline where he touched the ball down for five points. Following the final whistle, the three generations of Quinnells took a moment to savour the occasion and walked slowly from the pitch, with the exception of Steele, who was running off to find one or two of his mates to let them know he had scored a try at the Millennium Stadium.

It was a great day and a proud moment standing on the pitch with my father, my brothers and my son, but the best incident of the day occurred a couple of hours after the match had finished. My wife, Nicola, and I were staying for all the post-match festivities so Dad and Mam were taking Steele back to Llanelli in their car. Part way home Dad asked Steele if he had enjoyed his day.

'It was fantastic, Grandpa, the best day I have ever had. I scored a try at the Millennium Stadium, it was brilliant.' According to my dad, a mile or two later Steele said, 'Grandpa, I've been doing a bit of thinking.' 'What about?' asked Dad. 'I've been thinking if they'd brought you and me on a bit earlier, we would have won that game.'

OFFICIAL SELECTION PROCESS

JOHN TAYLOR

'John was an outstanding back-row forward for Wales and the Lions. Always recognisable, with his long flowing hair, sideburns and bushy beard, he not surprisingly acquired the nickname "Basil" (Brush). Rather like the modern-day John Eales, John was one of the few back-row forwards who could also double up as a goal kicker. In the 1971 match against Scotland, he famously slotted home a last-second conversion from a seemingly impossible angle to win the match — a kick that was later described as "the greatest conversion since St Paul". John's club side was London Welsh. He represented them in the sixties and seventies, along with many other legendary names of Welsh rugby in that era. Capped twenty-six times from 1967–73, John also played in all four Tests during the successful Lions tour to New Zealand in 1971. Most rugby fans will know John from his commentary on ITV and for the Rugby World Cups. He has always been a great friend of mine and probably has enough stories to write a book of his own!'

It is quite incredible to those of us who played in a different era that even with assistants and television match officials to help them, referees seem to get it wrong just as much as they always did.

But the modern player will get no sympathy from those of my generation. The only time we ever got a neutral referee was in the Five Nations Championship. When you played in South Africa, Australia or New Zealand, the man in charge came from the host country and almost universally they were blatant 'homers'.

Home referees were a legacy from the days when teams went to those countries by boat and it was totally impractical to bring in officials from neutral countries (although you would have thought it would have been possible to get an Aussie to New Zealand or vice versa). The truth, of course, is that they were very happy to extend home advantage to include the ref as well as the crowd and the pitch!

It usually worked but in 1971 the New Zealand Rugby Union met their match in the shape of Dr Doug Smith, the manager of the victorious Lions.

Doug was perhaps not the most sophisticated of doctors the world had ever seen. If we had anything wrong with us we would run a mile and find local treatment rather than submit to the primitive sports medicine he was wont to deal out, but he proved a clairvoyant and a wonderful politician/diplomat.

From the moment we arrived in New Zealand he would tell all and sundry that we were going to win the series 2–1 with one match drawn. We were there for over three months and he made his prediction everywhere from Whangarei to Invercargill. It always got a good laugh until we drew the final

Test in Auckland and he was proved right. He even had a bet on it, I believe. What people did not know was how hard he worked behind the scenes to make it happen.

The top referee in New Zealand at the time was a guy called Pat Murphy, but the Welsh contingent felt he was an out-and-out homer because we had toured New Zealand two years before and he had refereed both Tests. To be fair, we would never have beaten the All Blacks in 1969, but on top of a crazy itinerary we also had to contend with Murphy's rulings – to us he was a nightmare and we never wanted to see him again let alone play under his jurisdiction.

The system for selecting Test referees on Lions tours in those days had a peculiar mechanism to give the visitors some sort of input. In the early provincial games (we played ten matches in New Zealand before the first Test) the NZRU would make sure all their top referees got a game. They would then select a panel of three and the Lions management made the final choice.

Murphy was on the panel for the first Test. He had been very sympathetic when he had refereed the tourists earlier in the tour, which made some of us suspicious. With him were a relative newcomer, Dr Humphrey Rainey, and John Pring, who had refereed a number of internationals but was nowhere near as experienced as Murphy and very definitely behind him in the pecking order.

Rainey stood no chance because he had refereed the 'Battle of Canterbury' – we had lost three players in the mayhem and midway through it Rainey had told the captains he was going to follow the ball and it was up to them to sort everything else out.

The Welsh contingent were convinced Murphy would show his true colours in the Test and urged the management to resist the pressure in the press and from the NZRU to accept their 'top' man. We opted for Pring and he rewarded us by being about as straight as a New Zealander can be at home.

We had no hesitation in asking for him again in the second Test and, despite losing, went for him again in the third. Murphy was on the panel for both of those as well but was left fuming on the sidelines.

The NZRU were not happy either and upped the stakes in the build-up to the vital final Test. If the All Blacks won they would tie the series – a draw or a win for the Lions would create history with a first-ever Lions series win on New Zealand soil.

They threatened to take Pring off the panel – no referee had ever officiated in all four Tests on a Lions tour before – saying it was unfair for him to monopolise matches to such an extent, especially when their number one referee was in his prime and raring to go. They even suggested it was an insult to Murphy and the NZRU. Many would have succumbed to the pressure but at this point Dr Doug played his finest hand.

'Take your point,' he said with a poker face. 'Why don't you get Murphy to referee the final provincial game [against Bay of Plenty the Tuesday before the last Test] and if he does a good job, we'll be happy to have him for the Saturday as well. But just in case it's a disaster, or he gets injured, leave Pring on the panel as a back-up.'

They fell for it hook, line and sinker and agreed that if Murphy refereed the final game, we would be able to decide who took on the Test. On the Tuesday in Tauranga I was sitting next to Doug as the T and Ws (the Tuesday and Wednesday boys) set about completing a clean sweep against the New Zealand provinces, and I swear the game was no more than sixty seconds old when he turned round and passed a sheet of paper to the chairman of the NZRU. Written on it in bold capitals was 'REFEREE FOR THE FINAL TEST – JOHN PRING'.

We emerged with a draw – the NZRU and Pat Murphy were left seething and John Pring remains the only man ever to have refereed every Test in a Lions series.

RAM RAID

JEFF PROBYN

'I first met Jeff when I joined Wasps in 1989. He was in the England squad and was a bit of a latecomer to international rugby, making his debut at the age of thirty-one in 1988. But he went on to become a very successful prop for England, winning thirty-seven caps and playing in the 1991 World Cup. He toured South Africa with the World XV in 1989 and was a member of the very successful Wasps team that won the English Courage league in 1990. Jeff was quite slight for a modern-day inter-national prop but he was so effective in the scrum and was able to get underneath quite a few of his opponents. I suppose it was due to some of his exceptional scrummaging techniques that quite a few of the props took to cutting off their shirt sleeves as they believed Jeff was so low in the scrum that he would use them as leverage! Jeff used to run a furniture business and still comments on the game, writing in various newspapers. He has never been afraid of a little controversy whenever there is an opinion to be made. Certainly he will always be famous for his part in the front row with fellow international forwards Brian Moore, Paul Rendall and, towards the end of his career, Jason Leonard.'

I was involved with the England team in the eighties and nineties, during which time they introduced overseas training camps for the squad. I'm not too sure who to thank for this inspirational idea, but I would certainly shake his hand if he ever makes himself known to me. Warm-weather training in the amateur era, or as the boys called it, 'a late Christmas holiday' – fantastic.

The trips used to take place in January, and with the UK in the grip of winter we would board a flight, in the early days, to Portugal and subsequently to Club La Santa in Lanzarote. The change of venue might just have something to do with the story I'm about to tell.

In Portugal, we trained hard and played hard. Each day the fitness coaches would put us through our paces with endless physical exercises designed to increase our strength and endurance. At times I remember being so exhausted I would wonder why I had decided to accept the trip. Then I would remind myself that the session would end at some point and later that day (and every day we were there) we would all be in one of the several bars the resort had to offer, feeling no pain, sipping the drink of our choice, and telling a few lies.

On the last night, most of the boys were packing early in preparation for the flight home the following day. All rugby tourists will tell you it's a wise move to pack bags well in advance of departure. This technique removes the possibility of a last-minute scramble for clothes and toiletries when the brain might not be quite as quick as it could be – or in layman's terms, trying to pack when you're pissed.

I was putting the finishing touches to my packing when a knock came on the door. I walked over, turned the handle and with the door open no more than an inch it was hit with extreme force from the other side. As I jumped out of the way, Gareth 'Coochie' Chilcott, a committed member of the front-row union, burst into my room. He had a maniacal expression on his face and a fire extinguisher in his hand. He moved with greater speed than he'd displayed in the previous few days of training and 'extinguished' every item of clothing in my suitcase and kit bag.

As quickly as he had arrived he disappeared, out of my room and down the corridor in search of more victims, one of whom was the team physician, a gentleman called Pat England, who was actually flying out that night to assist with an important operation back in the UK. By the time Coochie reached Pat, he had emptied several extinguishers and was actually holding the final pair, one under each arm, somewhat reminiscent of Rambo. He fired simultaneously into Pat's suitcase and directly at the man himself, who was wearing an expensive looking suit ready to leave. I have a vivid memory of bumping into Pat in the hotel corridor and hearing him complain to anyone who would listen, 'How am I going to fly back in this state? Every item of clothing I possess is covered in white wet foam,' which obviously included the rags he was wearing.

At the final count, Coochie had managed successfully to assail twenty-one rooms, an achievement similar to Usain Bolt's recent sprint records, inasmuch as you get the feeling it will last for a very long time indeed.

EXCRUCIATING PAIN

MICHAEL BURTON

'A true legend of the game with Gloucester, England, the Lions and the Barbarians, Mike managed to get his finger in every pie going. He was the first man to get sent off for England, which he did while playing prop in the original "Battle of Ballymore" in 1975, and he always has fantastic stories to tell. He now runs a successful corporate hospitality business and is not only a true gentleman but a lovely man to work with.'

The 1974 Lions tour of South Africa had been a roaring success. As the wagon train rolled into East London for the match against the Leopards, we were confident that another win would be on the cards, despite the fact that the Leopards had been on their first overseas tour to Italy rather recently, and were expected to offer reasonable opposition.

On arrival in the township, the Lions party soon sensed an atmosphere of friendly combat. The stadium was a good one, the pitch had an excellent playing surface, and there were 15,000 people present, including 500 whites, who required special tickets in the years of apartheid to get them into the ground.

Before the match, a group of smart drum majorettes did some marching to the rhythm of a lively band, and the local Lord Mayor presented Willie John McBride, our captain, with a baby leopard. Willie, always the diplomat, gratefully stepped forward and grasped the youngster in his hands, at which point the excited cub emptied the contents of its bladder all over the front of Willie's Lions shirt and pristine white shorts, leaving a nasty smell that was to rise regularly at every scrummage on a steamy hot afternoon.

The match was going very much the Lions' way, and at the scrum our powerful pack had pushed the Leopards off every ball they put in. Indeed, they won just one scrum all day. Despite this, they tackled manfully and put up fierce resistance throughout, finally succumbing 56–10.

Five minutes into the second half, and now fed up with being pushed about, the Leopards' loose-head prop, and my opposite number that day, took exception to this treatment, and finally decided to stand up and do something about it at the next line-out. Clearly eyeing me up, I was aware that this big, aggressive South African, who looked and played like Marvin Hagler, was about to land a haymaker on the chin of yours truly. Using typical Gloucester guile, I ducked, and thus the whoosh went over my head and impacted on the right cheek of one Christopher Wayne Ralston, who was locking the scrum that day with Willie John McBride. The strength of the punch was extraordinary, knocking Ralston flat on his back, burbling bits of blood from a nasty cut.

McBride was a considerate and caring captain, and as the light of day appeared to re-enter the prone Ralston's world, Willie John asked him in that rich Ulster brogue, 'Are you all right now, Chris?' to which Ralston replied, in classic west

London tones, 'The pain is excruciating.' On hearing this, Stewart McKinney, an Irish flanker who was playing at No. 6 that day and who had hitherto shown great concern for Ralston's welfare, snarled, 'If he can pronounce a word like "excruciating", there can't be much wrong with him. Why don't we get Uttley on to replace him, and get on with the game?'

A PARDON FROM THE GODFATHER

GRAHAM ROWNTREE

'Graham is a legendary Leicester figure who, along with Richard Cockerill and Darren Garforth, was part of the inimitable ABC club, named after the letters they wore on their front-row shirts. He made his debut for England against Scotland in 1995, and everyone will remember Graham for his fifty-four caps, as well as for the state of his prop's cauliflower ears! He has given everything to Leicester Tigers and England, and is a good guy on the rugby circuit – a real professional and very passionate about his sport. Not an attention seeker by any stretch of the imagination, Graham is blossoming into a highly successful coach both with England and the Lions.'

One of the most enjoyable aspects of international touring as a relatively young player was the opportunity to get to know the boys from other clubs, and work out what made them tick. This is actually extremely important for the success of a tour. As I have experienced with the British and Irish Lions, both as a player and most recently as a coach, it is critical that the side gels as quickly as possible to ensure the team hits the ground running.

Of course, the other aspect is that when you train and play with other club players, you get an inside knowledge of their psyche, which comes in handy back home during the regular season!

This was true of the England tour to South Africa in 1994. I played with rookie Lawrence Dallaglio in the midweek team, which contained a few up-and-comers – John Mallet, Simon Shaw, Damian Hopley, Lawrence, me and my evergreen front-row companion, Graham Dawe, who was thirty-five years young at the time.

Fast forward one year, and we were taking on Wasps at Welford Road. Lol was established as the new kid on the block, following his success with the World Cup-winning England 7s team, and not surprisingly, he went on to win his first international cap that season.

We were a young Leicester pack back then, who had grown up together, and basically we were mad for a ruckus. With such players as Cockerill, Garforth, Johnson and Back, all marshalled by our leader, Dean Richards, it was widely known that we never took a backward step when it came to physical confront-ation. We always relished taking on Wasps, who never let us down in that department – how could they when their captain was Dean Ryan, who had also captained the 1994 midweek team in South Africa, and he was always first over the top, leading the charge. During the course of the game Lol found himself over the top of the ball at the bottom of a ruck with the Leicester foot soldiers in attendance. Happy days! Please wait your turn for a piece of the pretty boy from London. Suddenly, an all-too-familiar Midlands voice boomed out, 'Leave him!' We all looked round to see the Godfather himself, Dean Richards, looking on disapprovingly.

For a split second we were worried that Deano had gone soft in his advancing years. Heavens above, whatever next? It turned out that Deano had taken a shine to Lawrence and admired the young star in the making. So it was that Lol got a 'pardon' from the Godfather, and I can assure you, in all my years at Leicester Tigers with Dean, I didn't see that very often.

Despite this let off, the intense rivalry continued for the next twelve years, Leicester v Dallaglio.

This was born from the absolute respect we had for the man. A true competitor and warrior but, above everything else, a massive pain in the arse. In my time at Leicester, the Tigers spoke of only two people when we played against Wasps: Simon Shaw – what an irritation he was at maul/line-out time; and Lawrence – what a total nuisance he was from start to finish and in every single department. That was the ultimate compliment to a player in my book.

The one thing that everyone always points out about Lawrence is how he had the ability to control the referee with his relentless ranting and nagging throughout the game. I always felt sorry for any international referee around the millennium, who had to deal with the endless chat from Lawrence, Matt Dawson and Martin Johnson – like having tea with a bunch of housewives.

Following another bruising first leg of Heineken Cup back-to-back pool rounds in 2004, when Lawrence was interviewed post match on TV, he suggested that our methods at breakdown time were not 'totally legitimate'. How dare he? What insolence! We played that clip on a loop prior to every training session the following week – we even played it in the dressing room before we ran out for the return game, such was his ability to wind us up!

As you'd expect in such a tight game played between the two most successful English teams in the professional era, emotions were sky high. Lol had upset the entire 'Leicester massive' with his well-chosen comments. The Welford Road crowd was salivating. Our game plan was straightforward – we wanted retribution, and we queued up to deliver it upon our visiting guest, Mr Dallaglio, at the breakdowns. In typical fashion there was not one word of complaint, not one utter of a wince. At one ruck, as my feet stood on his legs, he looked up at me saying, 'You'll have to do better than that, Wig.' Having taken everything we could give and more, we gave up on our target about halfway into the game – he simply wasn't going to break. And you know what? Even though we won the game, that still didn't shut the bastard up!

KNOCKING HISTORY INTO TOUCH

FERGUS SLATTERY

'For me, Fergus was symbolic of rugby. I always looked up to him. I would have loved to have played alongside him, who wouldn't? That era was packed with great guys and his perform-ances in that wonderful 1974 Lions Test series against South Africa was monumental. They must have been terrified when they saw his name on the teamsheet, as every opposition must have been in all his sixty-one matches for Ireland. Although I missed his playing days, I'm lucky to see a fair bit of Fergus in rugby circles these days.'

William Webb Ellis is a man famed throughout the world as the inventor of rugby, who also became an English Anglican clergyman. This much we know is true. Since 1987 he has become immortalised by the William Webb Ellis trophy, which is presented every four years to the winners of the Rugby World Cup.

I'm certain any reader of this book will have at least a passing recollection of a story concerning a lad called Webb

Ellis who picked up a ball and ran with it in the latter half of 1823 while a pupil at Rugby School. The rest, as they say, is history.

I spent many years researching the origins of the game, which, in hindsight, was probably a stupid waste of time, since it would have been much easier and far less time consuming to ask my great friend Willie John McBride. He was there at the time, after all. However, I concluded Webb Ellis was indeed involved, but most certainly should not be credited as the game's inventor.

The reality is Webb Ellis most certainly did walk out of the main school building of Rugby School in the autumn of 1823. In front of him he saw numerous boys participating in a game of football on the quadrangle, and when the opportunity came he caught the bouncing ball and began to run. This is the precise moment history tells us the game of rugby football was invented – incorrect.

Every forward who has ever played the game will tell you rugby football was invented exactly one and a half seconds after this particular incident when Roland Dimrumple, the school juggernaut, drove a squealing Webb Ellis into the turf, kicked him in the solar plexus and told him to 'keep his sodding hands off the ball'.

That, my friends, is when the great game of rugby football union was invented.

The Roland Dimrumple trophy presented every four years to the winners of the Rugby Union World Cup? Perhaps not.

A FAIR COP

PAUL ACKFORD

'Paul "Chief Inspector Ackers" Ackford was part of the Harlequins pack, and England team, that dominated for so many years in the late eighties and early nineties. I first remember seeing Paul at Rosslyn Park before he joined Quins. He was an athletic forward and made an incredible contribution to the England team, winning twenty-two caps. That was a team of real characters and Paul played his part. He also toured Australia with the Lions in 1989, playing in all three of the Tests in the winning series. It was Paul, if you remember, who was on the receiving end of that killer punch from Freddie Mendez in 1990. The punch was meant for Jeff Probyn and to this day I am not sure who comes out of that worse in the mistaken identity stakes. Paul is now a successful journalist for the *Daily Telegraph* and one of the voices of rugby.'

I first encountered John Eales, the wonderful lock forward who went on to win two World Cups with Australia, on the 1991 England tour. Eales was a youngster at the time, had barely started shaving, but he was already being talked of as a major prospect. Anyway, the first time I bumped into him was in one of the games leading into the Test. I was in the second row alongside Wade Dooley, and Eales was in the middle of the Queensland line-out, directly opposing Wade.

At the time our esteemed coach, Roger Uttley, had suggested that we all research our opponents and do some homework into what sort of people they were, so that we could have a psychological advantage over them on game day. Now, it became very clear that Wade had ignored this suggestion from Big Rog and had done no research on Eales whatsoever. To be fair, this was in the days when pre-game analysis amounted to a glance at the match-day programme an hour and a half before kick-off. Just for the record, it turns out that Eales was a talented all-rounder and played first-grade cricket for Queensland University. The word was that the kid was pretty lively on the rugby field as well and unless Wade roused himself he might be in for a torrid afternoon. On the morning of the match I took the matter in hand.

'Wade,' I said, 'this lad is really good. Unless you get into him early, close down his space, we might have a problem.' Wade just sat there, munching his breakfast. I tried another tack, deciding to flesh out Eales as a human being to give Wade something to get annoyed about. 'Listen,' I said. 'This kid is young and he's into graphic design.' Wade stopped chomping and leaned forward in his chair.

'Pardon?' he muttered.

'He's ten years younger than you are and he's at college studying for a Bachelor of Arts degree. Everyone says he's the next big thing.' Wade was approaching thirty at the time and, as a career policeman, was not too fond of students. He settled back in his seat and smiled.

Fast forward to the game. Eales won the first two line-outs

on his throw and, if memory serves correctly, had the nerve to pinch one of Wade's. That did it. At the next line-out Eales tapped back a ball, which fell just short of the Queensland No. 9, Peter Slattery. Like all good scrum-halves, Slattery retreated backwards and motioned to his forwards to get involved and clear up the mess. Eales bravely fell on the ball and was followed by half the England pack. Dean Richards was first to arrive, lying across Eales pinning him to the floor. I followed the foot soldiers into the thick of the action and was next to the breakdown, and then Wade arrived flopping on to the pile of bodies.

Poor Eales was trapped at the bottom unable to move, with his head and shoulders sticking appetisingly out of the heap. That was when I heard the dull thwack of Wade cuffing Eales mightily round his ears, followed by the now infamous Lancastrian roar – 'Take that, you f***ing art student!'

That wasn't the end of the matter, though. Later, much later, as the two teams socialised after the game, Eales, who had played really well, came up to Dean, Wade and me as we stood chatting.

'Not bad for an art student,' he smiled before offering to buy us a beer.

The second Test between the 1989 Lions and Australia has gone down in rugby folklore as the 'Battle of Ballymore'. We had lost the first Test in Sydney by 30–12 and the series hung on the second encounter in Queensland. 'Disgraceful' screamed the headlines in the Aussie papers after we had won a game that amounted to an extended brawl. 'The Lions' tactics were illegal.'

To set the record straight, after Robert Jones stepped on the boot of Nick Farr-Jones, Australia's scrum-half, which triggered the fight, the sequence of events went as follows. First out of the back row of the Lions pack into the skirmish was PC Dean Richards. Second into the melee was PC Wade Dooley. Third into action was Inspector Ackford, and fourth was solicitor Brian Moore. Illegal? It was the most lawful fight in rugby history.

STICKING TO THE GAME PLAN

MIKE TEAGUE

'For me, as a back-row player, growing up watching the England team of Teague, Winterbottom, Skinner and Richards was awe-inspiring. Mike always played with such quality and calculated ferocity. My best memories of him are his awesome perform-ances in the second and third Tests against Australia in the 1989 Lions tour, which quite rightly earned him the player of the series title. A true Gloucester man, softly spoken but with a massive presence, he always had time for everyone before and after a game. Still does.

'Mike sits in a very exclusive camp of Lions players. Having done so much to win the two Tests in 1989, he also came on against New Zealand in the second Test of the 1993 series, which the Lions won 20–7 – so he retired with a 100 per cent record for the Lions. Not bad. Can't quite say the same thing myself, thanks to South Africa's win in the third Test in 1997. Mind you, we were 2–0 up at that stage, so we won the series.'

There's no doubt in my mind that New Zealand is the hardest place in the world to tour. Rugby is akin to religion across both the North and South Islands, and plenty of Kiwi fans have forgotten more about rugby than most of the 1993 Lions will ever know. There is no such thing as an easy game in New Zealand, as we had realised by the time we came to play the unofficial fourth Test in that tour, against the New Zealand Maoris (a prerequisite for playing in this team is that you have to be of at least one sixteenth, i.e. one great-great-grandparent, Maori descent).

The first two games, against North Auckland and North Harbour, were supposed to ease us into the tour, but both matches had been very physical up front. The provincial teams were intent on giving us a good hiding to soften us up for the Test series. After two wins the pressure on the squad to perform was gaining momentum, as every opposing player wanted to get a piece of the action and make a name for himself.

Our captain for the 1993 tour was Scotland's Gavin Hastings, who had not only played a major part in helping the 1989 Lions to defeat Australia, but was widely regarded as one of the great ambassadors for the game and capable of getting the full backing of the squad for this extremely difficult tour.

A dressing room before the match is a unique place to be. Everyone has different ways of preparing for the game. Some players like to get extremely wound up and beat themselves round the head to prepare for battle, while others take a more placid approach and may read a match programme just to ensure they don't get too nervous or work themselves up into too much of a frenzy. Each to their own, I say.

The captain's role in the dressing room is always an interesting one. He is charged with saying those final few words to get the very best from his men. With a national team, a routine has usually developed under the incumbent captain. With England during Will Carling's leadership, the forwards would huddle together, grunting and eyeballing each other as sweat dripped down our furrowed brows, salivating at the thought of the great battle that was going to unfold. Meanwhile, the backs would sit around drinking cups of tea and patting each other on the bottom, and moan about the lack of creases in the shorts. You get the idea.

A Lions tour is very different. Having no well-established pre-match routine made the captain's job even harder. For instance, Gavin couldn't really, as he might have done in the Scottish dressing room before playing England, stir the blood with impassioned words conjuring up historic victories over the Auld Enemy on the field of battle (not many to choose from then . . .) because there were four Englishmen in the pack – Jason Leonard, Wade Dooley, Peter Winterbottom and myself. Wouldn't have gone down well, as Gavin well knew.

All the talk in the pre-match build-up had been about the significance of the haka to the New Zealand Maori and how they had devised a special version to face the Lions. It was, of course, a tremendous gesture that they had gone to such lengths on our behalf in honour of this wonderful sporting rivalry, but at the end of the day it was still fifteen players against fifteen players, and all the forwards wanted to do was go out there and get stuck in.

So there we all were, gathered round Gavin, eyes popping and covered in liniment, pulling our team-mates in tightly with such force that a rib could have snapped at any minute. Gavin's pre-match chat focused solely on the historical nature of the haka and its insignificance for the Lions that day. As the referee knocked for the team to come out, Gavin's passion reached its climax. 'Right lads! All they've talked about all week is their f***ing haka! Well, I say to each and every one of you, let's go out there and stick that f***ing haka right up their arses! Now, come on boys!' And with those words ringing in our ears we took the field at Wellington, ready to follow our captain's cry.

The game did not start well. In fact, it could not have started any worse. We conceded three quick tries in the first fifteen minutes. As we stood beneath the posts, I could see Gavin was struggling to add anything to the two mouthfuls of expletives he had given us after the first two tries were scored. This was when I saw the opportunity to support my captain and asked, 'Here Gav, when *exactly* are we going to stick the haka up their f***ing arses?!'

I'm pleased to report that we came back to win the game 24–20, but that comment provided a few laughs in the kangaroo court later that night.

BEAUTIFUL BERMUDA AND THE BLOODY BUSH
SIMON JONES

'Simon played rugby for Bath many years ago whilst pretending to be a teacher. He was lucky enough to go on a tour with the Barbarians to the Hong Kong 7s and enjoyed it so much he spent the next ten years touring with anyone who would pay the airfare. Eventually, the legs tired and, thinking he had better do something besides run around in a tracksuit, Simon obtained his masters degree in education at the University of West England and settled down a bit. He is now director of Ed Support Ltd, and a coach and trainer for the RFU. He is also a writer of rugby books and editor of the IRB coaching website: irbcoaching.com'

Beautiful Bermuda

A lot of people will have heard of the annual Bermuda Classic, where players over thirty-three years of age play fifteen-a-side rugby over the course of a long week. Bermuda is a very relaxed place, helped by the fact that travel around the island is done on hired mopeds or taxis and rarely exceeds the speed limit of 20mph.

In the early nineties, when the tournament was an even more relaxed affair than it is now, I was lucky enough to be asked to play for the England Classicals, an invitational team made up of former England internationals and a few mere mortals, such as myself, who had been close to a cap but weren't really good enough.

I was very keen to make a good impression, surrounded by all my heroes, but also found it hard not to slip into the more relaxed culture off the field, and so I did what most rugby players do at the Classic – consumed far too many 'Dark and Stormies' (rum and Cokes) and managed to fall off my moped. Not the best.

We won our first game and were celebrating fiercely when a couple of the Irish team who I knew asked me if I wouldn't mind playing for them the next day as they were short of a flanker. This seemed a great idea at the time and, having agreed, I promptly forgot all about it.

The next day was a day off for the England Classicals and we were taken out on a boat cruise around the island, stopping only for boozy games of beach volleyball in deserted coves. The sun was shining, the sea was warm and our sponsors were very generous with their supply of alcoholic lubricant to ease our aches and pains, God bless 'em.

It wasn't until around 5 p.m. that I suddenly remembered my promise to play for Ireland that evening in their game against the USA, kick-off at 6 p.m. I detest letting people down, so leaving the rest of the lads in a bar in the main street of Hamilton, and wearing only flip-flops, shorts and a stained T-shirt, I jumped out in front of a passing car, which screeched to a halt (actually, because of the speed limit, it eased to a stop). The driver was surprised by my panicky request but with the generosity shown by all Bermudians agreed to drive me to the stadium where Ireland were due to be playing.

I arrived with twenty minutes to spare and, pausing only briefly to admire the Americans tearing around the field doing intricate moves in immaculate tracksuits, I rushed to the Irish dressing room. There, in front of me, was the cream of Irish rugby in various stages of undress. 'Jesus, Jonesy, thank God you're here. You're our only back row!' was the slightly worrying comment from one of the team. With ten minutes to go before kick-off, the Irish lads had found me some boots (one size too small), some shorts (two sizes too big) and, in a very proud personal moment, presented me with an Irish shirt. Shortly after the presentation two other back-row players arrived, bringing the body count to fifteen and enough for a team.

With five minutes to go, someone suggested that we ought to go out and run through a few moves. The backs went one way and I followed the forwards. A practice scrum was suggested but one of the second rows said he couldn't because he had a bad back. So we all wandered over to the touchline to do some line-outs, ambling past some ferocious running Yanks who had, by this time, worked up a confident sweat. I took my place at the back of the line-out and the scrum-half said, 'Right lads, why don't we use names of Irish towns for our calls?' All agreed this was a fine idea.

'What towns will we use?' said the hooker.

'I know,' said one of the inspirational second-row forwards. 'If the town is in County Kildare, we'll throw to the front, if it's in County Clare, we'll go middle and if it's in County Kerry, it's to the back, so it is.'

'Brilliant!' It was agreed.

'Shall we do a practice throw then?' someone suggested. With one minute remaining before kick-off, this seemed a sensible idea, regardless of the fact that the only towns or cities I knew in Ireland were Dublin, Galway and Cork and I had absolutely no idea which counties they were in.

The scrum-half said, 'Right, you ready boys? Tralee!'

The hooker was about to throw the ball in when one second row shouted, 'Lads, hold on a moment! Is that in County Kerry or County Clare?'

A big row ensued and no one could agree which county Tralee was in, at which point the referee blew his whistle for the start of the game.

What followed was a vindication of all those who favour the 'less is more' approach in preparation for a game. The Americans had clearly worked too hard beforehand whereas we were fresh, and won by fifteen points.

So I can thus far boast a proud career record of being unbeaten in an Irish shirt.

Bush Pilots Association

Thirty years ago, I was lucky enough to be invited to play for a year in the Easts team in Brisbane, Australia. I had a wonderful time and managed to find a job selling advertising, which entailed much travelling around the country. On one particular occasion, I had to go from Brisbane to a town called Emerald, deep in the Queensland outback.

The only way to get there was either to drive for two days or fly on what was, in those days, called the Bush Pilots

Association, or BPA, airline. I was told this consisted of small, privately owned planes, flown and run by former Qantas pilots who had retired and were supplementing their pensions. I arrived at Brisbane Airport, which was fairly small back then, and after I'd checked in, the girl at the desk told me to go out of the terminal, walk around the runway and look for the small hut by the windsock on the other side of the airfield. There I found a sixteen-seater plane and a charming young lady in hostess uniform, sitting in a deckchair and holding a clipboard.

'Right mate, you're the last,' she said, ticking off my name, and she joined me as we boarded the plane. I was delighted to be seated right behind the empty pilot's seat, so I had a great view out the front window as well as the side. 'This'll be a great way to see the outback,' I thought.

There were only six other passengers, all reading and looking bored, waiting for the flight to go. We were wondering how long we would have to wait when a big Aussie at the back of the plane, who was reading a newspaper, shouted, 'Where's the bloody pilot, I'm fed up waiting!'

The other passengers and I were a bit surprised at his aggression but also sympathised with him as there was no one looking remotely like a pilot anywhere near the plane, which presumably meant we still had a fair wait ahead of us. The air hostess tried to placate the big man.

'Don't worry, Sir. I'm sure the pilot will be here shortly,' she said.

After a few more minutes, the Aussie called out again, proclaiming, 'I'm going to be bloody late for my bloody meeting. Where the hell is this pilot?!'

Looking nervously around for any sign of the captain, the

poor hostess replied, 'I am sorry for the delay, Sir. I can assure you he'll be here soon.'

A few minutes of uneasy silence went by and we were all very conscious of the angry mutterings coming from the back of the plane. Then, to our considerable consternation, the Aussie threw down his paper and shouted, 'F*** it, I'll fly the bloody crate myself.' He stormed up to the pilot's seat and started to flick seemingly random switches. The hostess, with a genuine look of panic on her face, asked him to stop, but to our horror, with a final flick of a switch, first one propeller and then the other started to turn! That was it as far as two passengers were concerned and they tried to bolt for the door, at which point the hostess started to laugh uncontrollably and explained to the panic-stricken passengers that the big Aussie was in fact the pilot!

Next time I drove to Emerald.

BONN VIVANTS

STEPHEN JONES

'Stephen Jones reached a first and only career peak with selection for Newport United, second XV of the great Newport club at eighteen. He played for Oxfordshire in the county championship while at Oxford Polytechnic, then on arrival in London as a budding journalist he joined London Welsh. However, he tells me that almost as soon as he arrived he had to retire as he was engaged by the *Sunday Times* as match reporter. Was it the honour of working for the famous paper? No, it was the £40 match fee. Stephen has now been chief rugby correspondent of the Sunday newspaper for twenty-five years, having won numerous awards including UK Sports Journalist of the Year, Sports Correspondent of the Year, Sports Story of the Year and Sports Book of the Year with *Endless Winter*. He has recently completed work on *Lion Man*, the story of Ian McGeechan.'

Was it the most doomed pass in all of rugby history? I was captaining my college team, Oxford Polytechnic, on tour in Germany. Oxford and Bonn are twin cities and in the seventies, as part of some kind of cultural exchange, Oxford sent a rugby team, some choirs, poets, city grandees and a Morris dancing squad to its twin to take part in a festival to promote links and goodwill. The Morris dancers, amazingly, managed to drink us under the table.

The Oxford Poly rugby team shared a coach with the choir of Magdalen College School, who were a bunch of twelve-year-old cherubs. We alternated our repertoires. They kicked off with 'Angels from the Realms of Glory' and we answered with 'Barnacle Bill the Sailor'. Their parents were appealing for calm when we were still less than ten miles from Oxford.

Frankly, it was amazing that the city link ever survived. The tour was carnage. Two of us were hosted by a Bonn RFC player. He was delightfully naive. On the first night, he introduced us to his girlfriend, Sally. 'I am the only boyfriend she has ever had,' he told us proudly. He then made the crass error of bringing her to the game. By the end of the trip, her boyfriend count had gone up just a little.

The Bonn–Oxford Poly game was remarkably good, considering the pre-match preparations, and we were leading by a point or two just before the end. As ever on tour, the match had that extra bite and we were holding on well. We were far from a great side – the Bonn team had West Germany internationals – but we were leading and, by our standards, playing heroically.

In the last seconds, I took the ball in open play. God knows why I ever considered passing it at all, God knows why I didn't stick it up my jersey and try to beast it up the middle – or hoof it to hell. But for a reason I have never understood, I threw out a long pass across the midfield off my left, weaker, hand (as opposed to my right, weaker, hand).

Even when the ball was intercepted, the danger seemed

minimal, because it was caught by their worst player, a tiny, almost mouse-like wing, who had been terrified of the ball all day. As he set off, our cover defence converged to smash him. Rick, our fast man on the wing, had him in his sights.

Suddenly, everything stopped – Rick, the rest of the cover defenders, the Bonn support runners, the ref, the world itself. Everything stopped, or so it seemed. Their wing had unleashed the most terrifying burst of pace I have ever seen on a rugby field, and I have seen all the fast men of the last three decades. Harriman, Guscott, Rokocoko? Forget them. The Bonn wing scored under the posts and around twenty minutes later the rest of his team caught up to congratulate him. And so, we lost.

After the game, the scorer, Jobst Hirsch, showed us a small sporting memento. It was an Olympic medal, bronze, won as lead-off man in West Germany's 4 x 100 metres relay team at the Munich Olympics, a few years earlier.

There is no moral to the tale, unless it is that you shouldn't go out with Sally. What coach ever had the foresight to tell you to make sure you don't get intercepted by an Olympic sprinter?

FIRST IMPRESSIONS
NIGEL REDMAN

'Nigel was a true Bath legend, playing 349 games over a sixteen-year period. He played twenty times for England between 1984 and 1997, starting and finishing with Australia. In 1997 he was touring Argentina with England when he got the call to replace Doddie Weir for the Lions in South Africa. Nigel made a massive contribution to that tour and was the proud captain of the midweek team against Orange Free State (a match the Lions won 52–30). Nigel is now a senior RFU National Academy coach and I'm sure we will see him coaching at various levels within rugby for many years to come.'

In the summer of 1983, aged just seventeen, I decided to leave my home club of Weston-super-Mare and join Bath, one of the country's top clubs. My first pre-season training session took place on a Monday evening in mid July. I climbed into my old white Ford Cortina Mark 3 with my mother's packed tea (consisting of four rounds of beef sandwiches, a packet of cheese and onion crisps, a KitKat and the compulsory pint of full fat milk) on the passenger seat beside me. My mother insisted I drank three pints of milk a day because it was 'good for your bones', and as a consequence I was carrying a little extra weight for my now strong frame to support.

On arrival at training it was noticeable many of the first-team players were missing; some were still on holiday, others strategically choosing to skip the running around in favour of getting stuck in when the rugby balls were introduced, some-time during the early part of August. There were some mutter-ings that Gareth Chilcott was due back from his annual pilgrimage to Bangkok later that week and a sweep was being collected on how heavy he would be. But one person who most certainly was in attendance was the club captain, Roger Spurrell. Roger was an ex-paratrooper and now nightclub owner. He had curly blond hair and a powerfully built upper body, and his fearsome and uncompromising reputation had filtered down to my old club. This was the man I had to impress.

John Davis led the session and it wasn't long before I began to question why we were running so much without a ball in sight. John played outside-half and was built like a marathon runner. Boy, did he love to run! Oddly, as the session got harder, a number of the forwards had to stop because of stones in their shoes. Poor lambs. Me, I would not stop for anything – at least, not until I was violently ill, that is. On the pitch. In full view. Not ideal on day one.

My journey home was one of reflection. Had Roger seen me vomit? Was he pleased with my first training session? Why had he not introduced himself? Did he know who I was? Reflection turned to indignation.

He should know who I was – I was Nigel Redman no less. I had played for England Under-19s the previous year, I had made the effort to travel to his club and he couldn't even shake my hand and say welcome. How rude! I decided to make a point of introducing myself to Roger during my next visit.

Wednesday came very quickly and I still hadn't recovered from Monday. The tops of my thighs were red raw with chafing and I ached all over. I slumped into my car minus a packed tea, much to my mother's disgust, but I was never going to make that mistake again.

It was a beautiful summer's evening in Bath and as I parked I noticed a few new faces, but still no more first-team players. Roger, however, was there once again. The Wednesday session was almost identical to Monday's (minus the vomiting) and afterwards I decided to make my approach. I walked over to where Roger was standing and extended my hand in greeting. Roger did not move a muscle. Intimidated? No way. Even if my hand did look somewhat odd stuck out in front of me. Onwards and upwards, though.

'Hello, Roger. My name is Nigel Redman. I played for England Under-19s last year and I have decided to drive up to Bath from Weston-super-Mare, where I live with my parents, to play for your club. And can I also say that it is an honour to be here and I am thoroughly looking forward to gaining a place in the first team and experience being captained by someone as inspiring as you.'

I remained standing there for what seemed like eternity while Roger formulated his response. I remember thinking, 'That went rather well,' as he tilted his head, eyeing me from my toes to my slightly thinning hair.

'I couldn't give a f*** what you're called or where you've come from, I couldn't give a f*** who you've played for. You are a fat bastard and don't talk to me again until you've lost a stone and a half in weight.' He then walked off in the direction of the clubhouse.

As Roger disappeared into the sunset I remained rooted to the spot. Should I stay or should I go? I knew the answer immediately. This was the place for me. There was now no question of retreating to my old club and my good friends. I was going to stay where I was and fight my way into this band of very special people, and discover the reason why they would put their bodies on the line for this man. It didn't take long to find out. And I've never once regretted that decision to stay.

If Bath was 'A' list, the same could not be said, unfortunately, for the national set-up in the mid eighties. The great second-row forward and captain, Billy Beaumont, had retired hurt and England were rudderless, shifting effortlessly from a Grand Slam to the Wooden Spoon in the space of three years. These were indeed desperate times.

In the autumn of 1984, I won my first cap against the touring Wallabies but was subsequently dropped for the next game against Romania. The selectors were changing half the team with every new match that came along, and it was clear they needed the stability of a leader who was going to be there for the long haul, somebody young and inspirational, someone they could build a team around. That's when the phone rang.

'Hello Nigel, Mike Weston here.' Mike was the team manager of the England Under-23s. He started to explain the situation England rugby was in and then went on to tell me that I was exactly what they were looking for to take the national side forward. Mike now had my full attention as he continued the conversation by saying, 'We have an England Under-23 match coming up and we want you to captain the team.'

'Wonderful, who will we be playing?' I asked.

'We want you to lead the side out at Twickenham,' was Mike's response.

'Brilliant. Who will we be playing?' I asked again.

'The team we've selected is as experienced a bunch as has ever played at this level,' said Mike.

'Unbelievable. Who will we be playing?'

'There are five internationals in the pack, including Dean Richards and Andy Robinson, and a back division of the calibre of Steve Bates, Stuart Barnes, Kevin Simms, Fran Clough, Rory Underwood and Simon Hodgkinson,' Mike said proudly.

'That's absolutely fantastic, but who are we playing?'

'Spain,' came the response, followed by a protracted silence from both parties.

'Spain?' I asked for the sake of clarity.

'Yes,' said Mike. 'It will be their first fifteen.'

'Well, whoopee do,' I thought.

'We want you to show us your leadership qualities and, in all fairness, we would expect you to come through and go on to lead England long into the future.'

Well, it would be a great experience, and I started to think about the way I would lead the team. I could lead by example. I was playing well at the time for Bath and I could strike out from the front and let others follow. Or I could be a great motivator and speak with clarity and emotion to rouse the team and inspire them to raise their performance to levels they never thought they could achieve. Oh yes, cometh the hour, cometh the man. I was ready for the challenge.

Game day came around quickly, and following our intense training and preparation, the team were ready for the match, and I was ready for my leadership challenge. As Nigel had promised, the team was a strong one with only one change to the original line-up. John Wells had damaged his ribs during a game against Bath on the weekend before the international and had been replaced at blindside by Tim Edbrooke of Exeter University. Everything was on track and looking good.

We arrived at Twickenham an hour before kick-off and on entering the changing room our outside-half, Stuart Barnes, came to speak with me. Stuart was an Oxford Blue and had recently joined Bath from local rivals Bristol. He put his arm around my waist and moved his head close so he could whisper.

'Look, I have listened to some of your team-talks during training and have come to the conclusion you should lead by example on the field and leave talking to the players to me.' Stuart obviously wanted a part to play. Fair enough. Empower the players.

'No problem,' I replied, and gave Stuart a manly hug.

Stuart was in full flow as the referee knocked on the door and called, 'Let's have you out now, England.' I looked around the dressing room one last time before pumping up my chest, picking up the match ball and leading the team down the tunnel and up the steps on to the field . . . surrounded by a completely empty stadium.

Well, the game went as expected and displaying inspirational leadership I led England to victory. We stuffed Spain out of sight, 15–12. Spain scored two tries and I showed calmness, clarity and high levels of communication and decision-making under pressure as I asked Stuart Barnes to kick five penalties.

It seems I was the only one who thought my display that afternoon was worthy of bigger and better things. I was dropped. In fact, I hold the record of being dropped by England about as many times as I have been selected. But I have always thought Mike Weston had tremendous insight and vision.

DEBT OF HONOUR

STEVE BOYLE

'Steve was a little ahead of my time, playing for Gloucester and England in the early eighties. In 1983 he was selected for the British and Irish Lions tour to New Zealand and he also played a number of games for the Barbarians. Apparently, twelve months prior to his first cap he was playing England "B" against Ireland "B" in Belfast. On reading the papers the next day he learnt that a fellow second rower had got into a fight and was facing a ban. He turned to his coach, Mike Davis, and said jokingly, "I've moved up the pecking order!" Mike was quick to reply, "That must move you up to at least tenth in line for your first cap now."'

The many years I spent on the rugby field seem like a lifetime ago. Here's a story that highlights the changing times, the difference between the good old amateur era, when I played my rugby, and the current professional regime. Those of you who play your rugby in the lower leagues, where you have to pay a match fee rather than receive one, will know exactly what I'm talking about.

In 1983 I was honoured to be selected to play for the

Barbarians at Rodney Parade, now the home of the Newport Gwent Dragons. The match was televised and broadcast to millions, the stadium packed out with supporters. I assume a reasonable amount of money was generated as a result of the fixture, not that the players saw very much of it.

Once the match was over, a member of the Barbarian committee was in the changing room, not to congratulate us on our performance or for continuing the Barbarian tradition of playing an open, attractive running brand of rugby. No, he was there to collect the shirts. His sole responsibility was to ensure none went missing. This was the amateur era and, if I'm being honest, I knew I would have to hand the shirt back. It was expected. I was, however, hopeful of some memento to record my first appearance as a member of the world's most famous touring team.

Having filled in my expense claim (8p per mile) I handed it in, only to be told it was not 75 miles each way from Gloucester to Newport, it was 48.25 miles, making a round-trip total of 96.5 miles, which came to the princely sum of £7.72.

I made my way to the clubhouse and ordered a beer, which I paid for myself (I must have had a crap game, since no one offered to buy me a drink). After that I progressed to the dining area and helped myself to pie and chips, supplied by the host club (whoopee).

Shortly after that the moment arrived. Geoff Windsor Lewis, who was and I believe still is secretary of the Barbarians, approached me and handed me a Barbarians tie and a Barbarians scarf. Fantastic I thought, this is what it's all about. I would wear my Barbarians tie with pride to work the very next day, and hope the occasional person would ask me if it was representative of anything so I could tell them about my debut for the Barbarians Rugby Club. I was thinking about all this when Geoff handed me a third item, an invoice for £24.00, covering the cost of tie and scarf.

I hadn't brought much cash with me, and having had my mileage claim knocked back I didn't have the required sum on my person, so asked Geoff if it was OK to pay by cheque.

'Not a problem, Steve,' he said. 'Make sure you put your cheque-guarantee card number on the back though.'

Happy days.

LESSONS LEARNED
ANDREW RIPLEY

'When I was growing up, all young No. 8s aspired to be Andy Ripley. The long hair, the headband, the high knee lifts (okay, I didn't manage to emulate *that* much of his game) – the man had presence and style. He was a fantastic No. 8 for England, winning twenty-four caps, and he was also a member of the victorious British and Irish Lions side to tour South Africa in 1974. Andy kept himself incredibly fit, winning the British *Superstars* competition and coming a very creditable third in the world *Superstars* event. Andy was diagnosed with prostate cancer and continues to battle the disease to this day with immense bravery, as you would expect from someone with such a strong personality. He is a real character of the game and he will be remembered by many as having outstanding natural talent.

'David Trick tells a wonderful story about Andy, which I think gives great insight into the qualities of the man.'

I first met Andy when both he and I were invited to play for Sandy Sanders' XV (past president of the RFU) against Paris University Club (PUC) in Paris. I was eighteen years of age and had just started playing for Bath. When the team assembled at Heathrow Airport, it rapidly became apparent the only person I didn't know was me; everyone else was a famous name from the world of international rugby.

On arrival at the Hotel Saint Jacques, the rooming list was read out and I found myself sharing with Andy.

Following the match on the Saturday (I think we lost but the result is not relevant), both teams attended a huge dinner held in a massive sports hall. Hundreds of 'stuffed shirts' and 'alikados' were there. At a certain point during the evening Chris Ralston, a giant former England second row, walked behind Andy Ripley, who was seated at a table, and poured a bottle of water over his head. Andy did not flinch. He did not even break the conversation he was having.

Several minutes later Andy left his seat, walked behind Chris, who was now seated at his table, and poured a carafe of red wine over his head. Chris, to his credit, didn't flinch either. What followed can only be described as indescribable – the biggest food fight the world has ever seen, absolute mayhem. Trays of desserts, which the boys found behind a curtain, were hurled across the room. Two of the top-table dignitaries were seen, stripped to the waist, holding huge round cheeses in front of their stomachs and running into each other. Bowls of spinach were poured on to the floor creating a green 'skating rink'. Truly, it was an appalling scene but one to which I did not contribute (honest . . .). I merely observed, with my mouth wide open. Inevitably, it wasn't long before a few of the boys found the fire extinguishers. At that point I felt a tap on my shoulder. There was Andy, who looked down at me from his great height. 'Now is the time to leave,' he said, which I was more than happy to agree to, and we disappeared quietly out of a side exit into the Paris night. By all accounts we left just five minutes before the Gendarmerie arrived on the scene. Had they come to question us, they'd have found us innocently sipping a beer in a nearby bar.

And what did I learn from this incident? The importance of timing and positioning, both valuable life skills – and of making sure that when the shit hits the fan, you are no longer in the vicinity.

The following morning, the team was due to travel back to Heathrow on a mid-morning flight. I awoke with a considerable hangover and looked across the room to Andy's bed, which was vacant. Oh dear! A quick glance at the bedside clock showed me I had exactly five minutes to get dressed, pack my bag and make my way to the airport (about forty minutes away). Needless to say, I didn't make it and ended up getting a seat on a plane departing later that evening.

Several weeks later, Bath were playing Rosslyn Park and I managed to have a chat with Andy prior to the kick-off. Not surprisingly, my first question was to ask why he had left me fast asleep in bed. Andy explained how in the previous night's food fight he had removed me from a situation that was quite obviously getting out of hand, one I had no control over and had never encountered before. 'As for getting out of bed,' he went on to say, 'that's something I assume you've done almost every day of your short life and not a thing you require my help with.' In a nutshell, it was my responsibility on that occasion.

Another lesson well taught, and indeed learnt.

HUMPH AND THE HIPPY
LEE MEARS

'Now established as one of the best hookers in international rugby, Lee is a solid bloke. He has been a great servant to both Bath, scoring on his debut, and England, winning thirty-four caps. More recently, he has played for the British and Irish Lions. He is very reliable and always at the heart of everything that is happening.'

At the time of writing, Leinster are the European champions, and have always provided stiff opposition in the competition. I'm not qualified to talk about the magic of Brian O'Driscoll in the Leinster back line, but I think I know a thing or two about forward play and so can comment on the Leinster pack, and in particular their front row.

On one occasion when Bath were playing Leinster, I was on the bench and Jonathan Humphreys, the former Wales hooker and captain, was on the pitch. His opposite number was Shane Byrne, the former Ireland hooker aka 'Mini Munch' due to a more than passing resemblance to former England bruiser, Mickey Skinner. At the risk of getting too technical, it's thought among the Bath forwards that if you do not hit the scrum hard and lock in the Leinster front row, more often than not they tend to stand up, particularly Shane Byrne. He had tried this tactic several times in this match, and as one of the scrums broke up Humph said to no one in particular, 'Someone needs to send Byrne a message.' All eyes turned to our resident enforcer, Danny Grewcock, who accepted the challenge and, fixing Humph with his thousand-mile stare, grunted, 'That'll be me then.'

I'm sure most readers will be aware what Danny looks like but for those of you who don't, I'll give you a brief description. He is a giant of a man, 6ft 6in tall and weighing in at almost nineteen stone. His hair is often longer than it should be and his chin always appears to have a minimum of seven days' growth on it – a modern-day Desperate Dan look-alike, you could say. Not that anyone would dare say that to his face . . .

Now Danny is a straight talker, but he is also a disciple of the 'action speaks louder than words' philosophy, and at the next scrum Danny sent a very direct 'non verbal' message through to Shane Byrne. The scrum broke up and Danny got up to follow the ball, which had been kicked out of play for a line-out. As he was running he noticed Shane Byrne sprinting alongside him. 'Fair play,' he thought. 'I can see why Shane is the Irish national hooker. I've given him one of my best shots and not only is he still standing, he's actually running like a spring chicken. He must have a chin made of granite. Full respect to him.'

As the line-out formed there was a delay due to the absence of the Bath hooker, Jonathan Humphreys, who was in a heap somewhat adjacent to the previous scrum. A bit of treatment from the magic sponge and Humph made it to his feet and completed the remaining minutes until half-time, albeit staggering around in a daze.

From memory, we were a few points down at the break and were deservedly receiving a fairly severe bollocking from our coach, former Australian hooker Michael Foley. He was picking on individual players and delivering his withering verdict on their performance. Given Michael's international pedigree at hooker, when he got round to Humph he just stared and said, 'Humph, what on earth has happened to you?! You've been bloody anonymous for the last ten minutes.'

Humph stared at Foley and then shouted, 'The f***ing hippy f***ing hit me!!'

It's these moments, when you are in the middle of a 'hairdryer' treatment and a comment is made causing the entire team to start laughing, that often bond the team and make the difference between winning and losing. Fortunately, Foley laughed along with the boys and delivered the remainder of his message in more light-hearted tone to a more receptive team.

Indeed, we went on to win the match, and Humph and Danny kissed and made up afterwards.

LE COQ SPORTIF

DANNY GREWCOCK

'One of my England team-mates for many years, Danny has won sixty-nine caps for his country. You would always want to have Danny on your team, because he is one of the nicest guys off the pitch but one of the toughest men to play against on it. We had plenty of battles when Wasps played Bath, and Danny was one of the guys you tried to wind up – he always had a short fuse, no doubt about it! He has also been a key member of two Lions tours and keeps himself in great shape.'

I joined Saracens from Coventry Rugby Club in 1997, and I knew immediately I was mixing in a different league. I was surrounded by players such as François Pienaar, Michael Lynagh and Philippe Sella. Others included England back-row legend Richard Hill and scrum-half Kyran Bracken, both of whom would go on to win more than fifty caps for their country, and Hilly would play an integral part in England's World Cup triumph in 2003. As I said, this was a very different class of player I was now mixing with.

I would like to take this opportunity to thank publicly all of these players for the influence they had on me during my time with Saracens. They never complained – and, believe me, there was a lot to complain about. Some of the training methods were neanderthal to say the least, but none of them ever moaned. They got on with whatever they were told to do and taught me many valuable lessons along the way. Sadly, the one thing they never taught me was how to avoid getting a yellow card. Still, you can't have it all.

All the Saracens players were members of a gym not far from the training ground in Southgate – which had some novelty value for the players, not least because we could go and get in the Jacuzzi after training. It was a mixed gym and the Jacuzzi was shared by males and females, another reason to make the effort to turn up.

One particular day we had been weight training at the gym and, following the session, several of us decided to check out the 'scenery' in the Jacuzzi. Sadly, it was empty. However, we had the rest of the day off so we selflessly decided to get in and see who turned up. I remember seeing the door leading from the men's changing room open and Philippe Sella walk out with a towel wrapped around his waist. He went over to the pegs on the wall, hung up his towel and walked over to the Jacuzzi, wearing the same suit he was born in.

Given the nature of rugby changing rooms in those days, this was not out of the ordinary. Players used to have a quick shower following a match to get most of the mud off and then climb into the giant bath along with all their team-mates. All naked, all male – it was the norm.

However, we were not in a rugby changing room and this was definitely not the norm. It was surely only a matter of time before a woman walked into the Jacuzzi. In fact, it was less than five minutes before two ladies arrived, hung up their robes to reveal their swimsuits and joined us in the swirling water.

You can imagine the scene. All of us were acting like guilty schoolboys, sniggering, giving each other knowing looks, waiting for the moment the ladies realised Sella – our very own *'coq sportif'* – was naked.

We looked at this rugby god to see what his reaction would be. Was he worried? Was he going to wait in the Jacuzzi until the ladies departed? Had he even realised he was the only guy who was not wearing shorts or trunks? Or was he just the coolest guy in the world – well, in north London at any rate? It goes without saying that Philippe Sella was, and remains, a true legend of world rugby. He always kept a calm head when playing, always seemed to do the right thing at the right time – an extremely talented player with total control. So how was he going to remain in control of this particular situation?

Following a few more boyish comments, Philippe decided that if he didn't want to look like a prune, then he had spent long enough in the hot tub. He stood up and walked towards the steps of the Jacuzzi, saying, 'Excuse me,' to one of the ladies as he walked passed her with his 'Agen tackle' no more than eighteen inches away from her face. He continued to the pegs, retrieved his towel and walked towards the men's changing rooms using the towel to dry his hair!

The boys looked on in stunned silence and waited for a comment from one of the ladies. I was expecting something like, 'Fair play, he's got a set of bollocks on him,' or 'I've seen a bigger prick on a whelk.'

One lady looked at the other, raised an eyebrow and said, *'C'est magnifique!'*

Those words identified her as good sport, a Saracens supporter and a connoisseur of all things French. Rumour has it she went out and bought a season ticket for her and her friend that same afternoon. Perhaps that's what Nigel Wray meant when he said Philippe would deliver great value for the club.

FAT, BALD AND ENGLISH
GARETH CHILCOTT

'Gareth is one of the true legends of Bath, England and England Supporters. In his prime "Coochie" was a svelte eighteen stone and was one of the hardest men I have come across on the field but one of the nicest and warmest gentlemen I have met off it (even though he did like to say, "You got to swat those Waspies."). In terms of the physical side of the game, I think it's fair to say Coochie gave as good as he got. If you ever wondered what a prop was like in the amateur days – Coochie was it. In *The Times* Gareth was often described as "uncompromising, a player who never took a backward step". A similar report in the *Sun* would probably call him "a dirty bastard". He was your archetypal front rower, technically excellent and undoubtedly the cornerstone of the Bath team that dominated rugby in the eighties. I first came across him when I was a young boy straight out of Ampleforth College, playing for Wasps, and realised that for people like Gareth, i.e. all front rows, the rugby ball was actually an inconvenience throughout the whole eighty minutes of a game. This was an important insight into the mentality of that unique breed.

'Gareth now runs a successful sports tours business and is a fantastic after-dinner speaker. It's fair to say that since retirement he has not spent an unnecessary amount of time in the gym. I do believe he has a treadmill in his garage, which in recent years has become a useful low shelf on which to store pots of paint and wood sealer.'

Since 22 November 2003 I have lost count of the number of times I have been asked, 'Where were you when Jonny Wilkinson kicked the drop goal to win the World Cup?' It's a question I never tire of answering.

I was doing some commentary work for an Australian TV network, Channel 7, on top of the Telstra Stadium, the venue for the final. It was an occasion and a night I will never forget. Either side of me, assisting with the commentary, were two genuine legends (and I mean that) from the world of rugby union.

On my right was the Australian second row John Eales. John was a member of the Australian team that won the second-ever Rugby World Cup, at Twickenham in 1991, and went on to captain his country when they won again in 1999 at the Millennium Stadium, Cardiff, conceding only one try throughout the entire tournament. Arguably the most successful Aussie captain of all time, John stands 6ft 6in tall and proved to be a most influential figure both on and off the field – a great player and a real gent.

To the left of me was Tim Horan, another Australian legend and key member of the successful 1991 and 1999 World Cup campaigns, and also the finest centre I have seen in my entire career (apologies to my old team-mate Jerry Guscott – you were a very close second!). Tim was a complete player, who always appeared to have every aspect of the game firmly under his control, ruthless in attack and formidable in defence.

As you would expect from three former partisan players, the early banter between John, Tim and myself was lively. Prior to the kick-off Tim had said how much he was looking forward to the game and thanked the England team for bothering to turn up. I replied saying it was a great pleasure and turning up had been made so much easier since we no longer required a criminal record to enter the country. (I think, or rather hope, we were off air at this stage – on reflection, we must have been because I'm still here.)

Even though the match took place 12,000 miles from home, I have such a vivid recollection of looking around the entire stadium, amazed at how many English shirts were on display. The English support was phenomenal, tens of thousands of expectant fans hoping for a victory on the other side of the world.

Everyone who watched the World Cup final will remember how close the match was, particularly the latter stages. Andre Watson, the referee, awarded a controversial penalty (I thought it was controversial, anyway, and so did twenty million English fans around the world) against England in the last minute of the game, allowing Elton Flatley to level the scores. The tension on the pitch and around the stadium was incredible, and the chat between the three of us had dried up. In fact, we were so wrapped up in the match at times it was difficult to remember we were there to commentate as we lost ourselves in our hopes and dreams about the possible outcome.

With the teams tied and twenty-five seconds remaining in the second period of extra time, Jonny received the ball from Matt Dawson and shaped up to take a drop kick, 'with his less-favoured right foot', in the words of BBC Radio Five Live commentator Ian Robertson. I make no excuses for quoting again: 'This is the one. It's coming back to Jonny Wilkinson. He drops for World Cup glory.' The rest, as we all know, is history. The ball sailed between the posts and seconds later the final whistle signalled that England were world champions.

So where was I?

I was standing between the two Australian icons of rugby union, John 'Nobody' Eales and Tim Horan. I was out of breath, I was f***ing fat, I was f***ing bald and, above all, I was F***ING ENGLISH!!

BIT OF A MAULING

JASON LEONARD

'With 114 caps for England, Jason epitomises the word "legend". He played his club rugby at Saracens and Harlequins. The statistics of his international career are too numerous to mention here, but a few of the highlights are appropriate, given his stature in the game. Actually, having seen him recently, I could have deleted the "in the game" in that sentence. At one time he was the world's most capped player and is still the most capped forward. He won five Grand Slams, and the World Cup, and took part in a victorious Lions tour (to South Africa in 1997). In total, he won five Lions caps. Oh, and he scored one try – in 114 games.

'I first met Jason when I had just finished playing for Middlesex Under-21s against Eastern Counties at Barking Rugby Club. I walked up to the clubhouse and Jason, who hadn't played in the game, had come in for a Sunday pint with his mates. He was surrounded by people but seemed to have time for all of them. Actually, he had a pint with all of them, which was an achievement in itself! Little did I know then that Jason and I would spend hours upon hours with England. He is my lifelong training partner. The two of us, along with Will Greenwood, used to get up at some ungodly hour, meet at Twickenham and put our bodies through hell to get in the right shape to play for

England. Jason turned out to be my room-mate on most occasions in the England set-up. We were two peas in the same pod really. A fantastic character.'

Honest, Guv, it wasn't me . . .

I have the dubious distinction of being the first-ever international player to be cited for violent conduct – not something I'm particularly proud of, but a fact.

England were playing Scotland in Edinburgh, and at a certain point during the match I was seen flying into a maul with a raised arm and moments later the Scottish captain, Rob Wainwright, was seen departing the maul backwards at a rate of knots. Rob was definitely 'dazed' and played no effective part in the rest of the game.

After the match, I was cited by the Scottish coach Jim Telfer for violent conduct and was asked to appear the following day at a hearing to be held at the Lensbury Club not far from Twickenham. It cast a bit of a shadow over my normal post-match victory celebrations, and the flight back to Heathrow was not the most enjoyable.

At the Lensbury Club, I was escorted to a room where the hearing was to take place. Only three people were present – Jim Telfer the complainant, Marcel Martin, a French Rugby Union official (a neutral), and me. None of us really had a clue about the procedure because it was the first time a case of this nature had been heard. So after some discussion it was decided to watch the incident from the various camera angles. In those days there were only half a dozen cameras at the game, so the 'evidence' was not as detailed as it would be in the current era, when thirty-plus cameras are utilised.

The incident was studied at normal speed, half speed and, finally, frame by frame. Luckily, from every angle, at the critical moment the incident was blocked, either by another player getting in the way or, in the case of one angle, the referee himself obscuring the view (things were looking good). I was also fortunate that a couple of cameras were on 'long shot', which meant they were useless in determining what happened during the particular maul in question.

At the conclusion of the camera evidence Jim Telfer looked at Marcel and said, 'Well, it's obvious Jason Leonard punched Rob Wainwright.' I referred him to one frame that clearly showed my right hand was open and not clenched in a fist.

'If I'd punched Rob, I would have broken every bone in my hand,' I said, and held up my hand wiggling all my fingers to make my point. 'No bones broken here.'

Jim said it could well have been an 'elbow chop'. My defence this time was to mention that I was 5ft 10in and Rob was 6ft 4in and you could clearly see I was in a crouched position as I entered the maul, so it would have been impossible for me to 'elbow chop' Rob.

Jim was not happy to say the least. He had cited me, he had made the trip from Edinburgh for the hearing and things were not going his way. In desperation he said, 'In that case, it could quite easily have been a forearm smash,' (which, funnily enough, it was).

'Look Jim,' I said, 'we've seen every available camera angle and there's no conclusive evidence against me.' Marcel Martin was forced to agree with my statement and the case was dismissed. Jim departed the room absolutely furious, knocking over chairs as he went.

By contrast I was cock a hoop. I had not only become the first person to be cited for violent conduct in international rugby, I had by definition just become the first person to get off a citing case without a fine or a ban.

As I was just about to leave the room Marcel spoke to me and said he wasn't happy. 'Jason, I think you've been a very lucky lad. You know you did it. I know you did it.'

Then, pointing at the TV screen, he continued: 'Just because I couldn't see it, it doesn't mean I don't know it happened.'

Flushed with success I replied, 'I wouldn't get upset, Marcel. Rob was a lot closer than you and he didn't see anything either!'

A sponge and hot towels

Since retiring from professional rugby, it's fair to say that I have been in regular demand to speak, eat and drink at a few sporting functions all around the UK. Being a very sociable animal, I am always happy to accept these invitations and share a few tales from my long and enjoyable international rugby career.

I was asked at one such sporting dinner if I had ever taken the field of play in an international when I was not fully fit. My initial response was to say, 'About one hundred and fourteen times.' I think the guy thought I was joking. He laughed but a look of expectancy remained on his face.

As I racked my brains I remembered a match I had played against Ireland at Lansdowne Road. I was recovering from an injury and had been rushed back into the squad at relatively short notice. To be completely truthful I was, in building industry parlance, 'carrying a bit of timber'. Clive Woodward had notified me in advance that I was going to be in the team and told me to get as much training done as I could. I did try hard, but the layoff had been fairly lengthy and I had done no training during it. That coupled with a few beers more than normal (rude not to) meant I was always going to be struggling.

As ever with internationals between the Irish and the English, the first twenty minutes of the match were played at a frenetic rate as the Irish tried to run us ragged and upset our game plan. It's fair to say I was beginning to blow a bit and it was around then I found myself ever so slightly on the wrong side of a ruck – funny that. The Irish lads have never been slow to take advantage of an 'open goal' situation like this and they trampled all over my prone figure, kicking seven bells out of me, and I was 'spewed' out of the back of the ruck, thanks to the boots of virtually every Irish forward.

I had managed to get myself off the ground, knowing my back was going to look like a road map, and was on my hands and knees when the English physio arrived. He didn't need to lift my shirt, he just parted one of the full length rips in it. Without the physio saying a word I knew I was in trouble when I heard him take a sharp intake of breath, followed by, 'Euggghhh!'

Play had moved over to the other side of the pitch and into touch, so both sets of forwards were waiting for me to receive treatment before the ball could be thrown into the line-out and the game could continue.

Now I must admit I've had my fair share of 'slipper' throughout my career, but this was a proper going over. I was struggling big time and was breathing heavily on all fours as I was being treated with the 'magic sponge' and a bit of antiseptic spray (which, for the record, is unbelievably painful when sprayed on to an open wound!). The crowd was relatively quiet as they also waited for my recovery and play to continue. At this moment an Irish voice from the crowd shouted out, 'Leonard, you don't need a physio, you need a f***ing midwife.'

PART TWO

TALES FROM THE BACKS

There are so many stories I could have picked about those lovable backs – secrets of the hair salon, the gruelling ten minute training sessions they endure (three minute warm up, three minute stretch down and the rest spent practising how to make sure their socks stay up, in case you are interested) or how they have perfected the art of standing back and watching others get the job done. But instead, I have plumped for three favourites which I am happy to tell over and over again. Which, in fact, is exactly what I do. Often. I don't seem to get invited out much these days. Odd . . .

Make that thirty

Rugby union has a fierce reputation for the controlled (most of the time) aggression that players take on to the field. However, there is nothing quite like the prospect of a derby match between two local teams to get the blood boiling. Given the two very different demographic backgrounds of the main clubs in London – the wonderful Wasps and the other lot (Harlequins) – this fixture was the one that we always looked forward to every season.

The two clubs are at the opposite ends of the social scale –

Harlequins, who were, in the amateur era, the self-proclaimed landed gentry of the rugby world – with their multi-coloured shirts, excessive bags of toiletries and frightfully posh accents prided themselves on being 'Champagne Charlies'. You could always see them out in Fulham or Chelsea with a Camilla or Jemima on their arms, and always driving the smartest cars. They just begged to be loathed by one and all. You only have to read the story of how each club came into being to understand the deep-rooted dislike that dates back all these years.

Harlequins were originally known as the Hampstead Football Club, but were renamed in 1870 when the membership was no longer purely a local one. A meeting was called and because the HFC monogram had to be retained, a dictionary was produced and, when the reader reached 'harlequin', he was stopped and the new name was born. An offshoot of this was that there was a split in the membership of the Hampstead Football Club and the half that did not form the Harlequins went off and formed a club known as the Wasps, who were seen as the upstarts of North London with an altogether more grounded feel about them.

Wasps were called Wasps largely due to the fashion of the Victorian period when clubs tended to adopt the names of insects, birds and animals. That's it really. No other reason. As a reasonably well-established club, Wasps were invited to join the Rugby Football Union and, therefore, were eligible to be founder members. And so they would have been had it not been for a calamitous mix-up that led to them not being present at the inauguration ceremony. In true rugby fashion, the team turned up at the wrong pub, on the wrong day, at the wrong time.

To be fair to Quins they had actively sought to change their playboy image in the early nineties and had a pack of forwards who on their day would have rivalled the best in the country. They included an all-international front row of Andy Mullins, Brian Moore and Jason Leonard, locked out by fellow England and Lions international Paul Ackford in the second row; and in flankers Peter Winterbottom and Mickey Skinner you had two of the most feared back-row players in the world. They also had Will Carling and Simon Halliday playing in the backs alongside David Pears (when fit) and Andrew Harriman, the noblest of noblemen on the wing. (Perhaps they were always going to struggle to shake off that playboy tag after all.)

Wasps had a far more urbane feel about them – England internationals Paul Rendall, Jeff Probyn and Dean Ryan were playing upfront, whilst the backline included Steve Bates, Rob Andrew, Chris Oti, Damian Hopley and Huw Davies, so we weren't exactly shortchanged out wide.

The ferocity from the kick-off on derby day was always incredible, and this very memorable match was no different. The Wasps back row was Mark Rigby, Dean Ryan and Buster White, and they went headfirst into the contact situation like their very lives depended upon it. The pride of the black jersey was all-consuming, and an inspiration to everyone involved. I came on as a replacement in the second half and I was so fired up. There I was going toe to toe with my boyhood heroes and now great rivals. This was no time for adulation, however, and I knew I had to make an impression from the off.

The first part of the play I was involved in was when Will Carling took a switch ball back to the forwards and, like any good flanker, I pounced on him to try and stop him in his tracks. Now Will wasn't always a permanent fixture in the Quins side. He would often pick and choose his games according to form and fitness (his opposite number's form and fitness, of course!), but here I was with the England captain coming at me and I managed to scrag him to the floor. Given that it seemed Will's *raison d'être* was to try and stay in one piece in between internationals, it was obvious he wasn't very keen on going to ground. Having got him there, I could hear my forwards screaming, 'Hold him down Lol, do NOT let him get away!!' It's not very often that you get the chance to do the Mexican hat dance all over the England skipper, and this was an opportunity too good to be missed. I understand this is what is termed by management consultants as 'Low Hanging Fruit'. (Don't know where I got that little nugget from. Too much time with Clive?)

What followed was a thud of studs, feet and hooves that wouldn't have looked out of place in the Wild West. All hell broke loose and the referee blew his whistle as the ball was not coming out. As the two packs of forwards picked themselves up off the floor, breathing heavily, Will let out a yelp at the bottom of the ruck, and came up clutching his eyebrow which seemed to be oozing a not inconsiderable amount of blood. As the photographers trained their telescopic lenses on him, he pointed at the Wasps forwards and squealed, 'Oh, bloody hell, ref! Did you see which one of those rotters did this to me?!' Step forward Harlequins No. 8 Richard Langhorn, one of the two uncapped players in the Quins pack that afternoon, who mused, 'Could have been any one of twenty-nine of us, ref.' Quick as a flash the ref said, 'Make that thirty!'

This story has gone down in English rugby folklore for two reasons – partly because it served to lighten the brutal mood of an intense London derby for ten seconds – Wasps went on to win and take the annual bragging rites. However, this story is recalled on many occasions much more poignantly because just a couple of years later Richard Langhorn tragically died whilst undergoing a routine back operation, aged just twenty-eight. Langers was one of life's good guys and he left behind nothing but wonderful memories of his spirit, his remarkable sporting talent and a wonderful smile that would melt even the coldest of hearts. He was genuinely an inspiration to everyone, as were his parents who offered a lot of support to my parents as they both shared the experience of losing a child.

Richard had a keen love of all sports and so, in his memory, the Richard Langhorn Trust was established to provide sporting opportunities in rugby, skiing, basketball and sailing for disabled and underprivileged young people regardless of their age, gender, race, ability or background. I was very proud to be involved in the trust in its inauguration and one of the first events we undertook was to cycle to Paris in Richard's name. The Richard Langhorn Trust has brought smiles to many young people's faces, just as he brought smiles to all of our faces that afternoon at The Stoop and on many other occasions.

A taxing opening gambit

Prior to certain international matches, the players from both sides are often introduced to a dignitary, but what is said during those brief encounters is a mystery to most rugby fans. One classic story which has been told at numerous sporting dinners concerns Dewi Morris, the England scrum-half, and his meeting with Nelson Mandela prior to the South Africa v England international at Loftus Versfeld in 1994. This was the first clash between the two sides on Springbok territory since South Africa had denounced apartheid under the regime of the newly installed President Mandela.

It was an historic time for the English team to be in South Africa and the warmth of welcome for the tourists was exceptional. On the field the hospitality was not so warm. Games against the Free State, Natal, Transvaal and the South Africa 'A' team had produced mixed results for England, and the hype surrounding the first Test focused on the extent of the crushing victory the home team were expected to inflict on the visitors.

The pre-match entertainment was nothing short of spectacular. The world was watching South Africa, and they put on a stunning show whilst the teams ran out on to the field. One could sense that both sides were keen to get on with the game, but before that happened, the

145

entire Springbok and England squads were lined up on the pitch to meet President Mandela and his predecessor F.W. de Klerk. As they worked their way along the England line, Mandela warmly shook hands with each of the players as they enjoyed a once in a lifetime moment.

Rather like the line-up at the Royal Variety Performance, it is typical in these circumstances that some players get a shake of the hand and a smile, while others are asked a question which they obviously respond to. The team lined up in shirt order. Paul Hull was the full-back and the backs lined up 15–9. The forwards then lined up 1–8, so on this occasion Jason Leonard was standing next to Dewi Morris and was winding him up regarding his imminent meeting with the new president. He was saying things like, 'I'll bet he walks straight past you, Dewi, he won't have any interest in talking to you, the only chance you have of meeting the great man is if you can think of something to say to him that will capture his imagination. You need to engage him, Dewi.'

Jason could tell Dewi was getting agitated and nervous and was obviously thinking of a suitable question. As Mandela neared them Jason was hoping that he had got to Dewi and was intrigued as to what little gem might be forthcoming at the moment of greeting. Would Dewi mention the twenty-seven years Mandela spent in prison on Robben Island for leading the movement against apartheid? Would he ask him about the Nobel Peace Prize he was awarded in 1993? Or would it be about being elected President of South Africa in the first fully democratic election?

As they were introduced, Dewi puffed out his chest and uttered the immortal line, 'Mr President, do the cars in South Africa require tax discs?'

Jason, along with several other England players close enough to hear the question, was stunned to say the least. Do the cars in South Africa require tax discs? Where the f*** did that come from? Of all the questions you could have asked one of the world's greatest ever leaders, that particular one was not on anyone's radar. Except of course Dewi's.

To illustrate what a great man and diplomat Nelson Mandela is, he smiled at Dewi, turned to one of his aides and said, 'Well . . . do they?!'

A passing remark

A couple of days before the climax to the 1995 RWC final in South Africa, when François Pienaar led his team to an astonishing victory over New Zealand, inspired by the sight of Nelson Mandela in a Springbok jersey, the rugby world was 'looking forward to' the under-whelming prospect of the third place playoff between England and France. After a ritual humiliation in Cape Town in the quarter-final, where England were annihilated by Jonah Lomu and his New Zealand team-mates in a ferocious display that would haunt some of the players involved for years to come, the boys who had not been involved against the All Blacks had been cautiously optimistic that they would get a run out against the French a few days later. The collective squad effort had been immense to that point, and even though the match was a huge anticlimax, the feeling was that this was surely a good oppor-tunity to blood a few younger players and give them much needed game-time after six weeks on the road.

Jack Rowell, however, seems to have changed his mind before the game and dispensed with the idea of mixing up the team and introducing fresh faces. Instead he selected a very similar XV to the one that took the field in the quarter-final, with the exception of Tony Underwood, who had sustained an injury courtesy of that shy, retiring nineteen stone character who had lined up against him on the wing the previous weekend, and Dean Richards who had been 'rested'. Now I am always one to toe the party line provided I feel that I have been given a fair crack and opportunity, and I have no doubt that the players in the England squad felt the same; so when Rowell announced that he was picking the same team that had been defeated on the weekend, there must have been an overwhelming sense of injustice. Damian Hopley certainly felt that, and decided radical action was the order of the day.

The one up-side for Damian was that as Deano was being rested, he knew he had at least one partner in crime with whom to go out and find some medicinal lagers. The twosome grew significantly when Richard West, John Mallet and Tony Underwood all agreed that after the dinner that evening, as their team-mates headed back to an early night of tiddlywinks and Afrikaans pay-per-view, they would head out to catch some fresh air. One or two bottles of the Cape's finest blends later, they decided to head to Marilyn's nightspot – a hostelry that had been frequented with considerable aplomb twelve months earlier when England were on their summer tour.

The first indication that things were somewhat awry came as they walked up the stairs to the entrance, only to see Pierre Berbizier, the French coach, being carried out, considerably the worse for wear, by three of his players. A couple of raised eyebrows later, they walked into the main club to see the *entire* French squad in blazers, getting stuck into the local brew. Just to add even more confusion to the night, Deano then started speaking fluent French. By the end of the evening the group started to resemble a scene from *'Allo 'Allo!* with Pascal Ondarts as René Artois, Marc Cecillon as Roger LeClerc and Hoppers as Herr Otto Flick. The two French legends informed the England lads that they were under strict orders from their former team-mate and now coach (and probably at that moment in a coma) not to go to training and only show up in time for the game the next day. Inspired management in my book.

The majority of the French squad were in the club until at least 4 a.m. as Damian reports conclusively, because he didn't leave until

5 a.m. As the French captain, Philippe Saint-Andre, explained later, France had lost eight games on the bounce against England, so the squad all felt it was important to have a good night together and not worry about this losing streak.

The game itself was dreadful. The forwards struggled to establish any platform and with the backline receiving such sub-standard ball, Rob Andrew at fly-half – who had steered his team through the quarter-final victory with such a sublime drop goal to knock out the holders Australia – was forced to kick all evening. The end result was almost inevitable as England fell to their first defeat at the hands of the French in four years.

After the game 'Squeaky', as Rob Andrew is known (he was one of those guys who was always squeaky clean and could be quite annoying because every mother wanted to have him as a son and every daughter quite fancied marrying him; can't think why), was making his way out of the dressing room en route to the post match meal. He was visibly crestfallen to have lost such a proud record against a team he had been a constant thorn in the side of over the years. As he shuffled along replaying the game in his mind, a young England fan came up to him and said nervously: 'Excuse me Sir, but aren't you Rob Andrew?' Reaching for his pen to sign the match programme, the Wasps fly-half said, 'Yes, yes I am.' The fan then enquired, 'If that's the case, then do you know Jeremy Guscott?' Another affirmative response, 'Yes, yes I do.' 'Well then,' continued the young man, 'why don't you ever f***ing pass to him?!'

Even though Squeaky won seventy-one caps for his country and was undoubtedly at the helm of some of England's most successful moments in the eighties and through into the nineties, he was much maligned as a one dimensional fly-half. Mind you, I guess he didn't do a lot to correct that impression when later in the evening Jerry asked him to pass the butter and he kicked it forty yards in the air.

WHAT'S THE BLEEDIN' POINT?

WILL CARLING

'To my mind, Will is one of the best rugby players England has ever produced and one of the greatest captains, leading his country to three Grand Slams and a World Cup final. He won seventy-two caps and his record of fifty-nine, or however many, appearances as captain has only just been beaten by John Smit of South Africa. Will was the player who became the face of English rugby when it was on the rise in the late eighties and early nineties at a critical transitional period as the game moved into the professional era. Will took on the role brilliantly and, along with the help of many others of course, helped steer rugby towards becoming a far higher-profile sport in the mind of the public. An inspirational figure, he formed a fantastic centre pairing with Jeremy Guscott. His contribution as a player is often forgotten as people often just think of his captaincy (he was England's youngest captain since the thirties at twenty-two years of age), but his record was outstanding (as was, it has to be said, his ability to get into the frame of almost every camera shot during a match!).'

Running it up the flagpole

Becoming England captain at such an early age did have some disadvantages, lack of experience being an obvious one. However, I believed this could also work in my favour because I had not become too accustomed to the old traditional ways of doing things. I was always prepared to try something new, not necessarily revolutionary but perhaps just a change to the routine, which would make the English players think and cause a bit of confusion for the opposition.

I introduced one such idea on the eve of our Five Nations game against France in 1993. The pre-match meeting in the team room at the Petersham Hotel followed a traditional format, double checking line-out calls and back-row moves. As the meeting drew to its inevitable close I introduced my grand idea by saying, 'OK lads, before you make your way to your rooms for a good night's sleep I have an idea I'd like to try out in tomorrow's match. I just want to run it up the flagpole and see who salutes it.' Yes, I think I might actually have said that . . .

'For the past one hundred years or so every England team, indeed every international team, when kicking off, have lined up their forwards on the left-hand side of the field and kicked the ball towards them. What I would like to do tomorrow is kick off to the right. We can run through a few kick-offs to the right tomorrow morning so we get used to it, and with a bit of luck it will cause some confusion in the French ranks. Everyone happy with that?'

Just one voice was heard amid the stunned silence. In his deep, broad northern accent, the giant second row Wade

Dooley, 6ft 8in and a police officer with the Lancashire Constabulary in Blackpool, said, 'Err, Will, we always kick off left.'

'Yes I know we do. That's the point. By kicking off to the right we'll hopefully surprise the French and that element of surprise could give us an early edge.'

'But we always kick off left.'

To be honest, I didn't handle the situation particularly well. I lost it and in a frustrated, slightly raised voice said, 'OK, we'll just do what England teams have done for a century and kick off left. I just thought a bit of change would be a surprise, which might give us an edge, but don't worry, we'll stay as boring old England.'

With that one of the senior forwards in the room piped up, 'I've got an idea, Will. Why don't we run on to the pitch backwards? That'll really f***ing surprise them!'

End of meeting.

Ain't got time to bleed

Another magic moment followed a video we'd watched in the team room the night before one of our matches. There was usually a selection to choose from and on this occasion the boys chose the Arnold Schwarzenegger blockbuster *Predator*, a high-octane, science fiction, action and horror film, with the usual amount of gratuitous violence mixed in with excessive blood and guts.

I have to say the forwards absolutely loved it. Cheers echoed around the room as limbs were separated from bodies and the death toll mounted. At one point, Arnie, playing a character named Blain, was in a particularly bad way, having taken a bullet in his shoulder.

His ally, Poncho, looked at Blain's shoulder and said, 'Hey man, you're hit. You're bleeding.'

To which Blain replied, 'I ain't got time to bleed.'

This one-liner caused hysteria among the eight English forwards, and was repeated on numerous occasions during the rest of the evening and when the film came to its finale and Blain delivered his classic revenge line, 'Payback time', they went crazy.

Normal service was resumed the following morning, with all the players going through their normal pre-match rituals, the bus ride from the hotel to Twickenham, the changing-room banter tinged with nerves.

Halfway through the second half, with no more than one score between the two teams, 'Iron' Mike Teague, England's blindside forward, caught a stray boot in the face. As captain it was always my role to go over to an injured player to see how bad things were. I looked at Mike's face and saw blood streaming from a gash close to his eye.

'It looks bad, Mike,' I said. 'You've got blood pouring down your face. I think you'll need some stitches.'

Mike looked up at me and said, 'Will . . . ain't got time to bleed.' He then turned towards the Irish and came out with the immortal follow-up line, 'Payback time', before running back to his team-mates.

It's not often an England captain has been caught on camera pissing himself with laughter after one of his players has sustained a nasty cut.

THE BLEARY-EYED LION
ANDY NICOL

'Andy Nicol is a top man and great tourist with a wonderful sense of humour. I played against him many times both on the 7s circuit and latterly when he joined Bath, with whom he won the Heineken Cup. He won twenty-three caps for Scotland, captaining his country when they beat England in 2000, a game I tend to try to forget (I blame the rain). Andy went on two Lions tours, but that bare statistic does not even begin to do his record justice ...'

Representing the British and Irish Lions is the pinnacle of any player's career if they hail from these parts. We have all grown up with tales of the legendary Lions of 1971 and 1974. Willie John McBride, Gareth Edwards, Barry John, Andy Irvine and Ian 'Mighty Mouse' McLauchlan are household names.

My first tour was in 1993, when the Lions went to New Zealand. I was not included in the original selection but Scotland had been touring the Pacific Islands that summer, so I was flown in near the end of the tour as a temporary replacement for Welsh scrum-half Robert Jones. He had been taken ill and the management were awaiting the results of his blood test. Fortunately, the results were fine, but in the six days I was with the Lions, I managed to sit on the bench for the game against Taranaki in New Plymouth and get on for the last six minutes.

So my first Lions tour lasted SIX days and I played SIX minutes of rugby . . . and this was the longer of my two tours!

In 2001, again after being overlooked for original selection, I was asked to lead a supporters' tour around Australia. I expect many of you have been on such trips and know what happens – you drink, drink, drink and then have a couple more.

This was my training schedule for the three unforgettable weeks we were in Australia – I'm sure they were unforgettable, although I can't quite remember them. The 'training' started in Brisbane where the Lions, memorably, won the first Test with a mesmerising performance at the Gabba. We battled on, with no sign of letting up, through to Melbourne (where Australia levelled the series) and then to Sydney, where a huge four-day party rounded off the tour, and nearly finished off the tourists as well.

The amount of actual training I undertook amounted to a few runs along Surfers Paradise and the odd visit to a hotel gym for an executive work-out – sauna, swim and Jacuzzi. In hindsight, this was not text-book preparation for what was to unfold.

The tour group I was leading had secured a last-minute cancellation to climb Sydney Harbour Bridge on the Friday evening, the night before the deciding Test match. This is relevant because everyone has to be sober to climb the world-famous bridge. Indeed, you get breathalysed before you start the ascent. So, soberly, we were about to leave the hotel in Darling Harbour when I received a call from the Lions manager, Donal Lenihan, enquiring about my fitness.

Lying through my teeth, I said, 'I'm fine. What's the problem?'

He said, 'We have an injury in the squad.'

I said, 'Who's injured?'

He said, 'Austin Healey.'

I said, 'That's such a shame because he's such a nice guy!'

Anyway, I was asked to report to the team hotel at 10 a.m. on the Saturday morning to sit on the bench and be the replacement scrum-half in the deciding Test match, which was kicking off at 7 p.m. that night.

Now, not being in the best shape either physically or mentally, on arrival at the hotel, I went straight to see the management team to discuss my situation. I met with Graham Henry, the coach, Andy Robinson, the assistant coach, Martin Johnson, the captain, and Donal Lenihan, and basically asked them, 'You know what kind of trip I have been on, so why pick me?' They said they had scoured Sydney for three days and the only other scrum-half they could find was Gareth Edwards, who was fifty-five years old. They said it was a close call – I had won selection by one vote!

We arrived at Stadium Australia a while before kick-off with the series poised at one apiece. As ever with Lions tours, the travelling support was fantastic and it was an incredible place to be, with thousands of fans in red and gold creating a wonderful spectacle. Now you have to remember that everything that had happened to me in the previous twelve hours had happened overnight back in the UK. So my dad, back at my rugby club in Dundee, sat down to watch the game with all his cronies, about to tuck into a bacon roll for breakfast, totally oblivious to events affecting his beloved son. He said they watched as the teams ran out on to the field of play and lined up for the anthem. The Australians stood in line as the camera panned along them – John Eales, George Gregan, Daniel Herbert and Joe Roff, focused and ready for the kick-off.

The camera moved to the Lions – Martin Johnson, Brian O'Driscoll, Jason Robinson, eyes focused, every muscle and sinew bulging as they were in the shape of their lives, ready to play the game of their lives. The camera kept panning along the Lions replacements and there I was, standing at the end, bleary eyed, unshaven and out of shape. In Dundee, they all thought I must have won a competition to be the Lions mascot!

As it turned out, I did not get on to the field of play, which was just as well – the real mascot would have lasted longer than I would have done. Then to round off the most bizarre twenty-four hours of my life, when we returned to the changing rooms after the game, my number was pulled out of the hat for the drugs test! The other number to come out of the hat was 13, Brian O'Driscoll. Now what you have to do for a drugs test is fill a beaker with urine, but after a Test match of that intensity, dehydration was a major issue and Brian took two and a half hours to fill his small beaker. Having been on the piss for three weeks, I filled a bucket immediately!

Six weeks after returning home, I received a letter from the Australian Institute of Sport and it said:

'Dear Mr Nicol, I am delighted to say that the urine sample you provided at the third Test between Australia and the Lions at Stadium Australia proved negative and you were fit to play international rugby . . . but entirely unfit to drive a motor car!'

So the 'pinnacle' of my career, my record as a British and Irish Lion, stands at two tours and seven days, with six minutes of rugby.

MISTY-EYED MEMORIES
DAVID TRICK

'Tricky was one of the finest wings of his generation, playing twelve times for England at various levels and scoring eleven tries, and he has since gone on to become one of the best speakers on the after-dinner circuit. I met him as part of the legendary Bath side of the eighties, although he wasn't exactly a permanent fixture. For some reason known only to himself, he took eighteen months away from the game during this period to go "walkabout" in Australia, the USA and South America, playing just one rugby match for the Portland Pigs when he scored seventy-six points, thanked them for the game and moved on to Alaska to try his hand at salmon fishing.

'Tricky was always considered a crowd pleaser; if he wasn't entertaining the spectators by scoring tries emanating from his own twenty-two metre line (as he tells it – often), he would be found on the touchline chatting to them, invariably with his hands firmly stuck in the pockets of his shorts!'

Sizzling play

During the autumn of 2008 I was invited to be a guest at the twenty-fifth anniversary of the Wooden Spoon founders' lunch. Wooden Spoon is a rugby-based charity supporting children throughout the UK who are disadvantaged either physically, mentally or socially. I was delighted to accept, not least as I couldn't remember the last time I had attended a function when I was not required to provide a speech, conduct a Q&A session or an auction. I was going to be a guest and enjoy the event.

Within a minute of walking through the doors of the London Marriott, Grosvenor Square, I was approached by the deputy chief executive of the charity, my host Tony Richards.

'Thank God you've arrived,' he said. 'We've just found out that Jill Douglas has been called away by the BBC to do some work for the autumn internationals and she's not going to be able to attend. Would you please host the Q&A session with the rugby panel?'

It's amazing how your brain can be thinking 'bollocks' while the words, 'Not a problem, Tony, I'd be delighted,' come out of your mouth.

At the end of the session (which was a tremendous success, even if I say so myself), I asked the audience to show their appreciation for our star-studded panel as they left the stage. Suddenly, a lady in the audience requested the opportunity to ask me a question. With the benefit of hindsight I should have ignored her and walked off with the rest of the boys so I could get back to enjoying the evening as I had originally intended. However, I was mildly curious and somewhat flattered.

'Go on, ask away,' I heard myself saying.

'Do you know of any international rugby player who has drunk a can of beer and smoked a cigarette *while on the field of play* during an international match at Twickenham?' she asked. As soon as I heard the question, I realised two things. One was the identity of the lady asking the question – Jules Caplin, with whom I had worked twenty years previously and had not seen since. The other was the identity of the person she was asking about – me.

Seconds later I found myself telling the story to an audience of 400 people, knowing I was not going to emerge with an enhanced reputation.

It was 1978, England Schools Under-19s v Australia Schools Under-19s, and on the morning of the game the mist was as dense as any I had seen in my lifetime. Meetings were hastily arranged and the upshot was that although it was possible to play the match the following day, it could not be played at Twickenham. As you can imagine, both sides were desperate to fulfil their boyhood dreams and play at the home of rugby, not least because it might be the only chance we ever had to play at HQ. The decision was made to proceed with the game, the general consensus being that as the kick-off was not until 2.30 p.m., the mist would probably have lifted.

Time came and, if anything, the mist was even thicker, with visibility of no more than ten metres. The concession made by the match officials was to play with a light tan ball rather than the (at the time) traditional white ball. As I was soon to discover, this was not a helpful decision because the colour blended almost perfectly with the Australian shirts. Fabulous. I was playing right wing and from the moment the match kicked off I couldn't see a thing. I spent most of the first half wandering up and down the wing adjacent to the West Stand thinking,

'Where the f*** are they?' To emphasise the density of the mist, the record books show a 31–9 defeat for England, whereas the reality was actually worse. We were awarded a penalty kick at goal, I followed up the kick and arrived in time to see it drop a clear five feet below the cross bar. Noticing both linesmen looking skyward, I threw my arms in the air, shouting, 'Yes!' The linesmen looked at each other, raised their flags and awarded us three points. I subsequently learned that both officials went on to have distinguished careers, but not as match officials!

Ten minutes into the second half (and at this point I have to stress every word of this story is true) I was ambling around on the wing next to the East Stand and walked into my brother Paul and three of his mates on the pitch. They had started off in the stand, couldn't see anything, so moved to the touchline and still couldn't see so decided to get on to the pitch. Mike Dawson, one of the quartet, asked if I fancied a beer.

'Don't be so stupid,' I said, standing there in my England kit with the rose on my chest, the proudest day of my sporting life.

'How many people will be able to say they have drunk a can of beer at Twickenham during a match they were playing in?' he responded.

I thought for a second and decided he was right, and, to be honest, who was ever going to know? As he handed me a can of pale ale he asked if I wanted a cigarette.

'Don't be ridiculous,' I said.

'How many people will be able to say . . .'

'You're right,' I said. If I'm being honest, it was probably at this precise moment I realised I was never going to become an icon of the game of rugby football.

He handed me a roll-up, and there I was, playing at Twickenham, with a beer in one hand and a smoke in the other, as three Australians emerged from the mist. At the time I remember thinking, 'There are five of us and three of them. We've got a chance.' However, as I looked to my right, my brother and his three friends had disappeared back to the stands – I was on my own. I threw the can one way, the cigarette the other and as I could not see who was carrying the ball decided to tackle the one in the middle. As he went down he made an odd noise. Now this was not the sort of sound that indicated he had been on the wrong end of the most powerful tackle ever received. Rather it was more like a squeal. At the resulting line-out I felt a sharp pain in the fingers of my left hand and made a noise similar to the one I'd heard from the Aussie. I looked at my hand and stuck to my fingers was the cigarette. It took a nanosecond to realise I'd burnt him!

I've subsequently looked at various lists of possible injuries one can sustain on the field of play and strangely being burnt by a cigarette smoked by a member of the opposition is nowhere to be found. Until now perhaps.

A ballsy debut

I made my international debut on 19 March 1983 against Ireland at Lansdowne Road. I love saying 'international debut' because it implies you went on to win many more caps – I actually got a grand total of two, which, as I keep reminding people, is two more than most.

Having broken into the Bath first XV in 1979, I was fortunate to be in an ever-improving team, and that no doubt helped in my recognition by the England selectors. I should point out that I played right wing for Bath since this is relevant to the story.

We travelled over to Ireland on the Wednesday evening, which allowed us two training sessions on the Thursday and Friday prior to the match. At this stage, the nerves aren't kicking in and the overriding feeling is one of excitement at being part of a full England team, knowing you are going to be awarded a full international cap. As a matter of interest, I do have the same number of actual caps as Jason Leonard, although he played a few more times than I did. In rugby you are awarded one cap following your debut, unlike in football when a physical cap is awarded for every game played.

Having played four seasons of club rugby, on 19 March 1983 I was going to be the best right winger in the country, or so I thought at the time. At 10 a.m. on the morning of the match I was called into a little room in the Shelbourne Hotel where I met with two selectors who informed me I was now the best *left* winger in the country. John Carleton had not had the greatest of seasons and was not certain of his Lions place on the tour to New Zealand, which was being selected on the Sunday following the game. He had made this point to the selectors, and they had decided to allow him to play in his customary position rather than on the left, where he had been selected for this match. To be honest, I was not too perturbed because I was still going to make my debut, albeit in a position I had never played in before.

In the changing rooms just prior to kick-off, our coach Mike Davis gave me some last-minute advice. In those days, we did not line up for the national anthem, we stood in a circle. 'When they play the national anthem, do not look at the crowd, look into the eyes of all your team-mates,' he said. Unfortunately, his words only made me more curious and I felt I needed to at least glance in the direction of the stands. So I looked at the crowd and promptly shat myself. All those people, and many millions at home watching on TV, were going to witness any mistake I made – a terrifying thought. So I didn't start the game in a great frame of mind.

The match kicked off at 3 p.m. and for two minutes and thirty-five seconds I loved international rugby. I hadn't touched the ball, I could hear the roar of the crowd and I had a marvellous view! Then it all fell apart.

Ollie Campbell, the Irish fly-half, received the ball from a scrum and was about to put up a textbook kick on the English right winger John Carleton. Now Ollie is a very astute man and quickly realised John had played twenty-six times for England and was probably only one game away from his second British and Irish Lions tour, so he made the necessary adjustments and put up the kick on me. However, this was not just any old kick, this was the highest kick I have ever seen in my life.

There were 53,000 people at Lansdowne Road with tickets and somewhere in the region of 16,500 without tickets, all waiting for the ball to come into view. I shuffled around on the left wing doing what I thought I should be doing as a left winger, waiting for the ball to come into sight. As I looked skyward I could sense the Irish forwards, led by Fergus Slattery, charging towards me. I also have a vague recollection of the English forwards ever so slightly drifting off to my right and Peter Wheeler saying, 'Let's see how the little prat gets on with that one then.'

Some people believe I dropped that high ball, but I swear to you all that I most certainly did not. I firmly believe that in order to drop a high ball, you need to touch it and I got nowhere near the thing.

So my first touch of the ball in international rugby was when it caught me in the bollocks on the way back up. Sadly, this is all on BBC tape if anyone wishes to verify it. All the men reading this story will know when you've taken one full square in the crown jewels you have somewhere in the region of five or six paces before the pain really kicks in. I like to think I used those paces wisely. I ran towards our physiotherapist.

On the sixth pace I was doing a very creditable impression of a diehard Irish fan with fifteen pints on board, and collapsed to the ground. At the precise moment I hit the deck I realised it wasn't going to be my day. Having watched the ball reach terminal velocity and then felt the pain of it ricocheting off my knackers, I think it's fair enough to assume it could have ended up anywhere inside, or indeed outside, Lansdowne Road, so why, why, why, did it have to end up back in my arms?

Through the mist, the tears and the excruciating pain I could just make out my saviour, the English full-back Dusty Hare. I thought Dusty was looking at me, so I passed him the ball.

I'm sure on any other occasion during Dusty's illustrious career he would have caught that ball I passed to him, but for some inexplicable reason he decided to let it sail thirteen feet over the top of his head! I got to my feet, ran around Dusty and managed to put the ball down behind our own tryline for a five metre scrum. I got to my feet and realised I had just lost seventy-five metres of ground and fourteen team-mates.

Running on to the pitch that day, I had had no experience other than a few words of advice I had picked up from some of the other players prior to the game. The common theme was enjoy the occasion, savour every moment. 'Tricky, make the most of it. International rugby is so fast that before you know it the final whistle will have gone.' The game will be over before I know it? Let me tell you, that game lasted eight and a half hours. It was my international career that was over in no time.

THE F-FACTOR
CHRIS REA

'Chris played his club rugby with West of Scotland RFC and was capped thirteen times for Scotland scoring three tries. He was part of that very successful British and Irish Lions tour to New Zealand in 1971, which was the first Lions side to win against the All Blacks in nearly three-quarters of a century of trying. Picked as centre for the tour, he ended up playing mostly at fly-half due to other players' injuries. His career ended with a victory over England, 26–6, in the centenary fixture on 27 March 1971. He is a top guy and now works and is heavily involved with the International Rugby Board.'

Nineteen ninety-five was not a good year. Having presented BBC's *Rugby Special* for six years, dear old Auntie decided that she could do without me, and traded me in for a newer, younger model. It was therefore something of a relief, both emotionally and financially, when ITV offered me a job on their Rugby World Cup commentary team in South Africa. The fact that I was not a specialist television commentator, having learned my trade on the radio, which requires very different skills, was, in my somewhat parlous and impecunious position, of minor importance. I accepted with alarming alacrity.

My worst fears were soon realised, however, when I was told that I would be commentating on the pool match between Scotland and Tonga. My co-commentator would be Gordon Brown, 'Broon frae Troon'. No problem there. Gordon and I had played together for West of Scotland, Scotland and the Lions, and, along with legions of others in the game, I loved being in his company. No problem with the Scotland team, either. I recognised them all and was well versed in their back-grounds and careers. No, the problem was the Tongans. They are delightful people, except, that is, for their names, which present nightmares for commentators. The side selected to play against Scotland was no exception. Looking down the team list, my eye was drawn immediately to the tight-head prop – Fuko Fuka. Now it didn't take an Einstein to work out that this was not a name to roll comfortably off the commentator's tongue, and incipient panic set in. But help was at hand in the massively reassuring presence of the great Bill McLaren, who would be doing the commentary for the BBC.

There he was at the Tongan training session the day before the match, doing his homework as conscientiously as ever, and I made my way over to him.

'Bill,' I said, 'what do you make of this tight-head prop, Fuko Fuka?'

'Chris,' came the reply, 'you can be sure of one thing – I will get through the entire commentary tomorrow without once mentioning that laddie's name.'

How comforting was that! What was good enough for Bill McLaren was certainly going to be good enough for Chris Rea.

'Thanks, Bill – just what I wanted to hear,' said I, my mood immeasurably lighter and brighter.

Match day dawned, and Broonie and I took our seats high up in the stand. All was going smoothly – rather well, in fact – until, ten minutes into the match, right in front of the main stand, in front of the television cameras and in front of the entire watching world, this total pillock, Fuko Fuka, took an enormous kick at the Scottish captain and talisman, Gavin Hastings. Hastings was poleaxed. General uproar ensued and the cameras turned their full glare on to the culprit, for whom there was no hiding place. Nor was there any escape for the hapless commentator, but with a flash of inspiration I turned to Broon.

'Gordon,' I said, 'the Tongan tight-head prop, a little indiscreet with his boot, wouldn't you say?'

'Aye,' came the response. 'Silly Fuka.'

MORE THAN JUST PLAYERS

DAVID WALSH

'David has a wonderful command of the English language (I am sure he says the same about me) and it is no surprise that he has been names sports writer of the year numerous times. He co-wrote my autobiography (with me, in case you were wondering) and has a wonderful way of bringing things to life, whether they're happy or sad. He clearly has a passion for rugby, but across all sports David is an amazing writer in terms of his ability to put the reader exactly where he wants to be – right in the heart of the action.

'I asked David if he would contribute a favourite tale or two that reflect what he sees as the magic of rugby. He didn't disappoint. To me, these next two stories act as a wonderful and inspiring respite from some of the antics we've had up to now. I hope you agree.'

The Singing Lions

Perhaps it was the family background – chapel-going and God-fearing miners on each side – but Cliff Morgan was a pretty special No. 10 and has never been thought of as just another fine link in the chain of great Welsh fly-halves. You could claim, and it is easy to do so, that he will also be remembered for the brilliance of his commentary describing that extraordinary Barbarians try, scored by Gareth Edwards against the All Blacks in 1973. But to think of Morgan solely in terms of his wizardry with the ball in hand or his eloquence before the microphone is to diminish him. He has stood for the rugby of our childhoods; the scent of wintergreen in an overcrowded changing room, an acceptance that the game mattered more than the result, conviviality in the bar afterwards, and the understanding that friendships would outlast careers.

What he remembers most from his first cap is the moment before the match at the Arms Park when his rival No. 10, Jack Kyle, put an arm across his shoulder as they walked on to the pitch and said, 'Cliffy, I hope you have a good day.' That meant more to Morgan than anything that happened in the afternoon's battle against Ireland. You see, Morgan knew that if you didn't enjoy the bits that came before and after the game, you were missing the point.

They cherished him in Ireland – a fly-half who didn't try to kick the ball to death – but nowhere was Morgan more admired and more loved than in South Africa, where he played the most beautiful rugby for the 1955 Lions. That squad achieved a remarkable 2–2 series draw but, again, it was Morgan's charisma off the pitch as much as his genius on it that made him an iconic figure in South African eyes.

His great rival on the field was the Springboks' splendid flanker Basie van Wyk. At a critical moment in the first Test at Ellis Park, Morgan raced on to Dickie Jeeps's pass and with the elasticity that was his trademark, bent his way round Van Wyk and flew past full-back Jack van der Schyff to score a wonderful try in the Lions 23–22 victory. But Morgan and Van Wyk exchanged Christmas cards for years. It is hard to write that and not feel a sense of sadness at some of the things rugby has left behind.

As the 1955 Lions gathered at Eastbourne for the fitting of blazers, most of which were too long in the sleeves and too wide in the shoulders, laughter broke the ice and soon they were talking about the kind of Lions squad they would like to be. Nowadays psychologists and sports scientists are paid to stimulate these debates. The 1955 group decided they would be 'The Singing Lions' and appointed Morgan choir-master with use of the hotel piano. Cliff accepted his new responsibility enthusiastically. In a squad that contained four pianists, a guitarist, a trombone player and a drummer, the choirmaster had more than half a chance and with his life-loving nature, it was no surprise that so many wanted to follow him. Before they left the British Isles, the squad had practised singing English, Irish and Scottish songs in English, Welsh songs in Welsh, and, in what turned out to be Morgan's masterstroke, they learned to sing a South African folk song, 'Sarie Marais' in Afrikaans. Not just that, they performed it in four-part harmony. There was no more direct route to the hearts of the Afrikaner than to sing 'Sarie Marais', which the Lions did minutes after their BOAC Argonaut plane landed at Johannesburg Airport. They also gave a raucous rendition of the Welsh song 'Sospan Fach' and performed numbers from their Scots, Irish and English repertoire. South Africa was entranced. Nelson Mandela would be one of many thousands of black rugby fans who would support the Lions at Ellis Park in that first Test and before a match was played on that tour, the *Rand Daily Mail* declared the 1955 squad to be 'the greatest ever Lions team', which the players themselves could only attribute to their singing.

That 23–22 victory in Johannesburg is rightly remembered as one of the great Lions victories and perhaps only those who stood behind the tourists' goalposts in the final seconds of the match will fully appreciate how easily the match could have swung the other way. In injury time, the Springboks scored their fourth try and as the conversion was from halfway between the right post and the corner flag, Van der Schyff was fully expected to edge his team 24–23 ahead. But when 90,000 of your compatriots are willing you not to miss and the winning or losing is in your hands, a kick can be problematical. Van der Schyff miscued, the conversion went wide by seven or eight yards, and the match soon ended. As the Lions stood on the pitch, one part exhausted, one part shell-shocked, the Swansea prop, W. O. Williams, put his arm around Morgan and said, 'Cliff, I'm glad we went to chapel last Sunday.'

They had been to St Colombus Presbyterian in Johannesburg where the minister, the Revd Emlyn Jones, was from Pontrhydyfen, the same Welsh mining village that offered to the world one Richard Burton. Having come from a home where chapel came before everything, Morgan had known of Revd Jones before his departure for South Africa. At their first visit to his church a week before the Johannesburg Test, Morgan introduced himself to the minister and he and his fellow Lions were invited to attend chapel the day after the

Test. About a dozen or so from the party of thirty-one went to St Colombus that Sunday evening, the Lions congregation being made up of Protestant, Catholic and dissenter. The Welsh members of the group were well used to having *gymanfa ganu* (singing festivals), and when Revd Jones invited the players into the vestry for a little *gymanfa ganu* after the short church service, the offer was accepted. Unlike anything any of the Lions had seen before, this vestry was more like a fully fledged concert hall and by the time the players got there, it was standing room only. A woman was already sitting at the piano, a man at the organ and when the Lions began to work their way through their collection of hymns, the crowd was swept along by the passion and joy of their singing. The night was a wonder, enjoyed by both players and their audience and as it ended, a man known to Revd Jones came on to the stage.

'Emlyn,' he said to the Revd Jones, 'I can't let this occasion go without talking to the boy,' he said, referring to the twenty-five-year-old Morgan who still only looked about eighteen. The fly-half hadn't a clue who the man was but it soon became clear that he was Francis Russell from Tonyrefail near Morgan's home village Trebanog. In fact, Russell's sisters had taught at Morgan's village school and Russell had worked for Morgan's grand-father, Isaac Christmas Morgan, in the mines. But that wasn't what Francis Russell was cut out to do – he was, by nature, a wonderful tenor and would make his reputation at Covent Garden in London and at many of the world's most famous opera houses. He had then moved to South Africa but was going blind and because of this, no longer sang in public. Touched by the willingness of the Lions to sing for the faithful at St Colombus Presbyterian, Russell agreed to sing for the tourists, performing 'The Blind Ploughman'.

With emotions swirling, there was nothing for the Lions to say. After thanking Francis Russell, Revd Jones said it was time 'to let the boys go'. But his congregation was thirsting for more and they shouted for the Lions to respond with one more hymn. And so they sang 'Cwm Rhondda' which most people knew and an unforgettable evening had the ending it deserved. Can you imagine such a scene happening on tour today? All that spiritualism, the sharing of emotions, the wonder of music as a dismantler of barriers, it all came to pass because Cliff Morgan was more than just a special fly-half.

Fruitcake

There was a time in the ten years before rugby union embraced professionalism when attitudes changed and the old amateur game was diving for cover. We're not talking only about the passing of brown envelopes in dark corridors but of players wanting to train more seriously and of fitness levels rising to new heights. This had, of course, much to do with the arrival of the Rugby World Cup in 1987 where players from around the rugby world gathered in one place and learned from each other. Southern hemisphere countries carried the torch for the more professional way and for the first sixteen years, the cup stayed south. Nowhere was the professional game slower to catch on than in Ireland where old habits were dying hard. It wasn't that Irish players weren't serious about their rugby or indifferent to the need for physical fitness, they just weren't as serious or as fit as their rivals. That period from the mid-eighties to the end of the nineties wasn't a good time to be an Ireland player. Sure, there were one-off performances scattered here and there, back-to-back victories over England in 1993 and 1994, but bad days were more common and there were just too many crushing defeats. Perhaps from those desperate experiences some good came because when Ireland finally got the hang of professionalism, you could say that no team in world rugby gained more from it.

But there were casualties, good players and outstanding professionals, who had the bad luck to spend their international careers in the green jersey just as Ireland lurched through the twilight zone. Brendan Mullin is one obvious example, Simon Geoghegan is another. Geoghegan was a particular case because his insatiable desire to be good for his country drove him to try things that just weren't possible; not in the Irish teams of that time. The uninformed thought he was 'a headless chicken' when the truth was that few people thought more about the game, and fewer still were as professional as he. There were the usual training evenings with his club, first London Irish and later Bath, and on his free evenings you would find Geoghegan sprinting on the running track at Battersea Park with a harness fitted round his waist, from which a long rope stretched out behind him attached to a tyre. It was an exercise to help explosiveness and at the time it reflected a level of dedication that wasn't at all commonplace in the Irish set-up.

Though he was born in England, Geoghegan's father had come from County Galway and as a kid, Simon spent summer holidays in the west of Ireland. Whether it was his dad's influence, or those times shooting the breeze in County Galway, or his own particular, you might say unique, make-up but Geoghegan felt Irish. When he and his school mates attended an England/Ireland match at Twickenham, he was the one who secreted a tricolour into the ground and then unfurled it to his friends' consternation at the moment of an Ireland score. If that was a little cheeky, it was a sign of things to come. Geoghegan would never be afraid to challenge others, especially those who ran Irish rugby during his time, and on one depressing occasion he would receive a one-day ban from training with the Irish squad for complaining publicly about the amateurishness of Ireland's approach. Perhaps that contrariness was the most obvious sign of his Irishness but, whatever, it was there and joining London Irish was a natural next step for him after leaving school.

If playing for his country brought more grief than glory, there were enough dashing runs and fine tries to demonstrate that his was a special talent. Everyone remembers the 1994 score at Twickenham when he swept around Rory Underwood, and beat Jon Callard's tackle to score brilliantly in the left corner and help Ireland to the most unexpected victory. Geoghegan didn't just score that try, he pinched the move from Bath, where Brian Ashton was backs coach at the time and introduced it into the Irish set-up. The switch from London Irish to Bath should have given Geoghegan a stage worthy of his talents but a persistent foot injury hampered him and would prematurely end his career. Even so, his tries-to-games ratio for Bath was impressively high.

There is a story told about Geoghegan that is so mad you can hardly believe it but it is absolutely true and as much as anything he did on the pitch, it tells about his character. One evening after training at Bath, Geoghegan was returning with a friend to London by train. At Swindon, about 300 Millwall supporters got on the train and happened to seat themselves in the carriage that previously only Geoghegan and his friend had occupied. Millwall had played a Coca-Cola Cup game that evening and had been beaten 3–0 by Swindon Town. Remember, this was the amateur era and Geoghegan had left for Bath from the London law office where he worked and on the return journey he was still wearing his lawyer's suit and tie, as was his friend. 'Take off your tie,' Geoghegan said to his pal as soon as he saw the Millwall crew come into their carriage, 'we don't want to antagonise these blokes.' They each removed their tie, opened the top button of their shirt and tried to be invisible. Though the Millwall fans sat all around them, none of them actually sat alongside Geoghegan and his friend and for the first half an hour or so, everything was fine.

Then, perhaps it was the after-shock of a 3–0 loss to Swindon kicking in, but a number of the Millwall fans started to get restless. They were out of their seats, taking light bulbs from their fittings, plunging the carriage into darkness, then restoring the light. Toilet rolls were used as missiles and one of them found a fire extinguisher which he used like it was a machine gun. All the time Geoghegan and his friend kept their heads down, attempting to stay beneath the radar. What was remarkable were the ages of the Millwall fans; the majority were in their thirties and forties and they all looked like they had seen action in the days when football hooliganism was something to write home about. At Reading two policemen got on the train and walked down to the carriage containing the Millwall fans; by this point, some damage had been done and a number of passengers had been terrorised. The policemen stood at the door of the carriage, looking through the glass panel and as they did the Millwall fans chanted anti-police slogans. It was a challenge that the two policemen, almost certainly wisely, chose not to take on. Without even opening the door to the carriage, they turned and walked away.

Shortly after the train departed Reading, trouble found Geoghegan. Before the Millwall fans had gotten on, Geoghegan and his friend had ordered teas and two slices of fruitcake from the guy pushing a food trolley through the carriage. Geoghegan hadn't eaten his cake, and it just lay on a paper plate in front of him. It became the cheese that attracted the mouse but, in this case, the mouse was fortyish, stout, balding and very obviously menacing. With the fake good humour you some-times see in Hollywood psychopaths, he stood over the Geoghegan table, stretched his hand until it hovered over the piece of fruitcake and said, 'Think I'll 'ave this.' Through the eyes of Geoghegan's pal, it seemed a reasonable request. The bloke was probably very hungry and it was clear Geoghegan wasn't going to eat it. Let the bloke have it and be gone.

Geoghegan saw it differently. Instinctively he caught the Millwall's fan's hand at the wrist and said quietly but with undeniable intent, 'If you touch that cake, I'll take your f***ing head off.' Geoghegan's friend thought it was the craziest, most stupid route to self-induced homicide that anyone had ever taken. But the thing was the look in Geoghegan's eyes; it said that if the bloke persisted in trying to take the cake, he was going to be hit and it wasn't going to be pretty. All Geoghegan's friend could think was that this guy was going to shout for his mates to come and sort out Geoghegan and he, who wanted no part in this madness, was going to be beaten to death simply because he was in the wrong place at the wrong moment. But there was the thinnest seam of cunning running through the wall of pigheadedness and that was Geoghegan's hope – that the bloke wouldn't want a punch on the chin and would back off. Of course he could shout for help but that would have

179

meant a loss of face. Geoghegan's challenge was to him, one-on-one – either he accepted it or he didn't. The bloke took a quick, furtive glance around to make sure none of his mates were aware of what was going on, and realising they hadn't noticed, he moved his hand away from the cake and silently retreated.

Though he concealed his fear brilliantly, Geoghegan was on a knife-edge. If the guy had persisted, he would have hit him for sure. What would have happened after that, he wasn't much interested in considering. His friend just thought that the fruitcake on the table was nothing compared to the fruitcake who owned it but, strangely, his admiration for Geoghegan increased. The train reached its London destination without any further incident and, there, about 200 policemen waited with truncheons which they used with some abandon on the Millwall supporters. It was a little after midnight when Geoghegan got back to his apartment on Baker Street. And as I write these final words, the opening lines of the classic Gerry Rafferty song spring to mind. I'll leave you to decide if they seem an appropriate address for one of Ireland's great and most loved wings. I think so. Go have a listen.

PACK YOUR BAGS
HUW DAVIES

'I first came across Huw when I joined Wasps in 1989. He was coming to the end of his career as I was starting out on mine. Huw was an outstanding rugby player, who played twenty-one times for England and numerous times for the Barbarians. He was a full-back/fly-half/utility back. Huw has the most incredible, dry, witty sense of humour and was a great tourist, always capable of lifting the spirits if and when a tour hit a bit of a lull. Huw would have played many more times for England had he not picked up injuries along the way. He was part of the successful Wasps side that won the league title in the 1989–90 season.'

In 1979 an England rugby union team toured Japan, Fiji and Tonga (this was the first time that a major rugby nation had visited that country). No full international caps were awarded and the tourists played under the name of 'England XV' rather than 'England'. The tourists won all their seven matches, scoring 270 points and conceding only 93. The first international against Japan was the only close game, with Japan leading 19–15 going into injury time – a converted try by Peter Squires snatched the win for England.

Just for the record, I was the leading tour points scorer with sixty points. The leading try scorers were John Carleton (nine tries) and Mike Slemen (seven tries).

I was possibly a surprise selection for the tour because I was only twenty years of age and still at university. However, I was going to make the most of the opportunity and fully commit to all aspects of touring. I trained hard and played hard – both on the pitch and off.

Anyone reading this who has ever been on tour will know there is only one golden rule and that is what goes on tour stays on tour – a concise statement with clearly only one interpretation. Since the story I'm about to share took place during the 1979 tour, I'll be breaking the rule but I've two reasons for believing that, in this instance, it's OK. First, there is a possible chance that after thirty years the statute of limitations has expired on the trip, and secondly, the only person it shows in a bad light is me.

Many rugby stories told by players past and present rarely have anything to do with the game and often involve alcohol – this is no exception.

It was the last night of the tour, and following a meal and a few beers, I found myself in the team drinks room at the hotel. On most tours with national teams in the good old amateur days, contact was often made with a local brewer or drinks distributor, and in exchange for vast quantities of alcohol, we would supply tickets for the matches – in my eyes, a fair and equitable arrangement.

There was still a lot of booze remaining (despite the not inconsiderable efforts of the boys) and I felt it part of my duty to see how big a dent I could make in it during the last hours of the trip. Various players came and went, although there was always one constant – Alastair Hignell, first choice full-back at the time. A double Cambridge Blue who had graduated a couple of years before I arrived, Alastair was a great sportsman, having also played cricket at county level for Gloucestershire. As the last night turned into the final morning, Alastair and I were the only two players left. We drank, we told stories, we drank, we reflected on the tour, we drank, we shared our hopes for the future, and we also drank.

At 9.45 a.m. Alastair looked at me and said, 'It's time to leave, collect our bags, and meet the team bus to take us to the airport for the flight back to London.'

We left the drinks room for the last time, Alastair walked to his bedroom, collected his two kit bags, which he had packed the previous night, took the lift down to reception and walked down the short drive to where the bus was parked. The driver placed his bags in the boot and Alastair climbed the steps of the bus, took his seat and looked at his watch, which ticked on to 10 a.m. – departure time.

Punctuality is important on any tour. If there's a team meeting or training has been scheduled for a particular time, without fail everyone has the option of being early or on time; to be late is just not good enough. The one should never delay the many.

Alastair was, relatively speaking, an experienced campaigner who had toured on several occasions and knew the importance of good timekeeping – hence the pre-packed bags.

I, on the other hand, was on my first 'proper' tour and therefore a bit naive. On arrival in my room a little past 9.45 a.m., I couldn't help but notice it looked like twenty monkeys had participated in an all-night party, the highlight of which must have been trying on all my clothes and kit and then seeing how far they could throw each respective item in any direction. It was absolute carnage, and this, coupled with the fact I was extremely pissed, caused me more than a little panic.

I found a maid who assisted me with collection of all my belongings and helped to stuff them into my two kit bags. Many items were still hanging out of various pockets and compartments of each bag as we made our way to reception. Outside of the hotel doors I noticed a golf buggy, loaded my bags into the area normally reserved for the clubs, sat next to a shocked-looking Japanese golfer and pointed towards the team bus seventy-five yards away at the end of the drive. Go go go go go.

He drove me to the coach. The driver shoved my bags into one of the side luggage compartments as I negotiated the steps into the bus. At the top of the steps was team manager Budge Rogers (a former back-row forward, who for many years held the record for the highest number of England caps). I have to say, during the previous weeks I had seen Budge on a daily basis, but had never seen him even close to the level of rage now expressed on his face. He absolutely lost the plot.

'What time do you call this?!' he exploded, and before I could look at my watch and work out where the hands were pointing, he continued, 'It's twenty past ten.'

'So why ask me?' I was thinking, as he proceeded to launch into, 'When I say ten I mean ten, not five past, not twenty past, not half past, I MEAN TEN! You've not only let yourself down, you've let your club down, you've let your country down and worse than all of that you've let your own team-mates down. Have you got anything to say for yourself?'

At this moment there were two important things going

through my mind. First was that I was going to fall off the steps as I could feel my grip on the handrail loosening somewhat, and being so incredibly pissed my legs were unsteady to say the least. The other was, if I had let so many people, clubs, indeed nations down, why were all the boys in my line of vision behind Budge crapping themselves with laughter, and trying desperately to stifle it by ramming their own fists into their mouths?

I decided an apology was in order (for the record, I actually have no recollection of anything Budge said to me that day, or any of my responses, but all the boys told me their own version of the incident during the next few years). But funnily enough I wasn't able to make it, because Budge had thought of a few more people, organisations, republics and possibly kingdoms I had let down. It's fair to say I was getting both barrels and then some. Each time I thought he'd finally blown himself out, he kicked off again, explaining that timekeeping and respect for fellow human beings were the essential rules one needs to abide by to progress in life.

Now at this stage I have a major problem, because I can sense that Budge is a touch annoyed by my tardiness, and his annoyance is probably only going to escalate if I piss myself in front of him, while swaying on the steps. Luckily, he stopped to draw breath and I took my opportunity.

I am reliably informed by every member of that 1979 England touring party to Japan, Fiji and Tonga that I said to Budge, 'Well . . . if that's the way you feel . . . you can . . . send me home!'

Apparently, the boys exploded with laughter, the bus proceeded to the airport for the flight home and I, thankfully, passed out.

Sorry Budge, sincere apologies.

However, it taught me a great lesson – don't ever spend the night drinking with Alastair Hignell. It will only lead to complications.

NUMERO UNO
JOEL STRANSKY

'A real cool, calm customer and a fantastically skilful fly-half, Joel rightly took his place in rugby history as part of the 1995 team who won the World Cup in South Africa. English fans will remember him for his contribution to Leicester Tigers, which exuded authority and gave his team real direction. He was always a threat on the rugby field and he proved he could kick a mean drop goal when the pressure was on. Incredibly, the one he knocked over to win the World Cup was only the third he'd ever kicked for his country – and the other two came earlier in the tournament.'

As the final whistle blew ending the 1995 World Cup final, I had an overwhelming feeling of relief that the job had been completed. We had been in camp for three weeks prior to the tournament starting and then a further four weeks of competition. Anyone who was at Ellis Park, Johannesburg, or watched the occasion on TV, will remember Nelson Mandela, wearing the No. 6 jersey, being introduced to the Springbok team prior to the match by our captain, François Pienaar, the man who wore the No. 6 jersey on the field of play. Many will also remember it was at this time we saw the birth of 'the Rainbow Nation' following Mandela's release from incarceration on Robben Island.

Everyone in the team looked around for someone to hug, and eventually the William Webb Ellis trophy was presented to François. In the changing room afterwards we had a couple of beers, and if my memory serves me correctly, a few bottles of champagne were popped to help with the festivities. This was a special time. Everyone present had been responsible in some way for making the dream a reality – players, management, coaches, medical staff – and this was likely to be the last time all those people would be in a room together without any outsiders. Magical.

We left Ellis Park on the team bus with our wives and girlfriends with the intention of going to the team hotel in order to get ready for the official celebration dinner later in the evening. The traffic was unbelievable. The whole of Johannesburg was gridlocked – well, definitely the area around the ground, anyway. The noise was incredible. Drivers in every car were blowing their horns, not because of the traffic jam, because of the victory. There were people on car roofs and bonnets, dancing and singing, even the police were in party mood, adding to the scene by waving borrowed flags and chanting. Just incredible scenes. After what seemed like at least an hour, the bus had moved no more than 800 metres and one or two of us were getting restless.

A few minutes later, François Pienaar, Garry Pagel (prop forward) and I left the bus with our wives, Nerene, Anna and Karen, and walked a few metres to the Rattlesnake Diner. The place was packed with people celebrating the victory, including the stairs leading up to the main dining area, where everyone was dancing on the tables and enjoying a massive party. What followed seemed like a scene from a movie. Word was passed up the stairs to the bar that three of the victorious Springboks and their wives were in need of a few beers, and several minutes later the beers were being passed from hand to hand down to us at the entrance. We spent the next hour talking to anyone who came up to us, enjoying this unique moment when every person was smiling, singing or dancing. Eventually, we decided it was time to return to the team hotel and that was when it hit us. For the first time in seven weeks we were on our own. For almost two months everything had been provided for us – food, training facilities, clothing and, most importantly, transport. We had not had to think about anything other than rugby and the ultimate goal of winning the World Cup.

Given our predicament, I sent François to the other side of the road and told him to start hitching. The traffic was now flowing a little more freely and the first couple of cars passed François with his outstretched thumb and continued on their way. Shortly after this two young guys, both driving Fiat Unos stopped. Our wives, Garry and I crossed the road and we all decanted into the two Fiats. In the first one, François sat in the front seat while Nerene, Karen and I squashed into the back, leaving Garry and Anna in the car behind. We asked the young lad if he would take us to our hotel in Sandton and he started to drive, all the while glancing to his left at François.

'It's you, isn't it?' he said eventually.

'If you mean François Pienaar, then yes it's me,' François replied. 'And behind you is Joel Stransky, who dropped the goal to win the World Cup this afternoon. Either side of him is my wife Nerene and his wife Karen.'

The guy was practically speechless. A short while later,

François asked if he wanted to see his World Cup winner's medal, which was around his neck under his shirt. I thought the lad was going to drive off the road as François handed it to him. He alternated between glancing at the road ahead and staring at the medal, and finally handed it back.

Soon both Fiat Unos arrived at our hotel and we invited our new best friends into the hotel with us, where they met several of the players and stayed for a few beers, after which we thanked them for the lift and left for the official part of the evening.

The interesting thing about this story is that we never found out our driver's name, and he never asked for a thing, not even an autograph. I have often thought about him and imagine him in a bar with his mates telling them about the time he picked up the captain of South Africa and the guy who dropped the winning goal, when they were hitching a lift back to their team hotel on the evening of the World Cup final.

Can you imagine the response? 'Yeah, of course you did. In fact, you forgot to mention the following morning when you picked up Nelson Mandela, Madonna and The Spice Girls, who'd been out all night partying and spent their taxi money.'

I'd like to say to that driver, I'm sorry, I don't know your name, but if you ever read this story, you now have all the proof you need.

HELP FROM THE YOUNG 'UN

MATT PERRY

'Matt's a guy I know very well as I played quite a lot with him in the England team. He played full-back for Bath and England and indeed the British and Irish Lions. Clive Woodward took a liking to Matt when he coached him at Bath and selected him for his first game in charge against Australia in the autumn of 1997, a game in which I was captain. He was always a very reliable and solid full-back – amazing under the high ball and he liked to run with the ball and counter attack. From a forward's point of view he was a fantastic guy to play with as he would always get you playing on the front foot and establish a real target for you.

'At twenty-three I think Matt became England's most capped full-back with thirty-five caps, overtaking Jonathan Webbs' record, and I'm pretty sure that is a record that still stands today. He also toured the British and Irish Lions in 2001 to Australia playing in all three tests. Unfortunately he got a back injury on that tour and that kept him sidelined for quite some time. He was very successful with Bath, battling against injury towards the latter part of his career. Matt was always one of those guys who was immensely well liked throughout the world of rugby. He now works near Bath for a management consultancy company.'

I often wonder if people who support rugby realise the sacrifices certain players make to play the game, sacrifices that are not often evident until they reach the end of their careers. Now don't misunderstand me. It's a privilege to play rugby, especially if it involves playing for a club like Bath or representing your country, or indeed the British and Irish Lions. In the modern era, players earn a living from a sport that was completely amateur just fifteen years ago and I have absolutely no complaints from my time in the game.

One of my first games for Bath was against Nottingham. In those days there were no team warm-ups. Players used to arrive at an appointed time (give or take half an hour), get changed into their kit, go on to the pitch and do their own thing for a while. They'd be back in the changing rooms in time to listen to an unintelligible team-talk from the captain and watch the forwards head butt either the walls or, if it was a big game, each other.

As a new boy I arrived early, complete with a bad haircut and acne, and in the changing room was immediately faced with my first problem – where do I get changed? I had an idea that players had favoured places, but being new I didn't know who went where. I decided on the far corner, which turned out to be 'owned' by the two Bath second-row forwards at the time, Martin Haag and Nigel 'Ollie' Redman. Martin, who had already arrived in order to give himself sufficient time to get all his strapping on, looked at me and said, 'You might want to move over a bit, young 'un [I think he learnt my name sometime during my third season with the club]. Ollie normally sits there, and believe me he needs a bit of space.'

A few minutes later Ollie walked in, a wonderful servant of the Bath club who was nearing the end of an illustrious career. He walked slowly towards me, dumped his kit bag and said, 'Young 'un, take my jacket off and hang it on that peg,' nodding towards a peg above my head.

At the time I wondered if this was some type of ritual, the new boy removing the jacket of the senior pro. I did as I was asked, and several minutes later I noticed Ollie in the physio's room where extensive work was taking place on both his arms. The physio was building up a sweat and Ollie looked in agony. I quietly asked Martin Haag what was wrong with him.

'Oh, he's had problems for ages. Both his elbows locked up years ago and more recently, his shoulders have started to seize up as well,' he replied.

'But he's our number one line-out jumper,' I thought to myself.

The game ended and, not for the first time, Ollie was awarded man of the match following an incredible display. We all returned to the changing room and after getting showered, he looked at me and said, 'Young 'un, get my jacket off the peg and help me on with it.'

I now knew it had nothing to do with a ritual. He was actually incapable of removing or replacing his own jacket due to the numerous injuries and operations he had endured throughout his career. He wasn't picking on me. I just happened to be the nearest person to him in the room.

Anyone who sees Ollie today, walking like John Wayne with his arms at a forty-five degree angle to his body, looking permanently ready to draw a couple of Colt 45s from his holsters, can be assured it's not part of a rough, tough image. It's merely a reminder of the toll fifteen seasons of top-class rugby took on his body.

Rather him than me.

PLAYING AWAY
DAMIAN HOPLEY

'I first came across Damian Hopley at the outset of our respective careers at the rather unglamorous surroundings of Wasps' old ground at Repton Avenue, Sudbury. Nicknamed "The Bishop" on account of his masters degree in theology from St Andrews University and subsequent postgraduate studies at Cambridge, I was amazed how he burst on the scene when he thoroughly embarrassed Will Carling on his Wasps debut. We came into our England careers at the same time and I'm very proud to have made my debut in the same match as Damian and to have played alongside him in the inaugural Rugby World Cup 7s in Edinburgh.

'We have remained great mates from those early days and share a positive outlook and love of life. During our careers we both suffered anterior cruciate knee ligament injuries and while I made a full recovery, Damian was forced to retire from the game aged just twenty-seven. However, that setback didn't end his involvement in rugby. After his retirement Damian founded the Rugby Players Association (RPA) and has been the driving force for players' rights ever since. This is an achievement of which I hope he is rightly proud. Oh, and he writes a bit in his spare time as well.'

The First English Rugby World Champions

Having played some 7s in my school and student days, I was greatly encouraged to hear that the International Rugby Board (IRB) had agreed to stage the inaugural Rugby World Cup (RWC) 7s in 1993. Extra training sessions in my local gym were inspired by visions of playing in Hong Kong and sampling the famous Asian hospitality and service culture. So it was to my eternal chagrin that the IRB announced the inaugural tournament would be staged at . . . er . . . Murrayfield in April 1993. Added to this, the stadium was halfway through a building programme and wouldn't actually be finished in time for the 7s, so that made the trip even less appealing.

Before all of that, we had the minor issue of selection to overcome. The RFU appeared to have given this event scant thought and picked a makeshift squad to play in a few tournaments in the run-up – such was their selection tool. This was very much viewed as a damage-limitation exercise from Twickenham HQ.

A few candidates were certain of selection from the outset. England international Andy Harriman was announced as captain very early on, and given his tried and tested credentials – a genuine 7s expert, Olympically quick (literally), very bright and even funnier – we could just about forgive him for being a Harlequin and follow his lead. The early season tournaments also unearthed one of the most underrated players of this era. Playing for Northampton Saints up at the Gala 7s, Nick Beal emerged as the player of the tournament in guiding his team to the title. Imagine our joy being sent up there as the England team only to be beaten by the hosts in the quarter-final. As Bill McLaren might have said, 'And I tell you, they'll be whooping and a-hollering in the streets of Galashiels tonight.' The final piece of the early jigsaw was Chris Sheasby, the darling of the Middlesex 7s, and one of the most phenomenal athletes to have played the game in the pre-professional era. Unfortunately, he wasn't afraid to tell anyone in earshot as much, so that helped to bring the team together around him.

We had the grand total of three training weekends leading up to the final selection in late March, but a few more likely lads had been staking a claim. From Northampton Tim Rodber (our other England cap) and Matt Dawson were well versed in the game – Dawson was a team-mate of Nick Beal's at Royal Grammar School (RGS) High Wycombe, and Rodders added some much-needed grunt up front. A former England schools team-mate of mine, Adedayo Adebayo, a tremendously dynamic defender and as slippery on the field as he was on the dance floor, was added to the squad, and was joined by my good self (utility player, versatile on the piano and, as a St Andrews University graduate, the Scottish interpreter) and my Wasps team-mate Lawrence Dallaglio. Fresh out of the Wasps production line of back-row forwards, Lawrence was blessed with tremendous pace and had been a member of the all-conquering Ampleforth 7s team that had dominated the schools circuit under the tutelage of John Willcox.

The final two members of the squad were relatively unknown quantities – Dave Scully, a 7s veteran and full-time fireman playing for Wakefield in the second division, and Justyn Cassell, the rangy back row from Saracens. Both had impressed tremendously in the trial weekends and we all had absolute faith in their abilities, even though I'm not sure that feeling was mutual.

Our management were the tried and tested England 'A' team

pairing of Peter 'Rosey' Rossborough and Les Cusworth, who, with his precocious talent, continually outshone us in the touch sessions before training. Our medical team were the ever-reliable Barney Kenny (along with Lawrence Dallaglio and Matt Dawson, he was a member of the 2003 Rugby World Cup squad) and team doctor, Paul Jackson, or 'Fat Jack' as he was known when he was the scourge of the Hospitals' Cup playing for St Mary's Medical School in the eighties.

Having been hastily thrown together, the squad was kitted out in leftover samples from HQ, and our first official engagement was not in Scotland, but at a civic reception in Hartlepool, for which we had been volunteered by the then president of the RFU, Danie Serfontein. We were already running very late when Danie pleaded with us to stay to hear the 'riveting' story of the monkey hanging, which I am going to give you in a very truncated (keeping with the animal theme) form to see if you can (a) see the point of the story, and (b) understand why anyone would think it would be of interest to us. The story dated from the Napoleonic wars when a French ship was wrecked off the coast of Hartlepool. The only survivor was a monkey, wearing a French uniform (presumably to provide amusement for those on board the ship). On finding the monkey, some locals decided to hold an impromptu trial on the beach. Since the monkey was unable to answer their questions, and many locals were unaware of what a Frenchman would look like, they concluded that the monkey was in fact a French spy. Just to make sure, the animal was sentenced to death and hanged from the mast of a fishing boat on the headland.

I rest my case.

Anyway, with this moving story ringing in our ears we

eventually left for Edinburgh three hours behind schedule. The journey was made all the more memorable by our enthusiastic coach driver and his remarkable collection of adult films – in fact, he seemed to be rather more intent on watching the screen than the road, and his Geordie commentary throughout the movie certainly added a new dimension to what, to be honest, was a rather weak plot.

At 1.30 a.m. we arrived at the very pleasant George Hotel in the heart of Edinburgh and headed to bed, eager to get our World Cup week off to a flying start.

An unusual aspect of 7s tournament rugby is that all the teams stay in the same hotel, which ensures that the *entente cordiale* is in rich abundance throughout the week. As I'm sure you will be aware, the theme tune to the Rugby World Cup is 'World in Union' and during that week we certainly got the opportunity to catch a unique insight into the idiosyncrasies of the other competing teams.

One of the highlights of the first day was seeing the unfancied Latvian team arrive for dinner wearing ankle length maroon trench coats, looking like extras from Monty Python's 'Spanish Inquisition' sketch. Having studied their strange behaviour closely from the comfort of our allocated table, I was convinced that they were secretly stashing the wonderful culinary spread inside their coats with a view to sending food parcels home. I may have been mistaken, but I'm sure that an entire salmon and a side of beef disappeared after some stunning sleight of hand that even Paul Daniels would have been proud of. On second thoughts, maybe they just needed a good feed.

The other highlight of this first day in camp was that, since it was my twenty-third birthday, Andrew Harriman decreed that I should take the chaps out on a local tour to get acclimatised and get the jet lag out of our system. Marvellous. I did confess to having some local knowledge as my brother, Rupert, had been a student in Edinburgh and I frequently came down from St Andrews to enjoy the glamour of big city life before retreating once more to Fife to recover.

The night was a huge success – dinner in the hotel followed by a large single malt in my honour, and then out into the streets of Edinburgh for some good old-fashioned ice breaking. All of this was above and beyond the call of duty for Queen and country, but manfully we soldiered on. For the sake of protecting the names of the not so innocent I shall not divulge what happened over the next few hours, but having run into the Irish team, who were equally hell bent on getting over their arduous journey, we settled in for a fantastic night and knew that, in Andrew Harriman, we had a captain who led by example on all fronts.

Andy's vision was exemplary, as he proved by convincing the management to shift training back to the following afternoon. The next morning was relatively slow, and it gave us all a shock when we encountered the entire Fiji and Samoa squads going out to train just as we were stumbling back in from our bonding session. Whoops.

Things didn't materially improve when we got the minibus out to the local training grounds of Stewart's Melville and the collective smell was unbearable. Not only were we suffering from the excesses of the night before, but Fat Jack and Barney had insisted we take a professional approach to nutrition – necessary, they said, if we were going to survive the gruelling schedule ahead of us. The tournament was being played over three days, and comprised twelve matches if you got to the final. So our diet consisted of Power Bars, bananas and energy drinks. Now, as all good endurance athletes will tell you, Power Bars have come on a long way since the early nineties when they tasted like cardboard and had devastating effects on your insides. Consequently, we tried to order a cabriolet minibus for the rest of the week, but settled instead for windows down at all times, rain or shine.

We arrived at the training ground to be told that the Scottish Rugby Union (SRU) had provided opposition in the form of teams from local clubs around the area – 'cannon fodder' or so we fondly thought. The team we played were from Edinburgh Royal High Former Pupils and things weren't exactly going to plan when we found ourselves four scores down at the end of the first half.

Les Cusworth was tearing out what little hair he had as some of the fundamental 7s lessons seemed to have been washed away with Caledonian's finest 80 Shilling the night before, and it's fair to say our form was, at best, underwhelming.

Captain Harriman pleaded for patience, and gathered the squad in for a few well-chosen words, and he asked some very direct questions of some of us. 'What exactly was in the cocktails you bought us last night, Hoppers? I feel like shit!' Truly soul-searching stuff. Our form improved gradually as we sweated the booze out, and by the time we got back to the hotel we all realised that it was time to get (mildly) serious.

Unbeknown to us, one of the local bookmakers must have seen us in action that afternoon, as we were priced as rank outsiders for the tournament at 35–1 with Fiji and New Zealand made clear favourites to lift the inaugural Melrose Cup.

The one addition to the squad, who was to play a key and unsung role in our unexpected success, was our liaison man –

George. The role of liaison man is crucial. He is the 'Mr Fixit' on the ground, arranging minibus pick-ups, dealing with any unforeseen mishaps etc – the best liaison men in the history of the game are those who operate under a shroud of secrecy and always deliver. I've no idea how they are allocated, but to have an elderly Scottish gentleman looking after the England team was the final piece of the jigsaw for the extraordinary week that lay ahead. Now, having seen the state of us after the first night on the tiles, George intuitively realised he was with like-minded rugby men, and made it his burning ambition to 'take out' the other liaison men one by one as the week went on by getting them on to the extensive range of whiskies in the hotel bar. And my word, did he take his duties seriously.

It was with much admiration that I came down to breakfast that second morning to witness George sitting there with eyes like piss holes in the snow, reeking of liquor and looking not unlike Grandpa Potts (aka Lionel Jeffries) of *Chitty Chitty Bang Bang* fame. As he tucked into his kedgeree and coffee, he proudly informed me that he'd seen off a handful of his counterparts the night before, and he was only just warming up for the week ahead. His party piece when on the turps was to burst forth into a rendition of 'St Andrews by the Sea', in his finest pub-singer voice. To this day I don't know if that was a tribute to my seat of learning or the only song to which he could remember the words when stocious, but this ditty became his standard rally cry from the bar when he had seen off another victim. With twenty-four teams competing in the event, we knew George had his work cut out, but his earnest Scottish Presbyterian upbringing and the whiff of a free bar were all the ammunition he needed to come through for us.

After all this build-up, the tournament could well have been an anticlimax – as previously mentioned, Murrayfield was undergoing an enormous amount of building work – but to be fair to the SRU, they had really gone to town in their planning and had the grand total of ONE catering van in for the entire three days to ensure the 40,000 fans were given a memorable culinary experience and real value for money. In the first game of the tournament, joint favourites Fiji, featuring the world's greatest ever 7s exponent in Waisale Serevi, took on the minnows of Latvia, whose toughest opponent to date had been the eagle-eyed hotel restaurant manager. For the record, the first try in the 1993 RWC 7s was scored by . . . Latvia, thus setting the tone for a remarkable few days.

Having come through relatively comfortable pool games against Hong Kong and Spain on day one, on day two we suffered our first defeat – to Samoa, who were the recently crowned Hong Kong 7s champions. However, we still made it through to the second qualifying pool stages of the marathon event – the complicated format had clearly been thought up by the IRB after one too many post-lunch Amarettos in Dublin.

We awoke on day three, weighed down with little expectation, but knowing that slowly and surely we were coming together as a team. In Harriman we had the tournament's quickest player by some distance, and in Rodber, Sheasby and Dallaglio we had a pack of forwards who were quick, aggressive and skilful. However, before we could even think about progressing further, we had to overcome New Zealand, South Africa and Australia in the second pool stages. We were delighted to see our prayers to the rain gods had been answered, and the steady drizzle had our forwards licking their lips in anticipation.

New Zealand had come into the event with a tremendously rich heritage in 7s rugby, and in Eric Rush they possessed one of the greatest 7s exponents the game has ever seen. Our only chance was to catch them cold and get off to a good start. We couldn't have written the script better ourselves and scored from three kick-offs in the first half, effectively closing out the game. Dave Scully's and Nick Beal's decision-making was outstanding, and Dayo Adebayo put in a sensational try-saving tackle on Eric Rush, after which the Kiwi captain limped off the field and took no further part in the tournament.

As you can imagine, the Scottish support (all seven of them) were dumbfounded by this result, and I must admit we even raised a few eyebrows among ourselves when we came off. Lawrence had been rested for the game, so we knew there was a lot more to come, and he had dutifully spent the fifteen minutes calling his bookie to see if he could still get 35–1 on us. You can take the boy out of Shepherd's Bush . . .

Our next opponents were South Africa. Their team contained a number of frontline Test players, including Ruben Kruger, Joost van der Westhuizen and Chester Williams. Again, we stunned the partisan home crowd with a 14–7 victory that ensured our passage into the semi-final knockout stages. 'Good grief,' I thought, 'any more of this and George will be lynched when he goes home tomorrow.' We knew things were starting to go our way when we heard the strains of 'Swing Low' being sung by minority sections of the crowd around the ground.

Sadly from my point of view, I had pulled a calf muscle scoring in the victory over South Africa, so was ruled out of the remainder of the tournament. As ever in sport, the show must go on, and even though I was devastated to miss out, I had tremendous confidence that this squad was destined for bigger and better things.

The tournament rules state that any replacement player must come from a pool of reserves, and England called up Michael Dods – that would be the Gala full-back and Scotland international Michael Dods. The thought of him sitting in his England kit on the bench, trying to hide under his cap, still makes me laugh to this very day. As he said when I saw him in the hotel bar later that night, 'Of all the bloody teams that could have picked me, I get f***ing England! It's the one shirt I can never wear again in my entire lifetime!' Priceless.

The semi-final was against Fiji, and this is where the forwards came into their own. Led by Field Marshal Rodber, they assaulted the big Fijian forwards. I'm not sure what the collective noun is for a head butt, but that's exactly what Messrs Rodber, Sheasby (careful not to mess up his own hair) and Dallaglio delivered at the first scrum. And when you've got a swede as big as Rodders' coming at you, there'll be only one winner. Without the ball, Fiji and Serevi couldn't play and, against all odds, England grew as the game progressed.

The so-called 'moment of the tournament' came in this game when Mesake Rasari, the giant Fijian forward, was hurtling down the wing and the only man who stood between him and the tryline was our agent Scully, playing sweeper. This is the classic 7s scenario, one-on-one rugby pitting the players in a head-to-head confrontation. Being a nugget Yorkshire fireman, Sculls threw himself head first into the charging Rasari with such force that it not only stopped the run, but knocked the ball free, and England went on to score a try at the other end en route to winning the game 21–7.

In the other semi-final, Ireland lost to Australia by a

last-gasp try from Willie Ofahengaue in the final move of the match to secure a 21–19 victory.

Suddenly, we found ourselves in the completely unexpected position of being in the inaugural Rugby World Cup 7s final against Australia, and as Scots up and down the land rushed out to buy green and gold jerseys, the support for the England team became ever louder and sweeter by the minute.

Once we had made the final we had an hour or so to recover, attend to any minor injuries, eat more Power Bars and take the piss out of Dodsy for his England kit. Coach Cusworth was in his element, talking to the players, ensuring everyone knew their roles going into the last match. He talked Daws and I through our water-carrying roles several times – he was clearly nervous.

The final was a classic encounter – and the age-old game of two halves. It is ten minutes each way in the final, as opposed to the seven of all the other games. Australia, including Michael Lynagh, Willie Ofahengaue, Matt Burke and David Campese, kicked off and when Andy Harriman skinned David Campese with his first touch of the ball, we knew this was going to be a pulsating game. A score by Lawrence and the sight of Tim Rodber outpacing Matt Burke to score England's third try of the half – all converted by Nick Beal – gladdened our hearts and ensured Australia had a hell of a job on their hands to get back into the game.

As they have proved so many times before, Australians never say die, and so it was that tries from Michael Lynagh just before half-time, then David Campese and Semi Taupeaafe in the second half brought the score back to 21–17. However, England dug deep for the final few moments and when the whistle blew we went into rapture about what we'd accomplished. Basically, a scratch side had come together that week and had ended up winning the World Cup – you couldn't have scripted it.

It was fitting that our very own 'Prince' Harriman was then presented with the Melrose Cup by the Princess Royal as the English fans (and players) went berserk. The lap of honour was terrific, especially seeing how many friends and family had made the effort to come up and cheer us on. In scenes reminiscent of *Escape to Victory*, I had visions of the England supporters rushing on to the field and covering us in overcoats and flat caps and smuggling us out of the ground and away from the baying throng of distraught Scottish fans. It was a remarkable occasion, never to be forgotten.

The formal part of the evening was an official dinner held at the Royal Highland Centre out near Edinburgh Airport. When invited to say a few words, Captain Harriman demurely announced that he would keep his speech as brief as Scotland's efforts in the main competition – they were defeated by Japan in the Bowl final 33–19. That set the tone for another splendid night out and I'm delighted to say that George was crowned the unofficial world champion 7s liaison officer at approximately 4.45 a.m. on Monday, 19 April 1993.

The Epilogue

One of the more enjoyable stories from that weekend was that Eileen Dallaglio – Lawrence's remarkable mother and perhaps one of the shrewdest operators I've ever had the good fortune to meet – put a cheeky wager on us to win the tournament at 35–1. She always told me she would have made a good England selector. How could you disagree with that intuition?

The ten commandments of touring

While our winning trip to Edinburgh may not have counted as a tour in the traditional sense, that aspect of the wonderful tapestry that is rugby does still live on, I am glad to say. But be warned, touring is a part of the game that is fraught with danger.

So, what makes a 'successful' rugby tour? As the British and Irish Lions proved on their courageous, but ultimately unsuccessful, 2009 tour of South Africa earlier this year, one of the primary concerns is how to finance such an epic journey. In economically challenging times, the truth is that no longer does every club have a wealthy committee member willing to dig deep and throw a few coppers in the kitty for the 'chaps' to 'head awf' to 'Honkers' for a week's jolly. Begging letters are penned, numerous fundraising events are initiated and distant members of the family hear from their long-lost rugby-playing relatives for the first time in years.

Among fundraising events, one of the tried and tested perennials is the sporting dinner. Once a quality guest speaker has been collared at a reasonably affordable price, the next crucial item is the auction of sporting memorabilia. The timing of this is critical and, as a rule of thumb, the later in the evening it can be left, the better. Just as the cheap house red begins to take its toll, so should the first item come under the hammer. The more refreshed the punters, the more enthusiastically they will pay up for what are usually items that have lost all their appeal by morning. At the Harlequins' City Dinner, one of the guests paid in excess of £12,000 for a weekend's trip to Johannesburg to watch the Lions playing South Africa in the third Test. As richly deserved as the Lions' victory was for an outstanding group of players, it was unfortunately a dead rubber since the Springboks had clinched the series victory the week before. I trust the successful bidder's wife was delighted by his news as she filed her divorce papers.

Once sufficient funds have been gathered, the crucial decision to be made is the destination of the tour. This is usually best taken by a small nucleus of senior players and committee members, with the possibilities being put to the vote. The club, however, must take stock of the aims of the tour. Is it intended to be developmental, an end-of-season knees-up, or simply an excuse to escape from the strains of everyday life?

If it is to be a developmental tour, the destination is all-important. When one has the task of bringing on up-and-coming talent in the game – something at which the English Rugby Union are notoriously poor – then one must gauge the talent within the side. On the back end of a poor domestic season it would be ludicrous to head off to the South of France with a group of Under-19s to play friendlies against teams such as Biarritz or Bègles. Rest assured, this will be an uneven contest – at the post-match function, as you down your third gallon of Pernod and finish your second bowl of pâté, your opposite number will introduce you to his wife and ten-year-old son. Beware of developmental tours and insist that the referee checks both studs and birth certificates before kick-off.

At the other end of the spectrum is the end-of-season jolly to celebrate the club's survival in the league. Assuming that the kitty is brimming with cash, the more exotic destinations may be pursued. Some of the best venues to which I have travelled are sun-drenched beaches where the standard of rugby, although relatively poor, is more than compensated for by the standard of living. A prime example is Bermuda, where the hospitality is legendary. Of paramount importance in any destination is the accommodation. If you are lucky enough to be 'billeted', you get more of a feel for the country and its people. Despite the apparent glamour of touring with an international side, it can be a very isolated existence, wherein the only thing you see of the country is a hotel room, a couple of bars and a lot of rugby pitches (though in which order depends very much on the individual). I am in constant awe of people who are generous enough to host rugby players from foreign climes. Knowing the rugby beast as I do, the last place I would want him would be in my home.

Assuming that the club has chosen their destination, the next step should be to look at the creeds, cultures and customs that the tourists might face. In using a religious connotation, I like to think of tours as a form of pilgrimage and when the two are compared there are striking similarities, such as uniformity in dress codes, the chanting of familiar songs and the sense of community and fellowship throughout. One of the few differences is that while a trip to Lourdes could miraculously culminate in the cure of an ailment, an international weekend in Dublin will inevitably result in a rapid decline in health. As with a pilgrimage to the Holy Land, a tour requires participants to show respect for local cultures and customs – in other words, the opposite of the much-publicised antics of Wasps RFC in the Cobra 10s in Malaysia in 1992. I'll leave it to my brother Phil to tell you more about the cheeky behaviour of the 'Kuala Lumpur Five' (who included, I might add, a future captain of the England rugby team who you can see on the cover of this book) but suffice to say that the following year the competitors were each issued with a list of dos and don'ts and the liaison officers breathed a sigh of relief as the tournament went off without so much as a bare shoulder.

If the tour is lucky enough to be travelling to the South Sea Islands, and Fiji in particular, they will be treated to a welcome like no other in the world. When England toured there in 1991, we had the considerable privilege of being put up in the Nadi Sheraton, one of the most beautiful hotels I have been fortunate enough to stay in. On arrival we were invited to a traditional *kava* ceremony. The elders of the tribe sat round a large wooden mixing bowl in which tree roots were washed in a muddy concoction. A small bowl containing the murky waters was then passed round the group, who were also seated. Before receiving the bowl and drinking, one had to clap three times to ward off the evil spirits and then drink the potion. While the taste takes some getting used to, a warm glow is soon experienced all over and the world seems a better place. The secret of *kava* is not that it is alcohol-based, as is widely assumed, but that it is actually a narcotic. After a few bowls of the stuff, when we got up to go, to a man we found our legs had ceased to function – much to the amusement of our hosts. Next night we got our revenge by sending them off to the local Guinness bar with Messrs Kendall and Leonard. We're eagerly awaiting the rematch.

Another element of the minefield that can be the rugby tour is the vexed question of who plays. When the Test side was announced to play Fiji in 1991, inevitably some members of the midweek team were aggrieved at their omission. This is always a dangerous time in the life of any tour. Strong management is needed to ensure that the players who are not selected are kept 'on tour', and do not derail the efforts of the rest of the squad to win the Test match that weekend. Sadly, this firm hand was lacking, as Geoff Cooke, our team manager, felt he could leave it to the experienced players, such as midweek captain John Olver from Northampton, to steady his troops and keep us on the straight and narrow.

John called the 'bitter and twisted club' to an inaugural meeting at 6 p.m. in the cocktail bar that evening. The venom that poured forth from the mouths of those who had been dropped or overlooked was a real eye opener for me as a relative newcomer to international rugby. Within no time, the cocktails were flowing, the knives were being sharpened and cries of 'Seven before seven!' rang out across the bar. An unrivalled sense of camaraderie was blossoming between the 'rusty bullets', as we were affectionately known, fortified by frequent visits to the bar. This was becoming a potentially explosive situation.

As the night drew on, the karaoke bar beckoned and we discovered with considerable glee that Geoff Cooke had divulged his room number to one of the boys, telling him to put a *few* drinks on his tab if needs be, to keep the spirits up. No second invitation was needed, and not a soul in the place was allowed to pay for a drink. The barmen ably assisted us by signing as 'Mr Cooke' throughout the night and the party went off the radar, with John leading the troops from the front. The now legendary cry of 'Shooters?' was heard every five minutes as he produced yet another tray of tequilas, and the entire bar was out of control. Come 2.30 a.m., as proceedings drew to a close, we were in no mood to stop the frenzy, so off we went into the night looking for mischief.

As we entered the Tropicana bar we noticed that the band had vacated the stage and, somewhat foolishly (how I rue that day), I let it be known that I could knock out a tune on the piano. No sooner said than we were up on the stage trying to get the instruments and the speakers connected for an impromptu gig. The hotel security guards were shooed away by our own security guards – Nottingham's Simon Hodgkinson and Gary Rees – as they convinced them in no uncertain terms that we had years of experience on the road and that this would be an unplugged version of our standard tour routine.

It was left to our roadie – Nigel Redman, a sparks by trade – to flick the switch and send our unique sound out live, all over the resort. We had Dewi 'Ringo' Morris on drums, John Olver on lead guitar, Jon Hall on vocals and yours truly on keyboards. The curtains drew back and with a cry of 'Hello Wemberrrley!' we struck up a distinctly poor imitation of the Blues Brothers. This lasted approximately four bars before I looked up to see an extremely irate Geoff Cooke standing alone on the dance floor looking like he was about to explode. He had been dragged out of bed by hotel security, who were powerless to stop our one night only Nadi gig, and our situation wasn't helped by the fact that his wife had just arrived from the UK that evening. Crikey.

I looked around and saw, to my horror, that the wiser and more experienced members of the band had quietly melted into the night, leaving me – sorry about this – to face the music. As I staggered back to my room, the full extent of my mis-demeanour descended like a ton of bricks and I feared that I would probably be sent home in disgrace the next morning, thus bringing shame on my family and a premature end to any ambition of playing international rugby.

The mood was lightened considerably by my room-mate, Nigel Redman, who, even though he had left the stage seconds before me, was now fully naked tucked up in bed, and had the demeanour of a man who had been asleep for hours (you can't coach that sort of touring experience). As he checked the coast was clear Nigel muttered, 'Tell you what, fair play to Geoff, being up with the boys at three in the morning.' I laughed myself to sleep and I can assure you that the ninety-minute punishment we got some six hours later taught me a very valuable lesson – I never got caught out again.

But enough of nostalgia and on to my ten commandments of touring. These should not be taken as gospel truths but merely as an aid to the well-being of the tour party.

The first, and undoubtedly the most important, commandment on any tour is: *Thou shalt not take thyself too seriously*. It has been well documented throughout the ages that rugby players have an inimitable sense of humour, which tends to prey on the shortcomings of their colleagues. On tour the herd mentality is rife, and God help you if you find yourself in the firing line. Once the merest chink in your armour is exposed the whole team will descend upon you like a ton of bricks. The best form of defence, both on and off the pitch, is attack. If you find yourself up against the proverbial ropes, just start swinging – verbally or otherwise. Fortunately, with so much going on on tour, there will always be another story to divert the herd's attention. A small tip is to be discreet, and if you're found out, don't fret. Another 'night after' story will soon emerge and your indiscretion will soon be usurped by one much worse than your own. Hopefully.

The second commandment is: *Thou shalt always honour drives*. A common oversight on most tours is the need to keep the support team happy. There can be nothing more damaging than upsetting the driver of the tour bus. He should be humoured at all times and the bus should be treated with the utmost respect. It is inadvisable to follow the actions of the members of one London medical school team, who when fuelled by snakebite and blackcurrant swiftly followed by rum shrub chasers, removed a urinal from the opposition changing-room toilets, put it on the back seat of their bus and used it liberally sans plumbing throughout the journey home. Funny at the time no doubt, but not quite so hilarious when they were jettisoned many miles outside of London with little money, and even less chance of getting back home for last orders.

Third: *Thou shalt keep the Sabbath holy*. One of the many joys of touring is the God-given right not to play on a Sunday. Be it strong religious beliefs or simply the mother and father of all hangovers, use this commandment wisely and always maintain a sense of moral perspective on the game.

Number four: *Thou shalt obey the manager at all times*. A vital element in the tour party is the manager. Usually a 'forces man', he wears his blazer with pride and is always happy to recall the good old days of capital punishment. Known affectionately to the troops as 'Rear Gunner', he tries to run the tour with military precision, and invariably fails. It is important, however, to keep in with him for it is he who allocates the billets and the beer kitty, and makes the all-important decisions about dress code. He always packs his boots (white laces compulsory) 'just in case' and can be found at the end of the night slumped in a corner, singing wartime medleys. Lest we forget.

Numbers five, six and seven: *Thou shalt not kill/commit adultery/covet thy billet's wife/daughter*. If adhered to strictly, these commandments tend to help tour morale considerably.

Number eight: *Thou shalt not steal*. While all tourists are encouraged to return from the trip with a memento or two, the infamous Willie Anderson incident should serve as a sharp reminder of what may happen if you get caught. The former Irish captain was detained in Argentina following a run-in with the local constabulary about a missing national flag. Three months later he was finally released to tell his tale and become a shining example to each and every tourist of what may happen if you're caught. Beware: Big Brother may well be watching you.

Number nine: *Thou shalt not bear false witness against thy neighbour*. This can be roughly translated as: 'Thou shalt not drop thy fellow tourist in it' if caught misbehaving on tour. If called to the kangaroo court and charged with heinous crimes, you should shoulder the blame yourself and not take anyone else down with you. Of course, this depends on whether they deserve it. An ancient tour maxim comes to mind: 'Don't shit on your mates unless you *really* have to.'

Finally, number ten: *Thou shalt not take the captain's name in vain*. Well . . . not within earshot, anyway.

RABBIT PUNCHED
SCOTT HASTINGS

'Scotty was a tough, wonderful centre who, at one stage, was Scotland's most-capped player. I played many times with and against him. He could certainly tackle and was always hard to put down when he was in full flow. A great tourist, he was a lot of fun to be with, always having a laugh and joke about things. Scotty was selected for the Lions in 1989 in what was to prove an historic tour of Australia. Having been well beaten by thirty points to twelve in the first Test in Sydney, the Lions made sweeping changes for the must-win second Test in Ballymore. The midfield had a total make-over with England's Rob Andrew, a late replacement on the tour, playing at fly half and Scott and Jeremy Guscott being paired up in a formidable centre partnership. Guscott and Gavin Hastings scored two excellent opportunist tries in a bruising and extremely robust encounter, which was to be dubbed the "Battle of Ballymore", thus setting up a thrilling winner-takes-all finale at the Sydney Football Stadium one week later. Incidentally, the Hastings brothers are the only pair of brothers ever to have played in a Lions Test match.'

With the series squared at one win each after our transform-ational victory at Ballymore, it was well documented by the extremely partisan Australian press that no Lions team had ever come from behind to win a Test series. The match will be best remembered for David Campese's back pass to Greg Martin, which was fumbled in the in-goal area, allowing Ieuan Evans to pounce and score what turned out to be the only try of the game. Bloody Brilliant!

Entering into the final quarter, the Lions were pressurising the Australians and had the throw-in at a line-out bang on the twenty-two metre line. In the backs Rob Andrew called the move that would surey seal the victory, and relayed the call to Robert Jones, who in turn called for off-the-top line-out ball from the forwards.

We had practised this strike move all week and reckoned we'd score from it. Brian Moore at hooker would throw an inch-perfect line-out ball to Wade Dooley, who would leap like a salmon to flick the ball down to Robert Jones. Off the top, Robert's fantastic spin pass would find Rob Andrew on the run. Jeremy Guscott and I, the centre combination, would run flat on to Rob's pass and, on the outside berth, I'd cut an angle away from Jerry's pass to pull apart our opposition centre pairing of Lloyd Walker and Dominic Maguire, which would leave my brother Gavin to steam in from full-back and carve his way through the middle to score under the posts. Simple.

The move was called 'bullet one', and with the back line licking their lips in anticipation of winning the series, the play was executed to perfection. Moore fired a peach of a ball to Dooley, who in turn delivered the ball on a plate into Jones's hands. Jones sent out one of his trademark inch-perfect passes to Rob, who took the ball at full tilt and with fast hands passed on to Jerry. At this point I made my dummy run to pull apart the Australians' centre pairing and a gap opened up as wide as the Gobi desert. This would be Gavin's moment of glory and the magnificently executed move would go down in the annals of Lions folklore.

Just as Jerry was about to deliver the scoring pass, a small problem became evident – no Gavin! Jerry was nailed by Jeff Miller and the move broke down. With the ball hitting the deck, the Australian fly-half hacked the ball down field and as I tore back to our own twenty-two, I shouted to Gavin, 'Where the f*** were you?!'

It later transpired that when Gavin started his run for the line, he looked up at the large video screens to see a rabbit running alongside him. Someone in the crowd had thrown the poor thing on to the field of play and Gavin got the shock of his life when he realised what was at his feet! He never got near the ball and our strike move was never executed.

The rabbit was eventually caught by Ieuan Evans (the second best thing he did all game) and the Lions went on to win the match 19–8 and with it the series. And yes, Gavin did get a new hat for Christmas. Good old Flopsy.

A DEAL WITH THE DEVIL

STUART BARNES

'The 1994 England tour to South Africa was when I bonded with Stuart. He was the general of that amazing Bath team of the eighties and early nineties, playing alongside Guscott, Chilcott, Hall and Redman. Stuart was unlucky to have played at the same time as Rob Andrew, which meant his international appearances were limited to ten. Perhaps, in truth, it was England who were unlucky that Rob and Stuart didn't play in the same team. Stuart is now the voice of rugby on Sky, and he still loves a wee flutter on the horses, and in the odd casino as well.'

Did you watch the second Test between South Africa and the Lions in 2009? It was astonishing, brutal, brilliant – engrossing viewing throughout. I don't believe dear old Loftus Verfeld has seen a Test match like it since the 1996 All Blacks won there to atone for their failure in the World Cup final the year before and clinched a first-ever series win for New Zealand on South African soil.

That 1996 game sticks in the memory because it was my first foray into commentating – other than a singular and sizzling Hong Kong 7s tournament the year before when a Kiwi kid called Cullen oozed onto the scene. A year later, Miles Harrison and I were crammed together in a sweaty sound booth in Isleworth, adding our voices to the compelling pictures coming in from South Africa.

Now, I am not a great one for lying about the whereabouts of the commentators. I am a useless fibber and besides, if I am in South Africa the gravelly Barnes vocal strains, originating from the Stellenbosch region, tend to be a giveaway. But that day the emotion, the passion and the power of the game overwhelmed me as I claimed the All Black fans were going berserk 'here in Pretoria'. The game transported me there, at least in spirit. And lo and behold, there I truly was, thirteen years later, in the main stand – really fighting to maintain a semblance of broadcasting sobriety as the intoxication of the plot and the violence reached its finale high on the rugby Richter scale.

Bruised and battered mentally, and just ever so slightly disappointed, my mind struggled to escape from the clutches of a thought: 'Just how great has been the development of the game from the early dawn of professionalism in 1996 to the quantum leap of 2009?' The 1996 All Blacks – the greatest Test team I have seen in their prime – would have been physically ravished by the fellows I'd just been watching, although the skill level is another matter. If the devil really is in the detail, the sport lacks some impishness. The basic skills, such as accurate passing and the technical point of a left winger carrying the ball under his left hand to enable him to fend off the cover tackler, have regressed from the high point of the mastery of Zinzan Brooke and Andrew Mehrtens. But as far as power, pace and fitness are concerned, we are not so much talking as screaming about a different and superior sport.

That night, tired from the exertions of calling the game, I cast my mind back a quarter of a century to, I think, but don't quote me, 1984 and an England v Ireland international at Twickenham. In those days, the match was a starter course (from the perspective of numerous committee men, who loved to bring their wives to the Big Smoke for a Saturday night on the tiles). The after-match function was nearly as big as the game. In this instance, it was probably bigger. We beat a pretty ordinary Irish team by the narrowest of margins and celebrated as if we had beaten the Springboks in Ellis Park.

Alas, in joy was born suffering. The next morning was the start of the new regime – the dawning of fitness on the fields of rugby. The management ordered the celebratory squad to be in the foyer of the Park Lane Hilton, from where we would take off for a jog around Hyde Park to clear the lactic acid from the system. Back then I thought this sounded like a milk and LSD concoction. Why eradicate it from the bloodstream? What did I know . . . ?

Me, I'd been on the bench, but if you don't get on the pitch, well you might as well get on the piss and I had done, doing my best to impress the heavy-duty forwards, if not the selectors, with my Bacchanalian stamina. So, the next morning, feeling like Death would feel if he lived, I crawled to the lift, only for my spirits to soar as the door opened to reveal the splendid sight of the late Maurice Colclough in his dinner jacket and cummerbund, the whole nine yards of cloth, with only a pair of Dunlop Green Flash tennis shoes to break the image of a scene from an F. Scott Fitzgerald novel. What a man!

The rest of the squad were slightly less rebellious in their attire but the smell of fresh red wine (very fresh in most cases) did not augur well. The squad set out from the shell-shocked foyer into the steady Sunday traffic of Park Lane, the pace sedate enough for all bar the prop forwards and a twenty-one-year-old replacement fly-half who had not known when to call it a night. The blinding acceleration of my imagination was replaced by the cruel reality of the legendary metaphoric wall into which even the greatest of marathon runners crash at somewhere around the twenty-mile mark. That morning one mile equalled twenty miles and, pathetic creature that I was, I head-butted straight into the barrier after only twenty metres – that would be halfway across Park Lane as a bus heading for Piccadilly veered to avoid running down the plodding specimen of decadence in front of it.

By the time I had made it across the road, the fat boys of the front row were a good thirty metres ahead of me and, given the state I was in, there was scant chance of catching up with them without suffering, and I was in no mood for some Sunday masochism. Ah, but was I not a fly-half? Not a great physical specimen but smarter than the average rugby player? Indeed, I told myself, hiccupping all the while, that was exactly what I was.

Let the rest of them cover mile after mile of Hyde Park. I would saunter down to the Serpentine under the cover of London's lovely foliage, rest awhile, join the squad at the tail-end of the run and sprint past them to finish in a respectable midfield position, a trick played frequently in early pre-season training with Bristol, where our full-back, Huw Duggan, and I would enjoy a soothing half of cider waiting for the squad to run their gruelling four or five miles.

On this occasion, a genteel Sunday-school teacher arrived at the lake at the same time as I did, with an impressionable party of tender babes. She was explaining how the swans on the lake were part of God's grand design when one of those hiccups I mentioned a few minutes back, developed into something unfortunately more lumpy.

'And that,' said the young teacher, before I could offer my apologies to the class, 'is what happens when the devil takes control.' If that young lady – now no longer so young – ever reads this, a thousand and one apologies. The devil was indeed in the detail of the contents that found its way into the Serpentine.

Those days are long gone, consigned to the realms of ancient rugby history and thank God, many might say, but you know, old and grey and ashamed as I am, I just wish the devil came out to play the game a little more often.

Here ends this sorry confession. May the rest of this book make for more wholesome reading.

FUNNIEST T-SHIRT COMPETITION
IAN ROBERTSON

'I didn't get to see my good friend Robbo play that often – well, never actually. I don't think I was born when he had to retire from the game following a knee injury. But I bet he was pretty good. He tells me he was anyway. To be fair, he must have been, having won eight caps for Scotland and Blues at both Aberdeen and Cambridge Universities to go alongside a club career at London Scottish. Robbo is one of those guys whom everyone knows. Wherever you go in the world of rugby, if you mention his name, someone will have a funny story to tell about him. Everything he does, he does for the right reasons. He is tireless in raising money for various charities and is great company on a night out, with a fair bit of stamina, too (for his age). And I never tire of hearing that particular piece of commentary on Five Live from Telstra Stadium, Sydney, on 22 November 2003.

'When I asked Ian to make a contribution to this book, this is how he proposed to start his tale: "I was covering the 2003 World Cup in Australia for the BBC, and during the very rare spare moments I had during the tournament was often found in my hotel room engaged in deep research to assist with a series

225

of articles I had agreed to write for various publications, as well as editing the definitive 2003 World Cup Annual. This was quite obviously a busy period for me, leaving very little time for social activities."

'Now, anyone who has ever met Ian will know the paragraph above is total bollocks, so I asked for the truth this time.'

Okay, I have to admit that the 2003 Rugby World Cup was special for all sorts of reasons but one memory in particular stood out for me above all others – dare I say it even eclipsed Jonny's drop goal in the last minute of the final.

On arrival in Sydney at the end of September, I spotted a story in the *Sydney Morning Herald* that there was going to be a prize of AUS$20,000 for the best T-shirt at the 2003 World Cup.

The possibilities were endless. Was it to be the funniest, the cleverest, the most outrageous, the most witty or what?

In shops all over Australia T-shirts appeared in the window throughout the first four weeks covering the first thirty-two matches of competition. None really caught the imagination as being very special.

But in the very final rounds of pool games with the quarter-finals just one week away suddenly one match and one T-shirt hit the headlines in every paper and every television station in Australia. This was to be my highlight of the World Cup.

The match was America v Japan at a town called Gosford – thirty miles north of Sydney. It was the final match in that group and neither side had any chance of qualifying for the knockout stages.

I wasn't even at the game but the BBC engineers phoned me

two hours before kick-off to tell me they had just seen the winning T-shirt from the World Cup. They reported that outside the ground they had spotted a fifty-five-year-old Japanese gentleman called Hirotake Kirasawa, who clearly had a wonderful sense of humour. He was wearing his T-shirt very proudly and had 300 more on his wheelbarrow to sell to the rugby supporters as they turned up for the match.

My BBC colleague described the T-shirt in graphic detail. The whole image was irresistible. I ordered half a dozen.

This T-shirt inevitably, and justifiably, won first prize. I accept that the concept was not 100 per cent politically correct. I simply report the fact. It was a white T-shirt with black lettering. On the front it read from the top:

"December 7th 1941
PEARL HARBOUR"

In the middle third of the shirt it said:

"August 6th 1945
HIROSHIMA"

Below that it said:

"October 27th 2003
GOSFORD"

And right at the very bottom of the shirt it said:

"**THE DECIDER!**"

Incidentally, for those of you with an interest, the score on 27 October 2003 was Japan 26 USA 39.

So finally it is now official. The two legendary stars of the 2003 Rugby World Cup in Australia were Jonny Wilkinson and Hirotake Kirasawa.

THE BRIGHT SIDE OF RUGBY

IAN WARDLE

'Ian "Chalkie" Wardle played with Bath until his early thirties when he returned to his "junior club" Walcot and became first team captain. His claim to fame is that he was half a best man for Jerry Guscott along with another lifelong friend and former bath player, Peter Blankett. Only Guscott would have two best men. He also accompanied Jerry a few years ago on an 800 mile walk in aid of Leukemia, averaging twenty-six miles a day for thirty days finishing at Twickenham during the half-time interval of an England v Australia international. The walk raised £250,000 and Chalkie lost two stone in weight, both of which he considers excellent results. Chalkie is also a keen tourist and has even played for Nigeria vets in a tournament in Dubai, a wonderful achievement when you consider he doesn't even know where Nigeria is on the map. Obviously another illustration of being in the right place at the right time.'

Unless you lived in Bath during the eighties or nineties you will almost certainly never have heard of me. My story in the first instance is about being in the right place at the right time and then goes on to the greatest tour anyone could possibly imagine.

I could blow some smoke up your backside and tell you how I used to play rugby for Bath in their glory days. This is true, although 90 per cent of my time was divided between the second and third teams, with the occasional first XV fixture when players ahead of me were injured or on international duty. Having said this, I should stress that Bath was a great club to be associated with, and in many respects it was irrelevant which team you played for because there was great camaraderie among all the players.

I'll just say this once – every word that follows is true and is a great illustration of what can happen if you are prepared to go with the flow.

One evening during the early nineties I was having a quiet beer, prior to several loud ones, in a Bath pub called The Hot Tub when the phone rang in the bar. No one seemed particularly interested in answering so I walked over and picked it up.

'Is that The Hot Tub?' enquired a voice.

'It is,' I replied.

'Are there any rugby players in the bar?'

'You're talking to one,' I said.

'Are you a forward or a back?'

'I'm a back.'

'Excellent news,' he said. 'My name is Mike Coley. I'm the manager of the England Classicals rugby team and we've had a late "cry off" from our next tour. Are you available?'

There were probably a few more words exchanged than this but not many. Cutting a short conversation even shorter, I said I was available and found myself at Heathrow Airport less than twenty-four hours later with a ticket in my hand, destination Bermuda, to take part in the World Rugby Classic Tournament. Until that moment I would have said things like that rarely happen to other people and certainly not to me. I found out later that, having heard Mike was short of a player, one of the Bath players, David Trick, had told him to ring the pub because there were always a few rugby lads in there having a beer on any given night of the week.

I was in the departure lounge mixing with players I had mostly only seen on TV – Dusty Hare, legendary full-back; Steve Smith, scrum-half and former England captain; Jeff Probyn and Paul 'the Judge' Rendall, the current England props but old enough to qualify for 'vets' rugby.

From that moment on, I have never laughed as much. The team obviously knew each other well, and they included me in everything. I honestly felt like a proper member of the squad within a few hours (isn't alcohol wonderful!). Often they just called out numbers instead of telling jokes since they'd heard them all before – apparently thirty-seven and fifteen are exceptionally funny but eleven is crap. Little things I picked up along the way.

Memories from the trip include the Irish team collecting twenty-seven stitches between them whilst in Bermuda and not one of them as a result of playing. Terry Kennedy had to have ten stitches in his knee after walking into a glass coffee table at 3 a.m. The best one was Moss Keane. He, along with the Irish squad, had been invited to a party hosted by one of the Irish expats at his villa. Needing to use the toilet and seeing a short queue, he decided to go back into the living room and out through the patio doors to relieve himself in the garden – an excellent plan, and one that would have worked perfectly, had the patio been built. 'Mossy' opened the patio doors and stepped out into fresh air, falling almost six feet, grabbing the curtains as he fell and taking them through the gap of the open door with him. Seconds later his red face (no change there) appeared at floor level as he tried to climb back into the house and rejoin the party, and presumably the queue for the conventional toilet. The result of his fall was nothing more serious than six stitches in one of his fingers!

The mode of transport in Bermuda for all the players was mopeds. Apart from filling in a form, paying for the hire and leaving a deposit, there was also the small matter of passing a moped test. I assume this was more for the benefit of the company hiring out the bikes than Bermudan law, as it entailed riding up a road with a slight incline, turning around and riding back to the starting place. Bob Hesford, a No. 8 for Bristol and England (and the funniest guy I've ever met), made it to the top of the hill, could not turn, so got off his moped, picked it up, pointed it in the right direction and came back down the hill. He passed his test because, in words of the examiner, 'he showed good initiative'.

We made it to the final of the tournament, where the opposition was the New Zealand 'All Blacks'. Although this was vets rugby (thirty-three years and older), it was the highlight of my rugby career; not only was I playing for 'England', but it was against the world's greatest team. In addition, it was going to be the one and only time I participated in a match when the national anthem was played prior to kick-off.

We lined up and respectfully faced the 'All Blacks' as they performed the haka. We then turned ninety degrees and faced the packed main stand (about 3,000 people) in preparation for our national anthem. Bob Hesford had supplied the tape and told the guy working the sound system it was perfectly cued up to start at the right place and not to mess with it. (At this point, feel free to get as far ahead of me as you want.)

I stood ramrod straight with the rose of England on my chest, the proudest moment of my sporting career, as the Monty Python classic 'Always Look on the Bright Side of Life' rang around the stadium.

The referee had one of the most impressive 'comb-overs' ever seen. I had watched him officiate in a couple of matches during the week and seen him at various functions, always noticing (difficult not to) those lengthy strands of hair vainly trying to cover his head.

He checked with the 'All Blacks' captain and the 'England' captain that they were both ready, and blew his whistle for the start of the match. At this moment, both packs of forwards ran towards the referee, tackled him to the ground and pinned him down. Steve Smith produced a pair of scissors from his pocket (essential equipment when playing New Zealand) and cut off all of the offending strands from his head, held them aloft for the crowd to see and then threw them into the air to drift in the wind and find a suitable grave, following years of fighting a battle they were never going to win. Suffice to say there was only one person who failed to see the funny side of this action.

The following night we called into the Swizzle Inn for a final blast of Planters Punch before flying home. Sat in a cubicle on his own was the referee. A few of the boys went over to have a chat. He said he had never been so angry in his life, but went on to say that for nearly twenty years he had always found out the direction of the wind and had stood side on to it in order to try to keep his hair covering his head. That morning he had looked in the mirror, smiled to himself and thought, 'Why didn't I cut the hair myself twenty years ago? Who was I fooling? Now I no longer have to worry about the wind. Did the people I talked to all these years look at me and think to themselves, "Does he think that I think that he has hair, just because it's plastered across the top of his head?"'

Steve Smith looked at the ref and said, 'You should know by now, scrum-halves have always been happy to assist referees!'

GONE FOR A BURTON
ALASTAIR HIGNELL

'Alastair Hignell won fourteen caps for England between 1978 and 1979 making his debut in a brutal game in Brisbane against Australia. He also won four double blues at Cambridge in cricket and rugby. I think he retired from rugby due to injury and to concentrate on his county cricket, going on to hit a thousand runs in a season three times. Alastair then went on to forge another career in journalism in which he was much respected, working on six Rugby World Cups and four Lions tours. Our paths have crossed on many an occasion being interviewed pre- and post match. He always knew what to say and when to say it. If you lost, he was always very sympathetic with the microphone. If you won, he was equally as excited as we were, being a passionate Englishman.

'Unfortunately, in 1999 Alastair was diagnosed with multiple sclerosis. He has been an active fundraiser since. His final commentary for the BBC coincided with my last game with Wasps for the 2008 Guinness Premiership final when Wasps were lucky enough to beat Leicester 26–16. I could see no more fitting way of finishing that game then by dedicating the victory to him because he epitomises everything that is good about rugby. He was also awarded the Helen Rollason Award at the

BBC Sports Personality of the Year awards in 1998. We wish him well with his continued fight against multiple sclerosis.'

Whatever were they thinking? In picking a twenty-five-man squad to tour Australia in 1975, the England selectors fell heavily between the two stools of confusion and condescension. They'd already picked twenty-eight players in a Five Nations campaign that had only avoided a whitewash with a 7–6 win over Scotland in the last match. Now, even though England had never won a series in Australia, they left fifteen full internationals at home, and set off for the land of Oz with twelve uncapped players.

I'm not complaining; I was one of them. The other full-back, Gloucester's Peter Butler, was also untried at Test level, while the four half-backs chosen for the trip had one cap between them, and one of the flankers, Steve Callum of Upper Clapton, had only ever played four first-class matches – for Eastern Counties.

It's hardly surprising that we didn't know what hit us either on the field – as prop Steve Finnane lived up to his nickname of 'the phantom puncher of Sydney' and laid out three Englishmen in the first week – or off it. Our own prop, Phil Blakeway, accompanied by a close-up of his bulging biceps and a headline about his brief spell as a heavyweight boxer, succumbed to a tabloid set-up and threw oil on the flames of an already brutal tour by claiming that whatever happened in the rugby, 'England wouldn't lose the fight!'

England may have had a heavyweight boxer in the party, but we also had both the president and vice president of the RFU who, and I quote from the Test match programme, 'are past masters at the fine old English art of extending hospitality. What is more, they are adept at following their countrymen's sinister drinking custom – an allusion that the erudite may appreciate!'

The manager of the tour was chairman of selectors Alec Lewis, while the coach was John Burgess, a short, stocky Lancastrian with a penchant for planting great big smacking kisses on the foreheads of his forwards. He also had an unbridled passion for rugby and such an unbridled love of his country that his team-talks swiftly degenerated into table-thumping, mouth-frothing jingoistic rants. At one point in a three-and-a-half-minute tirade, and I know 'cos I counted them, he managed to use the f-word twenty-seven times, while there were nine c-words and several 'bloodies'. The gist, of course, was that we had to tear into the f***ing Australians from the outset, fight fire with f***ing fire, get our f***ing retaliation in first, etc, etc.

To say the policy backfired is an understatement. It's also fair to say that the acute depletion of our ranks did not help our cause – for by the time England had lost the first Test, as well as two of the four warm-up games, a whopping 20 per cent of the party that left England less than three weeks earlier had been sent home injured, while another 20 per cent had spent a large chunk of the tour as walking wounded. The Aussies, it seemed patently obvious, were out for blood.

That was the background to my debut for England as a nineteen-year-old university student with less than twenty games as a full-back under my belt, coming into a patched-up side already one down in a two-match series with an Australian referee smarting from some pointed – and gleefully reported – criticism from the English coach, and an Australian opposition whipped up to boiling point by their own tub-thumper David Brockhoff.

With Brockhoff breathing fire in the Australian dressing room – no doubt reminding his team, in between the head-banging, the fist-pumping and the obscenities, that they hadn't won a series at home since beating the Springboks in 1965 – the first match that was to be dubbed the 'Battle of Ballymore' got off to a predictable start.

From kick-off, the first ruck started off with what looked like the whole of the Australian pack tap-dancing on the head of England prop Barry Nelmes and the whole of the England pack wading in to exact retribution. As the ball went into touch and the players eventually responded to Mr Burnett's whistle, Bill Beaumont trudged off the field for stitches to a head-wound and England hooker John Pullin prepared to throw in. But the ball sailed over that first line-out and bobbled forlornly in the middle of the pitch as both sets of forwards piled into each other. A penalty to England was reversed when the referee spotted England prop Mike Burton landing a head butt on the Australian hooker. Burton had sensed that the whistle had blown, but he also knew that he might never get a better chance to exact revenge on a player who had been one of our dirtiest opponents in the warm-up matches. 'He had to have it,' was an excuse accepted by all his team-mates, especially as the resulting kick at goal sailed wide.

Not quite so excusable was Burton's next act less than a minute later, a spectacularly posthumous late tackle on the Australian right wing following up his own kick-ahead, which the referee was more than happy to punish. Mike Burton became the first Englishman ever to be sent off in an international.

Inevitably, the incident has become enshrined in myth, legend and after-dinner story telling. On being told that he was being sent off for the late tackle, Burton is alleged to have made a plea of mitigation – 'Late tackle, ref? I got there as soon as I could!' And Beaumont returned to the field, head bandaged, to discover that he would spend seventy-eight minutes of his second-ever international appearance in the front row. When he heard the reason for Burton's dismissal, he is alleged to have looked at the clock, which now read two minutes past three, and remarked, 'He couldn't have been that bloody late, could he?'

Welcome to international rugby!

LIVING WITH LIONS ROOM-MATES

JOHN BENTLEY

'What can I say about John that he hasn't already said about himself over the years? Having played his first union match for England in 1988, Bentos turned to rugby league, where he became a legend of the game. He came back to union in 1996 with Newcastle, winning the league that year. Most rugby union fans will not only remember his performances, but also his outstanding contribution to the 1997 British and Irish Lions series success in South Africa, including his lead role in the "Living with John Bentley" – I mean "Living with the Lions" – DVD and arguably scoring one of the greatest tries we have seen on a rugby pitch against Gauteng in a midweek match. John still remains committed to rugby in Leeds today.'

I was a member of the successful 1997 British and Irish Lions tour to South Africa, which was an eight-week trip culminating in a 2–1 series win. On the assumption that not all readers of this book will have been on a rugby tour, I thought it would be useful to offer an insight into one aspect of touring, namely room-mates.

Since time immemorial, the captain of a touring party has had his own room and all the other members of the party share two to a room. There are several different theories on how room-mates should be selected. Should backs room exclusively with backs, thus ensuring we are able to share our extensive range of hair and beauty products? Or perhaps backs should room with a forward, to ensure that the forward would get his tea served to him in bed first thing in the morning? Do you place the bigger personalities on tour with the quieter members? As you can see, there are a host of different combinations, and then you also have to factor in that the players on a Lions tour come from England, Ireland, Scotland and Wales. It's a rooming nightmare.

Every time the tour moves on to a new destination, the room-mates are changed. When I think back to some of my 'roomies' in South Africa, I always reach the same conclusion. Ian McGeechan, the coach, must have adopted the method of putting all the names into a hat and pulling them out two at a time. I shared with the smallest, the biggest, the loudest (apart from me) and the quietest. Actually, as I sit here writing this twelve years on, it has occurred to me that maybe I was not the easiest person to allocate a room-mate to, and maybe Geech was just trying different options in the hope of finding a successful combination. Perhaps I should leave readers to make up their own minds.

Jeremy Davidson, Irish second row (five nights)

Without any doubt, the messiest man God ever placed on this

planet. As we walked into the room for the first time, I noticed the mid-brown carpet. However, for the next five days it was completely invisible because Jeremy covered it with every bit of kit and clothing in his possession. Obviously, this left the wardrobe free for me to hang up my own beautifully pressed clothes, but even in there he managed to cram clothes on to the shelves and strew a few more across the floor. I'm sure someone from the hotel cleaning staff paid a visit to our room each day, threw a few clean towels into the mix and left seconds later horrified by this crime scene.

Alan Tait, Scottish winger/centre (six nights)

Let's just say Alan wasn't the best flusher in the world. I do not need to be too graphic here but, believe you me, if he 'paid a visit' just prior to going training, which was then followed by an official function, the return trip to the room several hours later was not a delight. And while I'm on the subject, Alan, if you ever read this, when you finish shaving it would be appreciated if you could wash away all the bloody hairs you've just scraped off your chin and not leave them to bond with the surface of the sink.

Gregor Townsend, Scottish fly-half/centre (five nights)

'Share and share alike' is a touring motto – 'what's mine is yours' and all that. I didn't realise this was not extended to personal letters home. To be honest, if he didn't want me to read it, he shouldn't have left it on the desk in the corner of our room.

The letter was to his girlfriend (now wife) and halfway down the first page he wrote about a dream he'd had the previous night. In the dream he had visited her bedroom at home in the UK and was just getting a little amorous when he heard a noise at the bedroom window. Having opened the window, he saw her father hanging from the ledge. Looking at Gregor, he smiled and said, 'Don't mind me.'

When I saw Gregor later that day I asked him about the letter and the dream. He didn't speak to me for three days.

Keith Wood, Irish hooker (ten nights)

Given his position as hooker it will come as no surprise to find out Woody's shoulders are not all they could be. The intense strain they had suffered after years as an international front-row forward have left him in considerable discomfort.

The only position he can sleep in is on his back with a pillow wedged under each shoulder and then one more, as is usual, for his head. The result is non-stop snoring. Bless. Much to my chagrin, I consequently had seven nights with little or no sleep. After the seventh night I couldn't take it any longer and asked the team physio for some advice. On the eighth night, as Woody made himself comfortable with his now familiar pre-sleep routine, I was waiting in hopeful anticipation that my new tactic would be successful. As the snores started to ring around the room, I crept over to his bed and kissed him on the cheek. For the next three nights I slept like a baby.

As I found out later on in the tour, Keith spent our remaining nights together sat on the corner of his bed, staring at me and fearing what might happen next.

Best advice I ever had.

TEAM BONDING

CHARLIE HODGSON

'Charlie is a great northern lad and someone whom I have played with and against many times. A loyal Sale team man, he was critical to their success in winning the league title a couple of years ago. He has now won thirty-one caps for England but has had to play in an era dominated by Jonny Wilkinson, so his chances have been limited (mind you, his debut haul of a record forty-four points against Romania wasn't a bad start!). As a playmaking fly-half with an all-round game, he is up there with the very best – a real good guy to have in your squad and team.'

Practical revenge

A couple of years ago, *Rugby Club* on Sky had a weekly feature in which a couple of players from a Premiership club took viewers on a tour around their training facilities. For the visit to Sale Sharks, the two wingers, Mark Cueto and Steve Hanley, were selected as the front men, and since both these players consider themselves comedians, they spent a couple of days preparing for an entertaining show.

Jason Robinson has never been known for his height and so the first thing they did was to hang some four-year-old boy's clothes on his peg in the changing room. They chuckled to themselves as they showed the cameras the spot where Jason got changed every day.

They then moved on to where one of our props, Stu Turner, got changed. Stu had had a couple of games for England 'A' and was very proud of his kit allocation. He seemed to wear his England tracksuit bottoms every day! Cuets brought in one of his England rucksacks and left it by Stu's place. As they walked round with the cameras, they stopped at this spot and proceeded to take the mickey out of Stu not only for using an England bag (the use of any international kit is considered a bit of a no-no in any dressing room) but for its contents, previously put there by Cuets. They pulled out an assortment of sweets, chocolate bars, cakes and pastries to show everyone what his diet was really like. Stu could be quite sensitive when it came to his body shape, and he took huge offence when he saw the televised version!

A few weeks passed and everyone kept having a laugh at Stu's expense, much to his annoyance, so Stu decided it was time for revenge. Without telling anyone, he took a picture of Mark's pride and joy parked in the car park – a Porsche 911 – and sent an application off to *Autotrader*, with Mark's mobile phone number, to sell his car for a knock-down price! Mark was inundated with phone calls from people asking for information on the car he was selling. Obviously, Mark knew nothing about it and he spent hours angrily telling people his motor wasn't for sale. It took him ages to get the advert off the website. He had to prove he was actually the owner of the vehicle, and what made it worse was that he had to pay a fee for the removal!

Needless to say, Mark hasn't played any more practical jokes since then.

Kiss and make up

This short story comes from the Lions tour of New Zealand in 2005. It was early on in the trip and we hadn't had many training sessions together. There was a bit of an edge because everyone was trying to impress the coaches in advance of selection for the first game. The backs and forwards had split up in one session, so I don't know the details of the argument, but it seems there was a bit of a bust-up between Leicester and England team-mates Ben Kay and Martin Corry. From what we hear, the Leicester boys are always kicking off at club training, so it probably wasn't anything different for these two.

However, on the way back to the hotel after training, Denis Hickie, the Irish wing, stood up at the front of the bus and told us all in no uncertain terms that if we were going to be successful, it was essential to get on well together. He singled out Benny and Cozza and gave them a choice. Either pay $100 each into the players' kitty so we could all go out for drinks, or kiss each other on the lips for a few seconds. Given that they were both from Leicester (Leicester players are renowned for sticking together all the time) and are stingy as hell, Ben jumped on Martin and gave him the biggest kiss on the lips! I'm not sure that would have been my choice but hey, each to their own, and for the record, they looked great together.

IT'S THE TURNING-UP THAT COUNTS

DAVID DUCKHAM

'David Duckham is a top man, who is now very much involved with the Wooden Spoon charity. Watching footage of him playing in the early seventies, with his long blond flowing hair and unbelievably wicked sidestep, he was clearly a wonderful player – unfortunately, he played in an England team that often struggled, it has to be said. He won thirty-six caps for his country and famously established a brilliant partnership in the centre with John Spencer. He was also a part of the winning Lions tour to New Zealand in 1971. As I said, a top bloke and a top player.'

In April 1973, I captained my club, Coventry, to victory against Bristol at Twickenham in the final of what was officially known as the RFU Knockout Cup Competition (the then-unsponsored England clubs championship). The Bristol captain, also England captain at the time, was John Pullin, who left the field after about ten or fifteen minutes with a badly gashed lower leg. We were leading and well in control of the game but, with no substitutes allowed at club level in those days, Bristol were now down to fourteen and they started to play like men possessed. At one point, they missed a very kickable penalty, which could have brought the scores almost level. However, as the game went on, Bristol began to tire and Coventry won (can't remember the final score!) with something to spare.

At the after-match function, in a press interview I was quoted as saying that I'd felt embarrassed at the manner in which Bristol had stepped up a couple of gears after losing John Pullin and, at one point, got close to getting the better of us. Four days later, someone anonymously sent me a cutting from the *Yorkshire Evening Post* – a report of Coventry's victory with the sub-headline: DUCKHAM EMBARRASSED. Attached to the cutting was a note from the sender, which said, 'Having read the first paragraph of the attached report of your victory last Saturday, I can understand your embarrassment!'

The first paragraph read: 'David Duckham, Coventry's captain, admitted to being embarrassed after leading his side to victory against Bristol at Twickenham last Saturday in the RFU **Kockout** Cup Final.'

Just a few weeks or so before that, I played in a match that couldn't have been further from a source of embarrassment. In February (or March perhaps, I can't remember the exact date) 1973 – after the previous season's Five Nations series had been effectively abandoned as a championship when Wales and Scotland declined to play against Ireland in Dublin because of the potential threat of terrorist activity – it was England's turn to play over there and the RFU declared that the match would go ahead. The team was announced and we were told that we were free to choose not to play, without prejudice. (In fact, three players opted out and never played for England again.)

There was certainly some disquiet among the squad when we met for training a couple of weeks before the game, so I offered to ring my good friend Willie John McBride and ask him point blank what he thought. W-J's reply is etched in the memory for ever – 'David, you must come, don't let the terrorists win!' Enough said.

We did all our preparation in England and flew over on the Friday. At the airport we were whisked off the steps of the plane straight into a luxury coach, which was surrounded by police outriders carrying some heavy artillery. To make our party even more difficult to spot, a large sign on the windscreen of the coach read, 'England Rugby Team'! For the whole journey to the Shelbourne Hotel on St Stephens Green, right in the centre of Dublin, our No. 8, Andy Ripley, rocked back and forth in his window seat. When asked why he was doing this, he replied, 'I'm trying to make it more difficult for the snipers!'

Wearing England blazers and ties, we were met on the steps of the hotel by an Ireland RU official, who was heard to say, 'Welcome to Dublin, are you here for the game?' It was all quite bizarre. The Ireland team were also entrenched at the Shelbourne and we were all effectively under house arrest, England at one end of the hotel and Ireland at the other. That evening, we were quietly watching a feature film in our team room when the door slowly opened and there stood Irish flanker Fergus Slattery. He came in and calmly sat down beside me. Out of mild curiosity, I asked him the inevitable question, to which Slats replied, 'Our film is f***ing shite, so I've come to watch yours!'

We took the field the next day and received the most ear-splitting reception I can ever recall from the 50,000 spectators, every single one of whom were on their feet to welcome fifteen men dressed in white. It was a moment of such high emotion as to be very difficult to put into words. Suffice to say that several of us were reduced to tears, simply overcome by it all. But after the anthems the referee went and spoilt it by blowing his whistle to start the match. Ireland proceeded to kick the shit out of us for eighty minutes, and we lost (don't want to remember the score!). Somehow, the result didn't seem to matter as much as actually being there. I certainly felt immensely proud to be an Englishman that day. At the after-match banquet, John Pullin, a man of few words at the best of times, rounded off a short traditional vote of thanks to the opposing team with the immortal words, 'We may not be much good, but at least we turn up.'

EAT YOUR HEART OUT WILLIAM WORDSWORTH

JOSH LEWSEY

'Josh is just about the only man I know who could qualify for three or four different careers, in addition to professional rugby. He has been a wonderful servant to Wasps. To give you an idea of what Josh is like, his recent retirement from rugby coincided with his decision to make an attempt to climb Mount Everest. Most people when they come to the end of their careers head to the sun for a few weeks, but not Josh – taking on the highest peak in the world is much more up his street. Rather him than me – I plumped for the beach when I finished playing and I found that quite a challenge. Josh won fifty-five caps for England and was part of the very successful Rugby World Cup team in 2003 – his tackle on Mat Rogers in the final will go down as one of the best hits I've seen in quite some time. A top guy, he was part of that golden era of trophies that Wasps produced over the past ten years or so, and is an excellent ambassador for the sport.

'I asked him to pen a few words for this book, and just to prove he passed his English GCSE he came back with this. I'm not one to criticise creativity openly but I do think his scanning struggles a bit and his use of the iambic pentameter in a few of the verses is really rather disappointing. He has invented his own intricately rhyming stanzas, and in places his poetic rhythm is about as syncopated as Richard Hill on the dance floor. Still, he meant well.'

A Rugby Team: The Sum of the Parts . . .

2003 was the year,
Hopes were high and the mission was clear.

Woodward's men were favoured by most,
But pedigree is often a deceiving host.

Fifteen warriors with the red rose upon their chest,
Entertain? – Sod that, it's winning that's best!

So let's have a look at this band of merry men,
Introverts, obsessives, not all strictly gentlemen.

Props – the cornerstone of any team,
Our boys from Cornwall raised on clotted cream.

Golden Virginia was their vice,
Oh and for Vicks, a weakness for special fried rice.

But these tough men of most simple needs,
Weren't gobby but leaders in action and deeds.

'Shrek' was at two, this brilliant soul,
A 'Jekyll and Hyde' personality he had to control.

Shooting and killing is now his game,
Not a surprise from the background from whence he came.

This lovable joker was everyone's fave,
Great fun and company but most of all brave.

The Athlete and the Bludgeon in the engine room,
With this position of giants, designated extra legroom.

Johnson our captain's steely furrowed brow,
Ben's line-out 'bankers' like a reliable oiled plough

On such a stage we'd receive warnings of not changing
   routine,
But Ben wore some new gloves dropping a sitter – were they
   not clean?

So discard them he did and in humour he sought
As an articulate man he coped brilliantly we thought.

To the back row and the land of cheating thieves
But Back was too small . . . or so Rowell perceived.

Such rejection had hardened his drive and desire,
But as was shown, every team needs a dogged open-side
   flyer.

The imperious Dallaglio held the position of eight.
Ampleforth his school, but 'Street Law' was really from a
   Shepherd's Bush estate!

Professional was Hill, the last of the Musketeers,
But always joined Porthos and Aramis in drinking some
    beers.

So to the half-backs and the brains behind any great team,
A captain on 'Question of Sport' and the new 'Mr Clean'.

Old Golden Balls and Big Ears, we had the most settled pair
    around,
With the drop goal called 'piss flaps' not the most gracious of
    sounds (or smells? – Ed)

Jonny had actually missed four up to that point,
No panic yet, but was there something wrong with that
    famous foot joint?

He struck though when it mattered, using his less favoured
    right,
Perhaps playing the crowd, as this Saint would later contrite.

But credit too to Daws for steering the ship,
At its helm this mature, astute Nelson kept a soft but firm
    grip.

Centres to me should be chalk and cheese,
Greenwood the spell chanter, Tindall the strong breeze.

Will's conjuring and chatter were key to our play,
But without Mike's muscle our game plan was in complete
    disarray.

To the back and three of the most peculiar type,
The same and yet different – plover, woodcock and snipe.

Game birds they were, both lean, agile and fast,
But toughness and bravery matter more, before selection is
    passed.

So on foreign soil, win well we did,
For that moment at least a nation's woes it did rid.

Reflection of that day has not been much thought,
Life moves on and so it ought.

Yet years from now, when we're old and grey,
We can say that we did our bit on that wet November day!

THE MOON'S A LEAD BALLOON

PHIL HOPLEY

'Dr Philip Hopley is the better looking and more talented half of the Hopley brothers aka 'the Dangerous Brothers' who played at Wasps in the nineties. A qualified psychiatrist, 'the Doc' was a very talented footballer who played a major part in the success of the club and, most notably, in the Wasps team that won the Middlesex 7s in dramatic style in 1993. Phil has a fantastic sense of humour and there was never a dull moment when the Dangerous Brothers were in tandem on and off the field. As you will read in the following story, the Doc was a sensational tourist who zealously spread the Wasps gospel to all four corners of the globe. And West Hartlepool.'

A squad of keen young club players, an international ten-a-side tournament, the prospect of some winter sun, the chance of glory and an all-expenses-paid trip – oh, the joys of touring.

West London, 1992 – picture the scene. High-tech preparations were essential for pre-tour humidity and heat acclimatisation. Black bin liners were handed out.

'Right lads, get your tops off and put these on,' instructed 'One-eyed' Jim, our coach. 'Cut holes here and here, put them on under your training kit and get outside.'

'Fair play to him,' I thought, 'he has certainly done his homework.' Jim was no science teacher and without the assistance of the internet he had worked out how to raise core body temperature by three degrees. It made a cold, wet January night seem like a trek through a Borneo jungle in monsoon season. And so it went on for a few weeks, with practice on floodlit, rainy, but now artificially humid, winter evenings.

We arrived in Kuala Lumpur in good spirits, the words of club captain Mark Rigby having faded from ringing levels to a distant echo – 'Do us proud, boys, we're a club with solid traditions . . .'

The perks of touring include the opportunity to see far-flung places, meet the locals, dip the toe in their customs and traditions and break up the predictability of life back home. Our liaison man was brimming with pride that he had been allocated to the mighty Wasps. He took great pleasure in providing a guided tour on the coach journey between the airport and downtown KL, giving hints and useful advice about local food, places to visit and the set-up for the tournament.

As we checked into our very comfortable modern hotel, we tried our best to look unfazed by the sight of some impressively athletic figures from Western Samoa, New Zealand and Australia. We were doing reasonably well until the high-pitched, squeaky voice of young Laurence Scrase was heard to declare, 'Here lads, look at that lot. We're going to be mullered!'

Our progress in the tournament was modest despite the presence of a sprinkling of 7s experts who the following year would lift the Middlesex 7s trophy at Twickenham. Training went to plan, we didn't miss the bin liners and the starting line-up was selected. If memory serves, we beat enough of the minnows to get through to the knockout stages of the tournament on day two. The intense heat, humidity and poor visibility had very little impact on our progress in the nightclub that evening, and we woke dull and late the following morning before our showdown with the mighty Western Samoans.

I forget the final score but we were knocked out – in some cases, quite literally. At one point a free kick was awarded our way. I took the quick tap, popped the ball to my left, finding our captain, Chris Wright, and within a millisecond he, the ball and Brian Lima disappeared horizontally into a pile of crunching bones. The crowd winced and Chris was a long time getting up. Later, I was helpfully told by the referee that my effort had been less of a hospital pass and more of a mortuary invite.

We retired to the stands, pride intact but record and bodies dented, to bask in the wonderful warming late morning Malaysian sun and the solace and analgesic properties of a few ice-cold Singha beers.

Sadly, this is where my tale of a hitherto joyful jaunt turns into an international incident. It is a well-recognised fact that alcohol inhibits the senses, reduces mental processing time and increases erratic and risk-taking behaviour as it slowly takes control of the frontal lobes of imbibers. By mid-afternoon we had formed a strong bond with the lads from Manly RFC, Sydney, sat side by side, stripped down to the shorts, sharing the factor 8, many tall stories, a few more beers and, unfortunately, a large bottle of Jack Daniel's. Inevitably, when amateur rugby players are gathered together under such convivial conditions, even the most stage shy are miraculously converted into *X Factor* hopefuls, and predictably a singing contest ensued. Fuelled by bonhomie, good spirits – and not so good spirits in the shape of the JD – we entertained sections of the crowd, who willingly joined in our merry sing-song.

I forget at which point in our rendition of the well-known spiritual 'Swing Low Sweet Chariot' a small number of us dropped our shorts. Our keen liaison man quickly jumped to his feet, indicated in no uncertain terms we should make ourselves decent and then dashed off to ensure that our antics had not deeply offended. A brief moment of ill-judged revelry quickly turned into a long period of regret.

Again, I forget at which course during the after-tournament banquet that evening we were approached by our manager to be informed that matters had taken an unfortunate turn for the legal. Our drunken act had indeed offended local custom. Deeply.

Many will be familiar with that waking-up-after-the-night-before feeling – a mixture of confusion, disorientation and a sense that all is not well. Through the clearing fog, recollections seep back and eventually the memory clears. At this point, the emotional reaction ranges from mild regret to aghast disbelief at what has transpired. And so it was a knock at our hotel-room door woke my room-mate Mark Brown, aka 'Browny', and me the next morning.

'Come in!' shouted Browny and our manager Jim appeared.

'Where is Wrighty?' asked Jim. 'I need to speak to him urgently.'

Off we went in search of our diminutive but wholehearted captain. Jim had tried his room but had found the bed vacated. I thought it wise to check again since Chris is a small fellow, easily able to hide himself in nooks and crannies, and indeed there he was, sleeping fully clothed face down in the chair in the corner of the room.

An emergency meeting was assembled. A picture of three of us was going to appear on the front page of the national newspaper, and we were gathered for, excuse the pun, a debriefing. The journey to the police station, on a voluntary basis, was somewhat less jolly than the previous afternoon's party had been. I was selected for interview by the chief of police and was in no rush to correct his spelling mistake when he took down my name incorrectly, conscious for the first time that perhaps the wider media may take some interest in this turn of events. The three of us then returned to the hotel and were delighted with the support offered by our squad and members of the other competing teams – it's funny how derisive laughter can in a strange way be warming at these times. Later in the day it transpired that a photographer with a wide-angle lens had managed to pick up a couple of other miscreants, and so two more headed off for interview.

After much hard negotiation on our behalf by a relative of our liaison man, arrangements were made for us to appear in court the following morning. By this stage, the anticipated media interest was established. Funny how in all the years of travelling the world and watching CNN in a rather disinterested way, we were now appearing in one of their major news features. We arrived in an unmarked vehicle and were ushered into a waiting room dressed in our blazers and ties. At least Mark Rigby would be pleased with our appearance. Having had some experience of courtroom antics, I took it upon myself to advise the boys on decorum, manner of addressing the judiciary and strategy for appealing – straight guilty pleas, heavy on mitigation, apology and remorse. Our brief suggested that just one of the five should offer a sincere apology and I nominated myself. He said that the likely outcome would be a toss-up between imprisonment for a short period or a fine and immediate departure from the country. He finally said, 'It would be best if the judge is male.'

As we marched sombrely into the courtroom, Her Honour looked very frosty. We stood side by side in the dock, the charges were read and we entered our guilty pleas. The judge invited comment. I took the opportunity to speak, as clearly and calmly as I could, in order to apologise sincerely for our reckless drunken behaviour, for the negative impact it had had on those who had witnessed it and for the offence caused.

Her Honour seemed singularly unimpressed and said, 'Anything else?' At this point, and against all planning, Laurence Scrase, whose wobbling bottom lip had been causing me some degree of concern, cleared his throat and squeaked, 'We're really, really sorry . . .' His utterance came to a sharp end when the full weight of my fourteen and a half stone was transferred through the heel of my nicely polished right shoe on to the middle of the third and fourth toes of his left foot.

Her Honour asked to see the evidence. The clerk passed back a large unmarked brown envelope from which she then removed a series of high gloss 8 x 10 inch photographs. She was not amused. She went from picture to picture until she got to the fifth or sixth one at which point she paused, looked up and along the line of defendants. Her eyes alighted for a second on Mark Brown at which point she might have raised an eyebrow before continuing her scrutiny. The photographs were put down, sentence was passed quickly and we were ushered out into a waiting vehicle and taken straight to the airport and back to London.

Fortunately for us, outside the Muslim world, the media adopted the traditional 'drunken antics – public schoolboys – behaviour out of hand – letting off steam' view. Mark Rigby felt otherwise. Not our finest hour despite the chuckles that followed. We certainly learnt our lesson in 1992 and I hope that others in the game are now wiser than we were when it comes to balancing rugby, responsibility and too much JD.

NAMING NO NAMES – FOR HEALTH REASONS

JONATHAN DAVIES

'I would say that Jonathan Davies is one of the most talented rugby players to play the game. Also know as "Jiffy" to his team-mates, he started his career in rugby union and then was recruited into rugby league, latterly coming back to union. He was selected for Wales against England for his first rugby union international and I think he managed to score a try and a drop goal and was named man of the match in a Welsh victory. So not a bad start to international rugby then. He went on to win thirty-two caps for Wales between 1985 and 1997, and that's with having a stint playing rugby league in between. Having played for Neath, Trimsaran and Llanelli, he switched codes and clubs signing initially for Widnes. In 1991 he went over to Sydney to play for Canterbury then came back to the UK to Warrington. He also represented Great Britain and Wales and was named player of the year in 1993 and 1994 winning the notorious rugby league Man of Steel award.

'I played against Jonathan when he came back to play rugby union. After the birth of his daughter in 1995, rugby union had just turned professional and he went back to Wales and joined with Cardiff. Wasps played the Welsh team in the Heineken Cup and I believe Jonathan won it with a drop goal in the last minute of the game – he still had the touch even then! Jonathan continues to be heavily involved with rugby as an ambassador for the sport and most people would recognise his voice from his BBC commentary for both union and league. A huge influence on the sport and one of the game's top guys.'

Wales had travelled up to Scotland for a Five Nations international at Murrayfield (sadly, my legs had given up on me before it became the Six Nations). We knew in advance the game was going to be a dogged war of attrition up front. We thought it would be a turgid affair played from scrum to line-out, a forward-dominated match with little of the natural Welsh flair on show. We would have to compete and scavenge up front and play an unnaturally tight game. The impressive Scottish back row of Calder, Jeffrey and White was going to be all over the park, ready to mop up any ball spilled by the Welsh backs.

So, having decided on the game plan, we then needed to execute it – easier said than done.

Our scrum was under huge pressure from the off, and our front row employed every tactic they knew, both legal and illegal, to try to combat the power of the Scottish pack. After twenty minutes the Scottish onslaught was too much and they scored a pushover try. I think it was possibly the first pushover try Scotland had ever scored. It was certainly the first against Wales. Oh, the shame.

Our front row decided it was time to employ even more stringent measures to counter this offensive. Now, as a back,

I'm not certain what this entailed but I do know that on several occasions the two packs would break up and start fighting toe to toe!

Englishman Fred Howard was the referee, and following one particular scrum when once again we found ourselves being shunted back at a rate of knots, he blew his whistle and called our pack leader Robert Norster over for a chat.

'Bob, I'm not happy with your prop,' he said.

'Bloody hell, Ref, *you're* not happy with him?!' Bob replied.

I'd love to tell you the name of the prop, but I'm prevented from doing so due to personal health reasons.

I also well remember an incident that took place during a club game I played in south-west Wales. It was a club in the Swansea/Neath valleys but, again on health grounds, I cannot be more specific about location than that.

Our winger was quick but his electric pace was counteracted by his appalling eyesight. However, as long as he actually caught the ball we were in with a great chance of scoring. On this particular day, almost unbelievably, he latched on to a perfect pass from the opposition and made a clean interception. Having somehow secured the ball in his arms, he set off for the tryline.

We all knew it was going to be a try. Unfortunately, the spotty winger from the opposition did not and duly gave chase. After about thirty yards our winger turned his head, noticed (just) his pursuer and without breaking stride flicked a two-fingered V sign at him. Thirty yards later he flicked him another V sign and thirty yards after that he scored (before you ask, it was a very long pitch).

Having placed the ball neatly under the opposition posts, he turned to make his way back to our half and realised the winger had not stopped, indeed he was running straight at him at full tilt.

At the risk of giving away the venue, all I can remember is the ginger-haired spotty winger chasing our boy around the roundabout next to the swings, which were situated fifty yards beyond the dead-ball line, with the sole intention of trying to maim him permanently for displaying such blatant disrespect.

The action was taking place so far away from the field of play, I think even the referee decided it was out of his jurisdiction and let them get on with it!

VARSITY BLUES
GAVIN HASTINGS

'Gavin is quite simply a legend of Scottish and British rugby and one of the outstanding players of his generation. He won about a total of sixty-one caps for Scotland, twenty as captain, playing at full-back. He also captained the Lions on that wonderful tour to New Zealand in 1993, having played in all three Test matches in the previous tour to Australia in 1989. I first came into touch with Gavin playing for England against Scotland but he retired in 1995, just at the beginning of my career, so our paths never really crossed that much on the rugby pitch. He was a guy that was such a talisman for Scotland – I think he twice passed world records for the most points In an international match. He was also a member of that historic Scottish team that won the Grand Slam, beating England in the final game in 1990. A top guy, Gavin is hugely respected by all his peers, including myself. He is still heavily involved with rugby and was involved with the lions as an ambassador for HSBC.'

I know it remains a mystery to countless people how on earth I came to be a student at Cambridge University but it made sense to join a host of prominent rugby players whose careers were considerably enhanced by representing the most famous university in the world. Clearly it goes without saying that it was my absolute privilege to enjoy two wonderful years as a Land Economy graduate student at Magdalene College. This was the obvious academic progression for me, having obtained my first degree at Paisley College of Technology and had absolutely nothing to do with me being slightly above average on the rugby field. Promise.

The unique nature of rugby at Cambridge University makes it a magical place to train, play and study. It is awe-inspiring to be a part of an institution, steeped in so many aspects of academic, philosophical, literary and political history, that has given much to the wider world. The list of famous Cambridge alumni is endless, but to think that I inhabited the same lecture rooms and college bars as Samuel Pepys, William Wordsworth, William Wilberforce and no less than eighty-three Nobel laureates and fourteen British Prime Ministers, fills me with pride to this day. When you add Sir David Attenborough, Stephen Fry, Sid Waddell, Vanessa Feltz and half of Monty Python to that long list of high achievers, I still have to pinch myself to make sure I wasn't dreaming.

A host of famous rugby players came before and played after me, including the mercurial Mike Gibson and Gerald Davies, both Lions legends. The remarkable side that I was fortunate enough to win my first Blue with in 1984 featured many players who had either already won international honours or were bound for great success with their national sides in years to come. The 1982 Varsity match had announced the arrival of a young Rob Andrew and was the start of a glittering career that earned Rob seventy-one caps and two Lions tours. Outside Rob in the class of 1984 were centres Fran Clough and Kevin Simms, while our captain and wing was none other than Mark Bailey – all of whom went on to play international rugby for England.

The 1984 Varsity match against Oxford could not have gone better for us, and with everything depending on the outcome of those eighty minutes, we romped home by six tries to nil, outscoring the dark-blue enemy 32–6. After the match, both teams went to the Oxford and Cambridge Club on Pall Mall, and ate separately, which may seem odd, but given the polar spirits of the two sides, it made sense to let the winning team celebrate in style while the losing team commiserated and drowned their sorrows.

One of the greatest honours in my rugby life came to pass a few weeks into the New Year when I was elected captain of the Blues side for the remainder of the calendar year, including the 1985 Varsity match. Cambridge had gone undefeated since 1980 and this would be my moment to lead the team out at Twickenham and make history by winning six in a row.

By its very nature the Varsity match is one of the more peculiar sporting fixtures. While the build-up to the game is important and the coach and captain try to finalise their strongest combinations against a variety of oppositions throughout the year, it doesn't count for anything if the team doesn't perform at that one game, played in front of a capacity crowd at Twickenham.

I was finding my feet as a leader, and in the months leading up to the all-important game I imagined what I was going to say to my team-mates in the crucial minutes prior to leaving the changing room to take the field. We had trained together, played together and partied together for seven months and we knew each other's habits intimately. Rather than pre-planning my speech I decided not to worry about preparing notes but to wait and follow my gut instinct on the day. I would wait for the inspirational moment to arrive and bare my soul with some words of encouragement to push ourselves to new heights for this enduring cause. When the time came, I gathered everyone at one end of the vast Twickenham changing room, but instinctively I hesitated because it just didn't feel right.

My thoughts turned to all the great Cambridge men who had proved to be able leaders in their field. Should I quote Charles Darwin, author of *The Origin of Species*, who clearly hadn't envisaged the evolution of a creature such as our second row, 6ft 8in medical student Sean O'Leary? Or perhaps I should have looked into a more humorous approach by adopting some lines from ex-students John Cleese or Eric Idle?

I realised too late that my lack of preparation had not done me any favours. However, I still felt it would come together and so, realising that I needed to be front and centre, I got all my team-mates to join a circle round me, and linking arms. As I looked round to face and eyeball each and every one of them, it suddenly came to me – my spur of inspiration for my thirteen English team-mates and the Nigerian speed merchant, Andy Harriman. Eureka! We started into a rendition of 'Flower of Scotland'.

To this very day I don't know why I did it. Not surprisingly, the result of quite possibly one of the worst Varsity matches in living memory was Oxford University 7, Cambridge University 6. The Cambridge University motto is *Hinc lucem et pocula sacra*, which roughly translates as 'From this place, we gain enlightenment and precious knowledge'. How true that is – since that day, that song has never been sung in any changing room in which I have been captain!

TOUGHING IT OUT IN TONGA

JOHN DEVEREUX

'A former Welsh dual-code rugby football international, "Dev" is a top, top bloke – one of the first in a generation of high-profile rugby players that switched from union to league and back to union again. In rugby union, he played for Wales from 1986 to 1989 winning twenty-one caps and he toured with the British and Irish Lions in 1989. He went on to play rugby league with Widnes in England and also for Manly in Australia, getting capped in league for Great Britain and Wales. John became a coach after he finished playing but before that I came up against him a couple of times when he had a brief stint with Sale Sharks – he was a good hard running centre with great hands. He then finished his playing career with the club that he had started out with – Bridgend.'

My first tour with Wales was in 1986 to the Pacific Islands and featured matches against those giants of the world game, Fiji, Tonga and Western Samoa (as they were called in those days). Well, maybe they weren't giants in rugby terms, but they were certainly the most physical nations involved in world rugby. It was a brilliant trip, combining a lot of fun with some brutal rugby.

Before the second match – the Test against Tonga – we had the privilege of meeting the king of that country. We were in our kit and someone led us from the changing rooms (a small hut) to the top of the only stand at the ground (an open park bordered by numerous huts) where we all lined up and exchanged a few words with the king and shook his hand. He was a huge man, weighing in excess of twenty-five stone, and I remember Jonathan Davies, who was ahead of me in the queue, looking very formal as he bowed, took the king's hand and in perfect Welsh said, 'How are you, Fatty?'

We spent ten days in Tonga and it rained incessantly for nine of them. Unsurprisingly, match day was one of the worst weatherwise, of the entire trip. But we soon realised the weather was to be the least of our worries. At the first line-out, the tone for the match was set when our lock, Phil Davies, leapt for the ball and was floored by a cracking punch from his opposite number. As normally happens when events like this occur, a massive fight ensued. When the brawl reached its natural conclusion, the referee stepped in and called both captains together for a chat. Our leader and inspiration was Richard Moriarty, a second-row forward who played his club rugby for Swansea. Following a lengthy meeting with the referee, he signalled the team to gather round. 'The ref said if there's any more shit, punch the nearest Tongan to you,' he informed us.

I doubt whether that was an accurate reflection of the referee's message but we knew what Richard meant –

something similar to the famous Lions 99 call on the 1974 tour to South Africa, where, on hearing that number being called, Willie John McBride's men turned and smacked the nearest Springbok. We figured, in the spirit of shared responsibility, that if we all got involved, then it made it nigh on impossible for the referee to single out any one player for punishment. Although in reality, it was always going to be fifteen v fourteen. In every team there is always one member who manages to steer clear of trouble and for us it was our full-back Malcolm Dacey.

Not long after the referee's message had been delivered to each team, it became apparent the Tongan captain must have said something similar to his side, as an almighty fight broke out again. In his later published book, *Raising the Dragon*, my Wales and Lions colleague Robert Jones described the event as 'the worst brawl I have ever seen on a rugby field'. I can absolutely confirm this as being a very accurate description.

The Tongan prop, who bore a striking resemblance to the Incredible Hulk, whacked Billy James, who quickly took up a horizontal position. Within no time, he delivered a stunning blow to the jaw of Stuart Evans, who subsequently occupied a position next to Billy. Then it was the turn of Adrian 'Adolf' Hadley, who found himself on the wrong end of a monster punch and was snoring before he hit the floor, knocked out cold. The man-mountain was working his way through the Welsh team like a tornado through a forest!

While the carnage continued, the Welsh centre, Bleddyn Bowen, made a sneaky trip around the blindside of the Tongan prop and gave him his best shot. It may well have been Bleddyn's 'Sunday Best' but its effect was merely to irritate the giant front-row forward, who took off after Bleddyn across the pitch. Bleddyn reached the touchline, which was ringed with spectators, who were clearly loving the spectacle. They tossed Bleddyn back into the arena whenever he tried to breach their defences. Finally, he found a gap and ran off to hide behind one of the huts on the edge of the park and the prop gave up the chase.

Back on the field of play, Adolf was still snoring and an ambulance was called, which arrived in seconds as everyone in Tonga, it seemed, was at the match. The ambulance completed a series of spectacular wheel-spins in the mud as it veered on to the pitch towards our comatose team-mate. Mark Titley went with Adolf to the hospital. On arrival, Tilts was informed that all the doctors were at the match, so Adolf was treated by a nurse with some strong smelling salts and our two team-mates hitched their way back to the ground. All the taxi drivers were – you guessed it – at the match.

I remember it all as if it was yesterday. Sadly, the only tape we had of the match was 'lost' a short time after the squad watched it en masse at the team hotel and it has never been seen since. I have my suspicions about who the thief might be – I've narrowed it down to fourteen possibilities.

The final rugby score was 15–7. Far more importantly for this story, the final boxing score was Tonga 13 Wales 1! We all took on a Tongan and I'm delighted to reveal that I was the only Welshman to beat my opponent. However, as anticipated there were only fourteen bouts in total because Malcolm Dacey found himself, inadvertently, I am sure, behind a post for the duration – which perhaps sheds a little more light on the mystery of the disappearing tape . . .

EARLY TO BED
KYRAN BRACKEN

'I first met Kyran when he was at Stonyhurst and I was at Ampleforth, and we've gone on to become great mates. He was amazingly talented, and used to play at 9 and 10. Fortunately, we used to get the better of them, just about, although the games were always closely fought. We went on to England Under-18 trials and made it through to the final selection day. There were twenty-three players in that final trial and twenty-two were to be picked. I was twenty-third (despite scoring a try in the match – not that it still gets to me or anything). I was obviously very disappointed. Standing at the bus stop, waiting to go home, I was surreptitiously trying to wipe a tear from my eye when Kyran drove past, stopped, reversed and offered me a lift. He took time to talk to me when 99.9 per cent of other people would have just driven past, and I've never forgotten that.

'Following a very successful England tour to Canada in May 1993, Kyran won his first full cap against New Zealand in November that year. The all-conquering New Zealand squad had won every single game on that tour until they came unstuck against England. Bracken played a starring role, despite the close attention of flanker Jamie Joseph, and Jon Callard's accurate goal kicking ensured the Kiwis crashed to their only defeat of the tour 15–9.

'When fit, Kyran was one of the best scrum-halves in the world. His ongoing duels with Matt Dawson, and occasionally Austin Healey, were a real highlight. We were exceptionally lucky to have three scrum-halves fighting it out all at the same time. Who could forget the 2003 Rugby World Cup against South Africa in the pool match, when to my mind Kyran was undoubtedly man of the match. For a guy who was struggling to get on the plane, he made a massive contribution.'

I was delighted to win my first cap, beating New Zealand against all the odds at Twickenham, and spirits were extremely high for the Five Nations the following spring. After defeating the All Blacks, we were expected to win the championship outright – wrong! Losing to Ireland for the second time in two years, with Simon Geoghegan scorching his way through the match to give Ireland a 13–12 victory, brought about inevitable changes, but one thing that lived on in the team culture was the Tuesday night drink before we trained on the Wednesday in preparation for the game on Saturday. No Friday night or Sunday kick-offs in those days, so at least we had a set routine.

Our next match was away to France in the cauldron that was the Parc des Princes – a nice gentle game to get back to winning ways. Being the social envoy for the squad, Jason Leonard insisted on taking young Mike Catt and me to the unofficial team clubhouse for the Tuesday evening drink; many rugby fans around the world know the clubhouse by its other name – The Sun Inn in Richmond. Clearly not having had quite enough by last orders, Jason insisted on taking Catty and me off to the local nightclub in Richmond – the Park Inn – for a couple of fliers, as he likes to call them.

I showed all my dummying skills by slipping off to the gents after pint number God knows what, and sneaking out of the fire exit. Then I started the stagger up Richmond Hill back to the Petersham Hotel. Being a bright young lawyer, I decided the best way of covering up any misdemeanour was to climb up the fire escape, thus avoiding the management, who were no doubt ensconced in the bar, wondering how they could put even more drinks on to Rory Underwood's room bill. On my way to bed at approximately 3 a.m., I stumbled into the team room in the hope of finding some leftover sandwiches to try to soak up the alcohol. Barging through the door, I was horrified to see team manager Jack Rowell and backs coach Les Cusworth studying videos and analysing the French team. Given his agility, which he often displayed in moving out of the way of oncoming traffic in midfield, it was not surprising that Les turned round in time to catch me red-handed. Fortunately, Jack was too slow to see who it was, and before he could pull himself out of his chair I had scarpered up the stairs as fast as my little drunken legs could carry me. Big trouble.

As you can imagine, a restless night's sleep was not made any better when an emergency team meeting was called at 8 a.m. The smell of alcohol combined with the nervous farting from the forwards was truly eye watering. Jack Rowell stormed into the room like Darth Vader, with the coaching team acting as his stormtroopers.

Whenever Jack spoke passionately his chin and bottom lip quivered and you didn't know if he was going to burst into tears. 'I am truly disgusted that a member of the England team should come into the team room at just after three this morning, just days before the most important game of the Five Nations,' he said, chin and bottom lip working overtime. 'Will [Carling] is going to talk to you all and in the interest of honesty we want the culprit to identify himself while the management leave the room.' And with that Jack turned on his (remarkably small) feet and headed out.

Before Will could stand up and ask for the culprit to come clean, all eyes turned to Jason, given his reputation as the cultural attaché to the squad. Jason rose solemnly to his feet and in the silence proclaimed, 'Donchu fakkin' look at me . . . I got in at six!' You could hear the laughter up in Richmond Park! The ice and the tension were well and truly shattered and the incident was soon passed over. However, I had just three caps, and Mike hadn't even made his full debut, and we were given a proper telling off by Will for being out. Of course, Jason was immune to such chastising – he would have told Will where to stick it!

I still give Les an appreciative nod for not shopping me, even though these were the amateur days. For the record, we beat France that weekend in Paris 18–14, and Catty went on to win his first cap against Wales at Twickenham two weeks later, a game we won. From that evening on, though, we always made sure we weren't the last ones in!

WALLABY TALES

MICHAEL LYNAGH

'Michael Lynagh goes down in my all-time first XV, him and Nick Farr-Jones. The combination they made for Australia was fantastic. On his retirement, Michael held a ridiculous number of records – most international points scored, most international appearances in the position of fly-half – but he is still a very understated person, always happy to let other people have the limelight and take the credit for most of the work he put in. English supporters got to see his value at Saracens, towards the twilight of his career. He managed to orchestrate the only cup-final defeat I've played in at Twickenham. It was incredibly humiliating – we lost by about fifty-eight points to Saracens on the day and Michael was part of everything they did.'

Mere mortals

When I was contacted by Lawrence and asked to supply a story for *Rugby Tales*, my initial thought was to write something about an incident in a match, or maybe commit to print my version of how some memorable Wallaby tries were constructed.

However, as I sat down to bash out a few words on the computer, it struck me that this might be a little dull, and more importantly, here was the perfect opportunity to write about a team-mate and to let the world know, no matter how much talent one is blessed with, there will always be reminders from time to time that we are all mere mortals. And I can assure you, this story is entirely true.

The Aussies had completed a tour of Ireland and Wales. It's always a sad day when a tour comes to an end, mainly because the relationships you have forged over the past six weeks or so with your team-mates are very strong. But it's also depressing because for the duration of the trip, the players have had absolutely everything done for them. Meals and laundry are taken care of, accommodation is always of a high standard and the training sessions and matches are planned well in advance. For that period of time, the players live in a bubble, fantasy land. The end of the tour signifies a sickening return to normality.

As it happened, my reality wasn't too grim. It meant a flight to Treviso in Italy, where I was playing my club rugby at the time. In a way, I envied the boys who boarded a long-haul flight back to Australia for the summer break, but a few months in northern Italy was not going to be all bad!

One or two of the other players were planning to take the opportunity to have a short European break away from the rugby treadmill, and having arrived in Treviso, I was contacted by my team-mate, centre Tim Horan, who wanted to bring his wife Katrina and young daughter Lucy to Italy to take in a few sights. In particular, they were keen to visit Venice. So, in advance of his arrival I contacted a good Italian friend of mine, Francesco, who was born in Venice and is a great rugby fan. I asked if he could arrange the trip to Venice and show Tim and Katrina the beautiful sights.

At this juncture I should mention that, in my opinion, Tim was one of the most gifted centres ever to play rugby union. He was my team-mate in numerous internationals and he always seemed to do the right thing at the right time, devastating in attack with defensive qualities to match. However, for all that Tim was near perfect on the pitch, the same couldn't necessarily be said about him off it, as will become clear . . .

I collected Tim and Katrina from the airport and a couple of days later Francesco arrived early at my apartment to drive all of us to Venice, pleased to show off some of the sights the famous city had to offer. Now, at the risk of allowing you to get one step ahead of me in this story, I think it is only fair to let you in on one key piece of information – during the short drive the weather was not too kind, varying from overcast to the occasional heavy shower. These were not ideal conditions for a day of sightseeing but Francesco assured us there were plenty of indoor attractions for us to see if the weather remained inclement.

As we neared the heart of Venice, Tim was staring wide-eyed out of the car window in awe of the beautiful buildings. This was going to be a successful day, I thought to myself, he's already impressed and we haven't even shown him any of the good stuff yet.

A few moments later as we pulled up in Piazzale Roma and prepared to park the car, he uttered his first words in a while – 'Jeez, they've had some serious rain here haven't they?' As he said this, I noticed it had actually stopped raining and looked as though everything was beginning to dry out.

'I don't think it's been too bad, Tim,' I replied. 'It's looking good for the rest of the day in fact.'

'You're joking aren't you?' said Tim. 'They've had a shitload of rain here. Look at all the roads, they're flooded!' I stared in silence as he pointed out one 'road' with gondolas moving down it. 'Look at that, boats shunting up and down all the flooded streets,' he said.

Have I ever let him forget that comment? No chance, and now I've had the opportunity to share it with you.

1991 RWC quarter-final: Ireland v Australia

A couple of stories stand out from our victorious 1991 Rugby World Cup campaign, and both highlight the enjoyment we all shared in some of the darker moments of that ultimately victorious campaign.

They both centre around our quarter-final against Ireland, which we played on Irish home soil at Lansdowne Road. Our assistant coach at the time was a great gentleman of rugby called Bob Templeton, or 'Tempo' to anyone fortunate enough to meet him. Tempo had a phenomenal track record – he coached the Wallabies in twenty-nine Tests from 1971 to 1981 and I first encountered him when he was a coach for my native province, Queensland. He held that position for twenty-six years and his love of the game was infectious. Tempo was one of the most recognisable faces in Australian rugby up until 1999 when he died from a heart attack at the age of sixty-seven. Given his extensive knowledge of the game in the northern hemisphere, through his close links with Harlequins, he was a vital cog in our ambition to win the Webb Ellis trophy that year, and he deservedly received an MBE for his services to rugby.

Now Tempo used to get extremely nervous the night before games, and couldn't sleep at all well. The night before the quarter-final was no different, and Bob decided the best thing to do was get up and head down to breakfast, even though it was only 6 a.m. We were staying at the Westbury Hotel in the heart of Dublin, where the breakfast room was on the first floor.

As Tempo came out of the lift he was distracted to see a dishevelled figure stumbling down the street and literally pinballing off the walls as he struggled to make his way. On closer inspection, he saw that the inebriated man was none other than David Knox, the New South Wales fly-half, who was a member of the squad but had not been selected for the match-day twenty-one. David had therefore taken an executive decision to go off and sample the delights of Dublin on a Friday night. Knoxy was clearly the worse for wear, and, being ever so slightly mischievous, Tempo spotted the opportunity to have some fun at his expense.

He waited patiently for Knox to come into the hotel and get up to his room, lulling him into a false sense of security by allowing him to think he had got away with his pre-match revelry unnoticed. Tempo gave David about twenty minutes to make sure he was tucked up in bed and then called the room. The phone rang for what seemed like ages, and then a startled Knox picked up the receiver, gathering his intoxicated thoughts when he heard the assistant coach at the end of the line.

'Knoxy, it's Tempo here. Listen mate, Noddy [that was my nickname] is pretty crook with food poisoning and has been up all night. It's pretty unlikely that he's going to be fit, so you will be starting at fly-half in today's quarter-final. Just thought you'd like to know as soon as possible to get your head right.' Trying to muster up some enthusiasm after a skin full of Guinness was extremely tough, but Knoxy put on a brave face, thanked his coach and hung up. The Randwick fly-half then went into overdrive and ordered three pots of coffee, several gallons of water and two full Irish breakfasts from room service in an attempt to soak up the booze and sober up in time for the mid-afternoon kick-off.

With all his experience of rugby players, and being a wonderful man manager, Tempo waited just long enough for the terror to sink in, and called the miscreant's room ten minutes later. Unsurprisingly, this time he found the young fly-half full of beans and answering the phone with considerable gusto. 'Knoxy, Tempo here again. I was only winding you up about Noddy, but next time you get out on the juice the night before a game, make sure you get in at a reasonable time. You just never know what might happen!'

This is a great example of exactly why most players viewed Tempo as a father figure and revered the man who captured the true spirit of rugby union. It was a privilege to know the man.

The other story that stands out from that remarkable game came from one of the most unlikely sources among the players who took the field. History tells us that Ireland almost pulled off one of the most extraordinary victories in their proud rugby history. We had looked the stronger side, scoring two well-worked tries through the inimitable David Campese. However, the Irish fly-half, Ralph Keyes, had kicked very steadily all afternoon and had kept the Irish right in the match. What unfolded next was a thrilling climax to the game. With only four minutes of regular time left on the clock and with Ireland trailing by three points, a break by the home side resulted in the ball being popped into the hands of the charging Gordon Hamilton. The Ulster flanker from Ballymena, who had made his international debut earlier that year, stormed past David Campese, leaving him completely for dead as he sprinted forty yards before being caught as he grounded the ball over the tryline.

Hamilton was mobbed by his team-mates and a host of spectators in some of the most jubilant scenes Lansdowne Road had ever seen. From the far left, Ralph Keyes, almost inevitably slotted over the conversion with his metronomic boot to take his side into a three-point lead.

At this time, our captain, Nick Farr-Jones, was off the field due to injury, so I was captaining the team, and I gathered everyone under the posts to rouse us for one last attack. We knew there was only four minutes remaining of normal time to get back up the other end to rescue the game. This was a moment for clear thinking. However, one of our team wasn't thinking clearly at all. There is no doubt that in the history of rugby union, one Australian will go down as one of the most gifted players to transcend the amateur and professional era. His on-field position belied his talent and ability. He was a second-row forward who could kick goals and give and take passes like a centre three-quarter. He had guts, passion and ability, and so it was that he was nicknamed 'Nobody', because nobody's perfect. He was, of course, John Eales, one of the very few players to be involved in two successful World Cup winning campaigns during their playing careers.

So what was going through this future rugby guru's mind as he collected his thoughts in the aftermath of Gordon Hamilton's try? Was it the soaring leap he would make to try to regain possession from my high-hanging restart? Was it the

285

relentless chase he would give to put the maximum pressure on Neil Francis or Donal Lenihan to try to force an error from his opposite numbers? I can reveal to you that it was, in fact, none of these.

Given that this was the knockout stage of the event, the sides who lost in the quarter-finals would be exiting the competition and heading home the very next day. Now, John had put some clothes in for dry cleaning that morning, and when he stood under the posts as the Ralph Keyes conversion sailed between them, he was worrying about how he would get the laundry back if he had to fly home the next day!

Fortunately for John and his laundry, we managed to score from the ensuing kick-off, but now you know what exactly goes through the mind of one of the greatest rugby players ever to have played the game!

WASH-DAY BLUES

JEREMY GUSCOTT

'Jeremy Guscott is quite rightly regarded as one of the best players of his generation – and possibly any generation. He pretty much had it all in terms of skill, and added to that he could run like the wind, which is pretty useful if you are a back. It is not something that ever really worried me.

'Jerry made quite an impact on his England debut in 1989 with a hat-trick of tries against Romania, and he was subsequently selected for the Lions tour of Australia that summer. In true *Boy's Own* style, he scored a crucial try in the second Test victory, and the Lions went on to clinch a series win after David Campese gifted them a try in the final Test in Sydney. Couldn't have happened to a nicer bloke.

'Known worldwide (well, in Bath at least) as the 'Prince of Centres', Jerry retired from the game in 1999 with a thigh injury, having won sixty-five caps in total for England, played in three World Cups and represented the Lions in a very impressive three tours. Perhaps it was in a Lions jersey that we saw the best of him, and he achieved rugby immortality when his late drop goal sealed an 18–15 win that gave the Lions an unassailable 2–0 lead in the 1997 series in South Africa.'

My entire career in rugby was spent with Bath Rugby Club. I was born in the city and from the moment I started to play the game I knew I wanted to play for them.

My first representative match was for Bath Under-8s. We played on half the pitch at the Recreation Ground, and it seemed as though everyone I had ever met turned out to watch. Mum, Dad and my brother were on the touchline along with many other friends and relations.

Over the years a lot of money has been well spent on the drainage at the Rec. This expense has transformed the playing surface from the bog I played on that day to one of the best pitches in the country. Honestly, as I ran out for the match the mud was ankle deep (not ideal for someone who just wanted to run with the ball) and getting deeper as the torrential rain fell.

The first time I received the ball was a great feeling. I beat the first lad with a dummy, sidestepped the next two, chipped the ball over the head of the fourth and then caught it, ran under the posts and scored my first try in a Bath shirt. I couldn't believe how easy it was (a bit like playing against Scotland and Wales in my latter years!).

I ran back to take my position for the kick-off feeling pretty good, and I felt even better a minute later when the ball came my way a second time and I scored my second try. What an easy game – I scored tries and everyone cheered! Fantastic!

It was during the second half I had my first experience of rugby when the opposition have the ball (not such a great game). The biggest lad on their side was nearly five feet tall and must have weighed almost eight stone, and he was running straight at me! I didn't know it then, of course, but this incident was an early indication of what was to follow later in my career. I looked to my right and there was no one to be seen; I looked left and once again, no one to be seen. Years later, when playing for England against New Zealand, I was in a similar situation with a guy called Jonah Lomu running at me. I looked right for Will Carling – nowhere to be seen. I looked left for Rob Andrew – nowhere to be seen. On that occasion I decided to do what I had done during that first game for Bath. I shut my eyes and threw myself in the way of the oncoming 'monster'. Both outcomes were remarkably similar. I was pushed into the dirt as the attacker steamrollered over me.

The major difference between the two occasions was what happened following the humiliation of having someone run over me as though I wasn't there. In the Under-8s match the final whistle blew shortly after my 'missed tackle' and I stood on the pitch with tears rolling down my face. I was covered in mud from head to toe and crying uncontrollably when my mother, noticing my obvious distress, ran on to the pitch, put her arm round me and said, 'Don't worry son. I'll be able to get your shirt clean.' That did not happen against the All Blacks.

Can you begin to imagine how embarrassing it was to have your mother running on to the pitch to tell you all about the positive effects biological washing powder will have on your dirty kit? It certainly had an impact on me.

In later years when I played for England, one of my nicknames was 'Persil', which I believe had something to do with the fact that my shirt always remained white and clean during matches. Of course it remained white! The thought of my mother running on to the pitch in front of 60,000 spectators and millions of viewers on TV, putting her arm around me and telling me not to worry about the mud on my shirt was too much to bear.

BEAN SHOOTS AND LEAVES

DEWI MORRIS

'Dewi "the Monkey" Morris gave his heart and soul to England, winning twenty-six caps. I first came across him when Wasps played Orrell. Dewi was a brilliant team player and worked his socks off at his game, giving everything to the cause. He used to work himself up into such a state it would cause him to say and do the most ludicrous things on the pitch! And not too much has changed I'm pleased to say. He is now a very well-respected rugby pundit and commentator who gets overexcited because of his passion about England and about rugby. Who can blame him? I've got a bit carried away myself at times.'

My first match for the Lions was against North Harbour on the 1993 tour to New Zealand. Words cannot describe the honour you feel when you pull on the Lions shirt, and you know you are representing England, Ireland, Scotland and Wales.

My shirt was presented to me by Ian McGeechan, the legendary Lions coach, and I remember him congratulating me, telling me to wear the shirt with pride and to think of the players who had worn it before me. Gareth Edwards immediately came to mind. Fifty-three caps for Wales, three Lions tours and voted the best rugby union player of the twentieth century. No pressure there then.

As you can imagine, I was very nervous prior to the kick-off. I kept looking for reassurance from Rob Andrew and Gavin Hastings, both of whom had previously toured with the Lions and knew more or less what to expect. They and the other team members were very encouraging, and by the time the match started I felt as if I belonged and that I was an integral part of the team.

The word that best describes the game against North Harbour is 'ferocious'. They were the bully boys of New Zealand rugby and definitely wanted to rough us up prior to the Test matches. I remember that Richard Webster, the Welsh back-row forward, absolutely loved it. The opposition were constantly sledging him, using words and phrases I couldn't possibly repeat here. To be honest, I think Webby was just delighted that people were actually talking to him.

We fought fire with fire for eighty minutes and it was not a great spectacle – but for me it was a personal triumph. I delivered a constant stream of great ball from the set pieces and loose play. Our forwards were magnificent and that, in turn, made my debut a lot easier than it otherwise might have been. The final score was 29–13 in our favour and I was voted man of the match.

To make it even more special for me, my mum and dad were there to witness my first match for the Lions. In 1983 they had toured as supporters and ten years later they were touring again, only this time watching their son play, a proud and very special moment for all of us.

The post-match function was held in a large marquee by the

side of the clubhouse and I managed to get my parents an invite so they could see me get my award. I had already decided I was going to give it to my dad, partly because it meant he would have to carry it around New Zealand for the rest of the trip, but also to show him how much I appreciated the fantastic support he had given me throughout my career.

As the meal neared its end, my mind drifted off and I couldn't help but wonder what the award would be – maybe an engraved tankard, a beautiful piece of cut-glass crystal, or perhaps even a silver salver?

With the conclusion of the speeches it was my moment. One of the officials from the North Harbour Club stood up to announce the winner of the man of the match award. Rather like the ceremonies you see after cricket Test matches, the presenter spoke warmly about a couple of players from each side who had made significant contributions but just missed out. He then started to talk about my efforts that afternoon and at the end announced the winner – Dewi Morris. With applause ringing out, I felt ten feet tall as I walked towards the top table to receive my trophy.

We shook hands enthusiastically and he reached under the table and proudly presented me with . . . a Ken Hom Electric Wok!

A f***ing Ken Hom Electric Wok! For the first time in a long time I was absolutely speechless! The boys pissed themselves with laughter as I held it aloft all the way back to my seat. I couldn't even look at my mum and dad through sheer embarrassment. Needless to say, I did not give it my father. In fact, I sold it to our bus driver for $NZ20 and put the money in the beer kitty.

That British and Irish Lions tour was the last of the amateur era and nothing better signified this than the wok. Nowadays, it's a bottle of champagne, an engraved tankard, a kiss on the cheek from the sponsor's promo girls and a not inconsiderable financial bonus.

That said, I sincerely hope the bus driver and his wife are still enjoying the occasional stir fry.

EPILOGUE
BY CURTSEY OF HER MAJESTY

There is no doubt that becoming a world champion must be the pinnacle of every sports person's career. I am no different. The pride, honour and emotion I felt as the winner's medal was placed around my neck, coupled with the fact that I shared that moment with such an inspiring group of individuals, is something I never imagined I would experience when I occasionally let my boyhood dreams drift towards the possibility of wearing the red rose of England on my chest. Every one of us had worked hard to achieve our collective goal and there had been, of course, hard times, strains and stresses along the journey. But as I hope this book has shown, in rugby, no matter how hard you are working, how intense the training, how many sacrifices you have to make, there are also moments of pure entertainment.

And it is with that thought in mind that I want to tell you one last story – a story which I hope you agree encapsulates what this book is about. There is a serious side to playing rugby, there is a dedication required to win matches and tournaments and there is a responsibility to celebrate your wins appropriately – especially when the victory is in the World Cup final. We all knew we had to be gracious in our moment of glory and to celebrate along with the nation in fitting fashion. But you can never take the rugby tales out of the rugby players . . .

On our return to the UK after Sydney there were scenes beyond our wildest imaginings. The extent to which England's victory had touched the nation only really became apparent to us on landing at Heathrow. The police came to meet us off the plane and said that we weren't allowed to go outside as there were literally thousands of fans who had turned up to greet us. We were taken to an anteroom where the police informed us we would have to go out one by one to save the crowd stampeding. To be honest, a few sherberts had been had on the plane and we were tired and keen to acknowledge the incredible reception and then head home to our own beds. So we had a quick huddle and came up with an excellent solution to the issue of how to move things along.

We opened the door to the terminal and pushed Jonny Wilkinson out with the World Cup!

We couldn't believe our ears when we heard the reaction of the crowd – it was just astonishing. When we came out to face the camera flashes, the noise level lifted the roof off. It was crazy and wonderful and suddenly any tiredness had disappeared from each and every one of us. We savoured the moment. We later found out people had abandoned their cars (and cares) on the perimeter road around Heathrow and had run to the terminal building just to welcome us home. Our world had changed, and this was just the beginning.

The next time we all got together was on 8 December when O2, the official team sponsors, had organised an open top bus to take the entire squad and management on a procession through the streets of London, finishing in Trafalgar Square. I must admit that most of us were fairly sceptical and had serious doubts about anyone turning up, but the procession was going to be followed by a champagne reception at Downing Street with Tony Blair and then on to afternoon tea with Her Majesty the Queen at Buckingham Palace, so we couldn't exactly not turn up.

We met in the morning at the Intercontinental on Park Lane with our families, and exchanged stories of the madness that had ensued since we got home, and the press intrusion which was normally reserved for the lofty heights of celebrities and footballers. Jonny was the darling of the nation and even the slightest bit of news on the heartthrob triggered mass media hysteria, likewise Martin Johnson, whilst not exactly in the poster pin-up category – do you remember those Tetley adverts he later took part in? – was in huge demand as everyone wanted a piece of the man who had inspired our success on the fateful night in late November.

We were given a brief run-through of the day and the first task was to head to Marble Arch where, emboldened by a couple of glasses of Bollinger, we boarded the bus still terrified that the whole thing would be a damp squib. Why wouldn't it be, as the victory was over two weeks ago? Surely all the fuss had died down?

As the bus drove out of Marble Arch and turned right down Oxford Street we realised we had made a serious error of judgement on the clothing front. It was the middle of winter and we were catching our death on the top deck, dressed in only our light grey suits and the very distinctive tan shoes that Clive had picked out for us. Thank God the fashion police didn't manage to fight their way through the crowds and haul us all off to the Tower or the celebrations would have been very short lived. There was only one thing to do, and that was to get a few inside us sharpish to keep the body temperature regulated and take our minds off our natty attire.

The scenes we witnessed that day will stay with us all for the rest of our lives. As the bus made its way down Oxford Street, the pavements were full of supporters draped in the cross of St George and cheering us on. The joy on everyone's faces, including all of us on the bus, was incredible.

On Regent Street people were hanging out of their office windows shouting their support, and we stood there in awe of what was unfolding. As the crowd continued to grow, it took us a good hour to crawl to Trafalgar Square but we were determined to savour every second – we waved, cheered and shouted, all the while tucking into the beer and the 'Bolly' with reckless abandon. When we got to our final destination another blindingly obvious problem presented itself. Given that we had had a few and were suffering the effects, we discovered the bus had no 'facilities' on board. Jason Leonard – who comes from the old school of hard knocks – was more desperate than most to relieve himself, so in true Bear Grylls fashion, he adapted to the surroundings and found an empty bottle of bubbly to meet his needs. Gathering the boys around him to protect his modesty (he's a shy lad really), Jason proceeded to attempt to empty his bladder into the bottle. I say 'attempt', as he was clearly having sighting and control problems and half of the contents went down Lewis Moody's trouser leg.

Given that the eyes of 750,000 people, not to mention the cameras of the world's media, were trained on the bus, it was pretty amazing that Jason didn't get caught out, but this was a day for celebration after all, so perhaps the odd blind eye was turned.

We then enjoyed a champagne reception at Downing Street

where unfortunately Mike Tindall failed to convince the Chancellor of the Exchequer, Gordon Brown, that the bonuses for winning the World Cup should be tax free. But a good effort, I thought, on Mike's part.

Following that it was on to our date with the Queen at Buckingham Palace. It had been a whirlwind few weeks since winning the World Cup, but to be granted an audience with Her Majesty was the icing on the cake.

Perhaps the most important aspect of this wonderful final recognition of what the England team has achieved over in Australia was that it involved the entire squad, as indeed the whole day had. There were, of course, those players in the squad who had quite rightly captured most of the headlines, but there were others who may not exactly have stood in the spotlight, but who had played their part nonetheless.

In the early games against Uruguay and Georgia, the perhaps lesser-known players in the squad had more than done their bit and played their part in getting England through the pool stages. They then trained as hard as their team-mates in ensuring that no stone was left unturned in the pursuit of bringing home the Webb Ellis trophy.

One of these individuals was Mark Regan, a man who had made his England debut against South Africa in 1995 and had been ever-present in the England squad for the next eight years. 'Ronnie', as he was imaginatively dubbed by his Bristol team-mates, is a tough old West Country bruiser who loves the banter. He was always quick with the wisecracks; not many were funny, even fewer made any sense, but that was Ronnie's magic, and everyone loved him for it.

On arriving at the Palace, everyone was on their best behaviour and minding their 'ps' and 'qs' as we assembled in one of the many ornate anterooms. One of the footmen approached Ronnie and asked him if he would like a cup of tea. 'Yes please, babb,' came the all-too-familiar Bristolian reply. 'Earl Grey?' enquired the footman. To which Ronnie thrust out his right hand very formally saying, 'Mark Regan, very nice to meet you, Earl.'

Once we'd recovered from this classic Ronnie-ism we paid attention to what the palace officials were telling us. It was explained that when the men were first introduced to the Queen we should bow our heads and shake her hand calling her 'Your Majesty', whilst our wives and girlfriends should do the same but curtsey. Following that we should call her 'Ma'am'. Fair enough, makes sense. Even we could manage that I reckoned. It was all shaping up to be a perfect ending to a truly once in a lifetime day.

One member of our squad, however, was not as excited as the rest of us about our imminent meeting with the Queen. Our reserve hooker, Dorian West, was a staunch republican, and strongly believed in a state without a monarch. Dorian (aka 'Nobby') had been reluctant to go to the Palace and further voiced his misgivings on our arrival and at the formal briefing. As the behavioural protocols were explained Nobby began to get more and more put out and kept muttering under his breath about Oliver Cromwell having it right all those years ago.

The Queen arrived in the state room where we were having tea and getting as much cake inside us possible in an attempt to sober up after the excesses of the bus journey. Behind her were her famous corgis who all took a lot of interest in Lewis Moody's trouser leg, much to the amusement of Jason Leonard.

The formal introductions took place and, rather like at the

beginning of an international match, Martin Johnson accompanied the Queen and the Duke of Edinburgh round the room and introduced them to every member of the squad. She instantly recognised Jonny and Jason Robinson, both of whom had played pivotal roles in the final, and enjoyed some light-hearted banter with other members of the team. Jason Leonard, who is an old hand at meeting royalty, seized the opportunity and asked if he could apply to be a Beefeater when his rugby career was over.

As luck would have it, the last in the line of players happened to be Dorian West and as the Queen ceremoniously moved towards him, the players started nudging each other, desperate to see the show of defiance that Dorian had promised us all just minutes previously. The pressure built steadily, and glancing to my left I could see Nobby getting hotter under the collar with every step she took closer to him. The sweat was literally running off him when the presentation party finally arrived.

'And lastly, Ma'am,' said Martin, with due solemnity, 'may I present my Leicester team-mate, Dorian West.' Everyone craned their necks to see this historic moment where two worlds would collide and this working-class hero would single-handedly bring down the monarchy. However, instead of shaking her hand and bowing as he had been instructed, Dorian bent his knees and performed the daintiest curtsey of the day!

IT'S IN THE BLOOD

LAWRENCE DALLAGLIO

'Uncontrollably frank . . . A terrific book' *Daily Telegraph*

Powerhouse of English rugby, Lawrence Dallaglio's raw strength, determination and passion for the game runs in his blood. He lives and breathes rugby.

Three consecutive Prempiership wins and two Heineken Cups with his club Wasps, his England credentials are just as impressive with the 2003 World Cup-winning campaign and three Lions' Tours.

But Dallaglio's life off the field is no less compelling, filled with tabloid headlines and family tragedy. From the closed private persona to the intelligent, roguish charisma of his public face, Dallaglio finally opens up.

NON-FICTION / SPORT 978 0 7553 1574 1

LEGENDARY
STORIES OF BLOOD,
SWEAT AND BEERS